A Single Girl's Journey to the Greatest Love of All

MASTER OF SINGLE

NICOLE JONES

Master of Single
Copyright © 2021 by Nicole Jones

All rights reserved. No part of this publication may be reproduced, distributed, or transmitted in any form or by any means, including photocopying, recording, or other electronic or mechanical methods, without the prior written permission of the author, except in the case of brief quotations embodied in critical reviews and certain other non-commercial uses permitted by copyright law.

Tellwell Talent
www.tellwell.ca

ISBN
978-0-2288-3752-7 (Hardcover)
978-0-2288-3751-0 (Paperback)
978-0-2288-3753-4 (eBook)

TABLE OF Contents

ACKNOWLEDGMENTS i
PREFACE..iii
INTRODUCTION...1
CHAPTER ONE: Unmastered Me 7
CHAPTER TWO: I Do But I Can't..................................49
CHAPTER THREE: Being Single......................................81
CHAPTER FOUR: Blind Faith 95
CHAPTER FIVE: Best Friend or Bust........................... 103
CHAPTER SIX: Coming in Hawt................................... 119
CHAPTER SEVEN: Lover's Lane 139
CHAPTER EIGHT: To Ring or not to Ring 163
CHAPTER NINE: Charming is Alarming 177
CHAPTER TEN: The Guy with no Name..................... 187
CHAPTER ELEVEN: Single is the new Jame 199
CHAPTER TWELVE: The Rebound Guy...................... 213
CHAPTER THIRTEEN: Online Dating: Yea or Nay?. 231
CHAPTER FOURTEEN: But He's so into Me............. 239
CHAPTER FIFTEEN: The Things I do for the D 261
CHAPTER SIXTEEN: Hot Bitches and a Bachelorette 273
CHAPTER SEVENTEEN: The Greatest Love of All... 285
BOOK COVER SPECIAL CREDITS 321

To all the singles who have loved (or not) before, I see you…

ACKNOWLEDGMENTS

I dedicate this book to my mom, Margaret Rose Jones, 1930–2015, forever my hero, angel, beloved Mama Bear, greatest teacher, and chosen one.

Thank you for saving me from a motherless life and for sending me Dior, a gift from above (a Chihuahua/Jack Russell mix) adopted from the SPCA, December 7, 2016.

The blessing of us finding each other had you written all over it. Amen.

My beloved family, my sweet little sister, Dolisha, you are my favourite human, you make me so proud; my love for you is infinite.

Uncle Maurice, my aunties Raymond and Glenda, Sheldon, and family, you are each a beat of my heart.

I thank you and adore you, my core sister tribe—Ely, Judy, Betta, Stephanie, Patricia, Julie, Sophie, Marie Eve, and brother Perry—I couldn't imagine the journey without any of you.

To the ones I love and who bring me all the joy and

feels, the list is exclusive, and I trust the queens and kings on that list know who they are. Crown on!

To my biological mother, thank you for having the courage to give me life. And to my family, you are my roots, and after a lifetime apart, the blessing of meeting you is not lost on me.

God bless you.

Dearest mentors, teachers, coaches, and critics along my journey, thank you for contributing to my growth. I've learned something from each of you that's made me a better person.

To God, my angels, my ancestors, and spirit tribe: Thank you for always guiding me towards the light and for bestowing upon me the strength to keep moving forward, breaking the glass ceilings of my life. Amen.

And finally, to you, my dear readers, thank you for supporting my first book. I have no words to express my gratitude.

Disclaimer: If you aren't offended by some profanity, hard truths, a little vulgarity, and/or sexually explicit content, then enjoy the ride and the read.

See you on the sunny side of the greatest love of all.

PREFACE

Please note much of this book was written prior to the Covid-19 pandemic, and parts have been edited accordingly. Meaning a lot of my thinking was framed during a time when we were much freer to live, love, and lust among each other. That said, proceed with caution, and please read discerningly given the world's current circumstances. Thank you.

The first thing I wish to tell you is that I would never impose my thinking on you, nor would I negate your desire and path to finding lasting, meaningful love. My intention is to share what I know about going from being single and surviving to mastering my single life.

I adopted said mindset when I reached a certain age and, finding myself single, realized that I wasn't going to wait for someone to come along to make me happy.

That whoever my person is meant to be, he will arrive when the time is right. Period. No rush, no stress, no problem, and in the meanwhile, I got this. Instead of worrying about what I couldn't control, I would control what I could, and that was me.

NICOLE JONES

I would be responsible for my own happiness and not let my relationship status deter me from moving through the world, conquering and living my best, most glorious life.

I would become master of single. Crown on.

Let it be clear from the start that I love *love*, and I'm not trying to keep anyone single; in fact, I wish love for every single person who desires it. I value and recognize the power and momentum of true, relentless, core-shaking, worth-the-wait kind of love, and I think we can all agree that finding that special person to share it with is nothing short of a blessing and a small miracle. Especially given today's oversaturated social media, superficial, emoji-driven, sex-crazed, often moral-less society we live in. Just saying.

I've spent most of my life dating, in relationships, or recovering from them, and guess what? I'm still single, and thank goodness for that. To choose to be happy and content with yourself, some might say, is an act of valour because it challenges so many ideals that we think we must meet to be happy, and most end with being in a relationship. But it's not about being brave or having courage; it's about taking your power and owning it.

This book of essays isn't always for the faint of heart, but there is an endgame. They're meant to invite you into my journey towards what I perceive to be the greatest love of all love. As well, to challenge the narrative of what it means to be single.

Much like society has moved forward and evolved in so many ways, so too have singles in that we've far surpassed the old stereotypes and labels society once put on us. Such as being single means something is wrong with you or that you're not good enough or you can't be happy if you're single, blah, blah, blah, all so blasé, passé.

MASTER OF SINGLE

Singles today are a new breed of personalities: fearless, free, independent, happy, and loving it. We're wearing our individuality and status as a symbol of strength, not weakness.

Mastering your single life is a new and exciting movement, so grab your closest single friend, buckle your seat belt, and hang on because our time has arrived… and not a moment too soon.

What does it look like to master your single life? Answer: complete freedom, independence, personal growth, doing your work, and honouring the relationship with yourself. It's your opportunity to lay the foundation for the journey into who you are, who you want to become, and whom you may want to be with.

The bottom-line, hard-knock truth is that the relationship we have with ourselves is the most important relationship we will ever have the pleasure of experiencing.

If the definition of luck is "preparation and timing coming together," wouldn't you want to be the most prepared you can be for when the timing of your life presents you with your person?

Preparing yourself to become who you want to be is your work, and your single life provides the opportunity to do that work to become your best self for yourself, trusting that the rest will follow. I said this is a movement, but it's also a spiritual thing.

By now you might be asking yourself, "Who is this woman professing to have mastered her single life? And what qualifies her to write about this seemingly interesting subject?"

These are justifiable questions. After all, who *am* I?

Allow me to introduce myself. My name is Nicole Jones (not Nicki or Nic or any other version of my name unless authorized by me, thank you). I've always wanted to master something—an instrument, a third language, a relationship, or a sport, but as it turned out, I mastered my single life.

I'm a little bit of a rebel at heart with very traditional values and a lot of lover at my core. Proud of my Jamaican/Metis roots and being a child of adoption. I stand for justice and use my voice and my platforms for positive messaging to inspire, empower, and spread love.

I've endured many hardships throughout my life, and I'm proud to say that I'm a survivor of abuse, trauma, shame, and fear, coming out stronger on the other side. Amen.

Although my life has seen tough to terrible times, I've been resilient and able to find the positive. Even in my darkest days, I can recognize the many blessings in my life, as you will soon read about in the stories that make up this book.

I consider myself to be an ambassador of love and light and a peaceful warrior. I love freely, I shine my light on others naturally, and I choose my battles wisely.

My religion is love and intention. I believe I am the creator of my destiny, divinely supported and guided by God, the universe, and what I call my spirit tribe, including my many protective angels who art in heaven, lovingly watching over me. Amen.

I subscribe to the school of thought that the universe is full of abundance and is always conspiring with us to bring our dreams to fruition. But that doesn't mean you don't have to do the work. It's our job to support our dreams with hard work and a clear vision, and you can never be too specific with the universe; the clearer you are, the clearer the guidance will be.

Here's a good place to point out that hope is not a plan, action is.

MASTER OF SINGLE

Aside from being passionate about writing my first book and excited to add "author" to my credentials, I'm also a proud daughter, sister, best friend, godmother, and fur mama.

I'm obsessed with my sweet (debatable) doggie, Princess Dior. She's more of a D-I-O-R than a D-O-G. That's what she tells me anyway.

Like Mama, like "doughter," her attitude depends on your personality.

I'm a constant student of life, higher learning, and spiritual growth—a truth seeker and part of the light on my journey to my divine purpose is to be of service in this lifetime. I possess an artist's heart with a passionate soul and have enough empathy for the world.

On a simpler note, I'm a faithful, unapologetic fan of the *Real Housewives* (especially Atlanta) and bingeing on reality television. Some call it a guilty pleasure, but I have no guilt about it.

Speaking of pleasure, some of my favourite foods include poutine, lobster, salt-and-pepper shrimp, caviar, foie gras, oxtail, fried chicken, and a big salad is always a great palate cleanser.

I still love a great party, music, reading a good book, travelling, and making memories with friends and family.

Basically, I do what makes me happy, and I balance my pleasures with living a healthy and, most importantly, happy life as defined by me.

To support myself and Dior (pre-Covid), I proudly worked as the first-ever appointed master of ceremonies for the uberexclusive Four Seasons Hotel/Marcus restaurant here in Montreal.

It was a position of leadership and being the creator of all things five-star and magical in terms of guests' experiences. From setting the environment with music and entertainment to overseeing our guests' every need. Most importantly, I gave a piece of my heart to everything I did, which comes naturally to me and was a pleasure to do; in fact, I wouldn't have done it any other way.

Prior to that position, I was acting and working as a television reporter/host/producer, with my last assignment as a special correspondent for Canada's number-one national entertainment show, *etalk*. (#nationalgoals)

Today, due to Covid circumstances beyond my control, like so many others, I find myself having to reinvent myself, but the silver lining is that I'm free to pursue me, further confirming my belief that there's always a bright side if you look for it. Although I don't know what the future holds, my faith in my life is strong; it has never failed me, and I don't intend to lose faith now.

In full disclosure, I am not a trained psychologist, relationship expert, or therapist. My highest and most important training comes from the school of life, graduating with a degree in "master of single." I've paid attention to my life, and my lived experiences have shaped the messages throughout this book. I bring a lifetime of observation and learning from some of the world's best teachers, including my beloved mother, whose simple but powerful messages of "just love everyone, even when it's difficult," that "I am stronger than my circumstances," and "be kind, but don't let anyone mistake your kindness for weakness," are not lost on me.

I've also learned from my incredible tribe of family and "framily" (friends who become family) who have been some of my greatest allies, guiding and growing alongside me.

I have also benefited from years of personal work, seeking higher learning, and educating myself on how to become the best, most authentic version of me. I've learned lessons from countless spiritual leaders, teachers, and authorities who have influenced my way and from whom I've borrowed many a tool over the years.

These are world-shifters and mind-openers, like Dr. Maya Angelou, Martin Luther King Jr., Rosa Parks, Mother Teresa, Oprah Winfrey, Nelson Mandela, Iyanla Vanzant, Tony Robbins, Marisa Peer, Mel Robbins, Eckhart Tolle, don Miguel Ruiz, Gary Zukav, Brené Brown, Deepak Chopra, Simon Sinek, Dan Millman, Marianne Williamson, Barack and Michelle Obama, and so many more.

These eyes have seen a lot throughout my travels, and I've been fortunate to have access to and learn from some of the world's most influential and powerful individuals. How that happened, I have no clue (LOL). But I do know that being exposed to some of the richest people and most deprived people has helped shape my views on the world and only made me a more empathic, wise, compassionate, and aware individual.

My biggest takeaway is that money, as nice as it is to have, doesn't buy happiness, and that being poor is often a state of mind. I've known rich people who are miserable and disadvantaged people who are some of the happiest souls I've ever met. I've concluded that true, authentic happiness lives inside us and isn't determined by our affluence.

Which raises the point: men who try to impress me with their money never get far.

Like most women, I'm looking for substance, depth, and realness; things that money can't buy.

What would be attractive, however, is a man who approaches me with something to say and is interested in what I have to say.

To all single men I say this: the bar has been raised, and that's where you'll find us.

As a person who came from poor to humble beginnings and has worked hard for everything I've earned, I've finally realized that I don't need to keep up with the Joneses. I am the Joneses 2.0. Today I stand proudly in my light—empowered, optimistic, and strong for all, to uplift, encourage, and impress upon you a new day and a new way of seeing your single life as a life worth loving. And that confidence has nothing to do with the car I drive, my zip code, or what I'm wearing. That's all me, naked, standing in my truth. Priceless.

My allegiance to you is that no single be left behind, brooding in self-pity while waiting for the right person to come along. You might as well be watching paint dry. I'm here to invite you to join me in the now, to do all the things that please and excite you now—not tomorrow or maybe later.

Tomorrow is not guaranteed; today is our present, and that is a gift.

You will notice that aside from my people who have graciously given their consent for me to use their names, I don't name any of my suitors in the stories. This was a creative decision. These are my stories to tell, and they're strong enough to stand alone. I trust in my storytelling abilities to serve the truth of every story without having to put anyone on blast.

In the end, the men are not the lessons—the experiences are.

In fact, I hope that it only adds to your experience and taps into even more parts of your imagination.

As you flip through these pages and stories, I'll share what I've learned—the good, the bad, the embarrassing, and sometimes the cringeworthy truth, but I own it all. I've discovered that the best way to find peace, strength, and truth is to be still with myself and allow the light to fill the darkness, to be courageous enough to say, "I love all of me, and whomever I'm to be with will love all of me too."

But until then, I have me, and now we have each other.

There's also something to be said about having solid couples in your life; being around partnerships that you respect is a good reminder for your muscle memory of what a healthy relationship looks like, sounds like, and feels like.

One of my examples are my dear friends T and O and their beautiful union and wedded bliss—the epitome of black love and black excellence. And who doesn't love a wedding? This one was special and magical, reminding me that pure, crystalized true intention and love is indeed possible and does exist. To bear witness to each of them present and available for the other was nothing short of inspiring, and as a single woman, it's good to be reminded every now and then that love and partnership is only a unicorn away.

But wait… there's another kind of love to consider in the meantime, a different yet equally important and powerful love that can fill you in the most unsuspecting and glorious ways. It's what I call the greatest love of all—an idea we'll explore, one chapter at a time, as we access this underrated world of mastering your single life.

Have you ever asked yourself if you're happy in your life? Have you fully embraced the power that comes with being single? Or are you the type of person who's sitting suffering in silent, single sorrow, feeling low and lonely?

Are you lying to yourself and those around you because it's the polite thing to do? Do you put on a happy face even though inside you're scared, maybe even ashamed and feeling unloved? Have you ever felt that you're "less than" because you're not coupled?

I have, and that's why I know that to reverse those feelings, mastering your single life is the best path moving forward.

Today, sitting pretty in my forties, a woman who has been in love, hurt by love, blinded by love, mad at love, still believes in the power of love. I know now that there's more than one way to achieve love or happiness. Mastering your single life is not reserved for a specific age, gender, or generation. It's a state of mind, a lifestyle, and an attitude—if you dare—and I'm living proof that this theory works.

On my road to love, I've been the girl who would jump off a metaphorical cliff without a parachute if I believed the reason, dream, or person justified the jump and enriched my journey. May no potential partner, life experience, or opportunity to live my best life go unturned. When it comes to matters of the heart and love, I'm not law.

I jokingly and fondly compare my sex/love life to Oprah's weight-loss journey. We're both determined to reach our goals but with one exception—she wants to lose the weight, and I wouldn't mind a little extra weight on top of me at night. Ha ha! Love you, Oprah!

Joking aside, I consider myself qualified to write about this subject because I am the subject, my own niche market and, humbly, every single woman. I am master of single at your service. You know what they say: write about what you know. And this is what I know for certain.

You're welcome.

INTRODUCTION

LET'S TALK ABOUT societal pressures that come with being single. I'm a tough chick with a thick skin and wide shoulders who can pivot through a lot of the noise and nonsense. The kind of nonsense that often comes from unsolicited, unfounded personal opinions of strangers.

First tip: beware of toxic, nosy people trying to project their insecurities onto you; they're everywhere. Which is why doing your personal work is invaluable. The better you know yourself, the easier letting people's opinions roll off your back becomes. Those people (they know who they are) with opinions about your life but don't know anything about you can all humbly fuck off and take their opinions with them.

It's a new day for singles, a time to change the old narrative and for society to meet us where we are. The new conversation should be one that celebrates and respects our status, congratulates us, doesn't doubt, dig, or question us. Gives us the same consideration and support as we would give anyone else's relationship.

And singles, if you find yourself being judged for your status particularly by someone in a relationship, forgive their ignorance; they clearly didn't get the memo. Pivot left and keep it moving. Their opinion is not worth your time.

This is a tangible change that we can impress upon society. Let us stop judging or assuming. Instead, let's raise each other up, no matter the relationship status, and encourage the individual.

And for those in relationships, remember that before you were cozied up and coupled, you were single too.

So, if you can't say anything nice, save your opinions for yourself and talk about the weather.

Note: you'll notice that I tend to swear when I feel passionate about driving a point home but also sometimes just because it feels good. Sorry, Mom.

In the same breath, I'd also like to thank those people. Because society and their dumb-ass opinions about my status in part played a role in inspiring me to write this book. Someone had to do it, and someone had to say it.

Working in the service industry, often engaging with the public, I started to notice a pattern of behaviour that was quite alarming in its audacity. When asked if I was seeing anyone, I'd often get this perplexed "poor you" look from people (usually people in a relationship) when I'd answer that I'm single. It would be followed by either a consoling hand on my shoulder or a chin-up word of advice as if there was a problem I wasn't aware of.

I called shady bullshit every time; it was insulting to my single intelligence.

As bewildering as it was, I also found it fascinating how people could be more concerned about my relationship status than I was. What was it about me or my situation that people felt the need to pity? Do I look pitiful? I don't think so, and I wasn't looking at them and envying a damn thing. So, WTF? Really. It was wack. I didn't get it, and I certainly didn't appreciate it.

But like I said previously, when you're at peace with who you are, you don't allow people's opinions to get to you.

I arrived at giving zero fucks in my forties, and it's been brilliant ever since. By now, I'm like T-Fal—shit just slides right off me. What's even more hilarious is that those conversations usually ended with me making other people feel better about my status, as well as teaching them a lesson in minding their own damn business.

Never shy to confront their pity, I would ask them straight up if they were honestly sad or concerned for me because I was single. (#teachablemoment) Sometimes people pushed me too far with probing and stupid questions, like "Why are you single?" or "Are you really picky?" Other times I heard ignorant comments such as "Oh, you're intimidating. That's why guys are afraid to approach you." That always unnerved me. And the classic "How is it possible a girl like you is single?" Trust me, I've heard it all.

For some reason people can't get past the idea that a beautiful, intelligent, successful woman can be single and thrive in that. The look of confusion in people's eyes as they navigated their own misperceptions was priceless. I realized that their observation was a "them" problem and not mine to carry. The moral here is to beware; these types of people lurk among us dressed in sheep's clothing and will try to get in our heads and cast doubt where there wasn't any.

Shame on them!

Society, please stay in your lane. Just because you couldn't do it, don't for a second mistake a single's completeness and happiness with their relationship status. One is not dependent on the other.

Now, what else you got going on? (Insert hair flip).

It's time for singles to know just how powerful they are. Never operate from a place of fear or desperation; no good decisions come from that place. One of the worst things you can do is to get into a bad or toxic relationship, turning a blind eye to the red flags or making excuses for poor behaviour just to avoid being alone with yourself. It may be a quick fix in the short term, but in the long term it will become clear that it's not truly serving you. As much as I look forward to being in love again, I'm not willing to be in a relationship at any cost and neither should you.

Also remember that the way you treat yourself is a good indication of how you will let others treat you, which highlights the importance of practicing being good to yourself first.

One can also argue that it's important to know what you like but equally important to know what you don't like.

Some say finding love is like looking for that missing puzzle piece. If that's true, do you know how much time I've spent looking for puzzle pieces? Damn, if I had a dollar for every piece that didn't fit, I'd be nouveau riche!

On the flip side, my soul tells me that I'm not a puzzle. I am a complete, clear-to-see, fleshed-out, perfectly imperfect, vivacious woman. No missing pieces here! The whole idea of finding someone to "complete me" doesn't sit well with me. It feels like such a big ask to put on anyone and suggests that you're not enough on your own, when the truth is, you are.

What would be cool would be to meet that special person who complements me in my completeness—which is a totally different conversation—and that's the person I want to be with.

Be patient with yourself and your process, beloveds. You are worth the wait, and so will they be. In the meantime, there's so much living for you to do just by way of your status.

Another advantage of doing your personal work is that it prepares you to become a great *partner* as opposed to a *project*. A partner is a person who has done their work and is able and willing to contribute to another person's life in a healthy, solid, loving, reliable way. Someone who's open-minded and available, honest and present, caring and accepting. A person who pulls you forward and brings out the best in you; someone to lean on through the good and the bad and who makes you laugh even when there's nothing funny. They can be vulnerable in being perfectly imperfect and won't judge you for being the same. They see you and allow you to see them, and they're a positive driving force and a complement to your life.

It's a rare and special package, but I believe those souls exist, and only timing and preparation can manifest such a gift of a person in our lives. But if you've ever been in love, then you know it's worth the wait, and if you haven't been in love, I promise you that it's worth the wait.

A project, on the other hand, can be all kinds of a disaster waiting to happen. This person likely hasn't done their personal work and typically takes more than they contribute. They may be caught in odd patterns or bad habits and not know how to get out of their own way.

They project their issues onto you and/or the relationship, making their issues your relationship's problems.

A project may appear to be co-dependent, needing constant reassurance to validate their own lack of self-worth and insecurities. They might judge you because they judge themselves and tend to suck energy out of the room and fuel fear, which can lead to distrust in themselves and their relationship. Not good. Stay woke.

Raising your standards can make you feel like you have fewer viable choices out there in the once sea of possibilities.

It's true that good partners can be hard to find, but I'd rather fish in a pond filled with potential than flounder in a sea full of impossibilities.

Before we set off, I remind you of this: falling in love is great, but your best bet for staying in love is finding the love for yourself first.

Our journeys may be different, but any way you cut it, single is still spelled the same. With that, let us sail away into the uncharted waters with my first single-girl story and great adventure… Get your popcorn, and Lord have mercy on your eyes.

Ready, steady, single rocks… here we go!

Chapter One

UNMASTERED ME

OUR IDEAS ABOUT love, why we seek it, and how it shows up in our lives tend to vary over the years. My journey to defining love and getting to know myself started in my early single twenties. It was a time I'd describe myself and my life as wild and free, lost and found (ish), but mostly lost. However, I was never at a loss for having a good time... Then again, isn't that what your twenties are for? Having fun and thinking you know everything, only to realize you have a lot to learn?

This first single-girl story is exactly that: it unfolds in phases and covers many stages of being young and having fun, sisterhoods, taking risks, living carefree, and getting to know me. It also represents a time when my morals and values were put to task and my personal boundaries were tested.

It's all that and a bag of chips.

This season still reigns supreme as one of my most memorable, enriching, pivotal life experiences. A time when being a rebel ruled and moving through the world with the mentality of "the bigger the risk, the greater the reward" was a way of life. Little did I know that a series of supremely designed events would soon unfold. I believe that God and the universe can provide extraordinary things that our mere mortal minds can't even conceive.

Like the saying goes, "Make a plan, and God will change it from there."

Let me take you back to when it all began. Growing up, we didn't have much. I rarely got what I wanted but always had what I needed, but our mom made sure that we were always rich in love.

As a young athlete, there were times I would have preferred having less love and to get my Nike running shoes instead, but unlike the shoes, her love is everlasting. She was our rock, as most mothers are, and she kept our family grounded and together, as most mothers do.

You'll notice throughout this book I reference my mom a lot. That's because I had the best mom in the world.

She was a humble and kind soul, a lady of Caucasian persuasion who stood just under five feet tall. Mighty in her power and love, but trust me, you did not want to mess with her. She was also very tough.

In her defence—not that she needs one—she had to be tough. We were a wild bunch, and her toughness maintained controlled chaos in our revolving household, where she made family and education the cornerstone of everything.

Unable to have her own children, at a young age she dedicated her life to helping other kids and disadvantaged families, contributing to the welfare of primarily black children, where she recognized the need was the greatest. She did this in a largely white and French-speaking community, making her a pioneer for breaking the colour lines in our small town.

Over the span of twenty plus years until she got stomach cancer, the only thing that could slow her down. But up until that point, fifty-seven children and families passed through her door, and she was eventually acknowledged by the government and acting Prime Minister at the time for her contribution to the youth of Canada.

Out of them, I was the sole and blessed one to be adopted.

Once the household was stable, most of the kids would eventually go back to their respective homes, but I was in foster care.

I was five years old on that fateful day, visiting her home with a social worker to see if she would be able to keep me until someone adopted me officially.

When she saw me with my pretty braids with ribbons and those big eyes (her words, not mine) and heard of my situation, she knew she couldn't let me go back to wherever they were going to take me. That was the moment she made me hers and she became mine, saving me from a motherless life and fulfilling her dream of being a mother.

It was divine intervention at its best.

Our mother-daughter bond was like no other, rooted in a unique kind of love, knowing that we were meant to be. She possessed a heart bigger than her entire body, with such depth of wisdom, generosity, and compassion paired with an unwavering faith. She lived to be of service to others.

Growing up, she had a way of giving her opinion and

sharing her wisdom, but never imposing herself on me or telling me what to do.

When I became an adult, she told me once that although she didn't understand a lot of my choices, she was able to let me live my truth because she had faith that she had given me the tools I needed to be a strong and honourable woman. Trusting that would be enough for me to always find my way back to my light. And she was right.

Because of what she taught me, no matter how far I fell, I'd always find my way back to the light.

She was and will forever be the best woman I'll ever know, and it is my intention to carry on her legacy, however I can. One of my heart dreams would be to one day create my own chosen family.

But, despite her best efforts to protect me as a kid, a lot of bad things happened to me. Unbeknownst to her, I experienced things that no kid should ever have to go through.

Trauma that until now, I've only ever spoken about with my therapist and very close friends. Although I won't go into detail about it because that's for a different book, I will say this. My childhood showed me early on that not all adults do the right thing, and life isn't always fair.

From an early age I knew I was different, bearing an old soul with wisdom beyond my years, but it wasn't until much later that I began to understand my gifts or even consider them as gifts.

As a young girl, that same wisdom told me that I deserved better than the actions of some or the life I was dealt.

Eager to start my adult life, I left my parents' house at eighteen years old and a day to move in with my boyfriend. He was popular, good-looking, and I was infatuated with him, but in my parents' eyes, all they saw was a basketball player who smoked weed.

Technically he was my first serious boyfriend, and because I was of legal age, they couldn't do anything about it. I was just excited to finally make my own decisions, take my first steps to adulting, and have my own lived experiences. Of course, this was all to the absolute horror of my mother.

That relationship eventually ran its course, and that's when my life really began.

Picture this: rebel me with no one to answer to, attitude for days, and giving the world body, face, and you're welcome all over the place.

In my youth I was beautiful. (#humblebrag) I mean, I still look great, if I do say so myself, but young Nicole was a fire you couldn't put out.

A dangerous combination for a rebel girl with no direction and nothing to lose.

It was a rough start into adulting. It came with a lot of confusion, disillusionment, and figuring shit out along the way.

Thank goodness for the morals and values my mom instilled in me, because honey, for a long time they were the only things I owned outright. When I was lost, I especially held my values close to my chest. They were often my saving grace through a lot of difficult times.

That's why all that I do, minus the things no mother wants their child doing, is for us.

She sacrificed her entire life to help others, and I always told her that when I succeed, we succeed. I could hear her voice the whole time I was writing this book, asking me, "Nicole, are sure you want to write that?" … and I'd answer back, "No, Mom, I'm not sure, but I'm writing it anyway." The truth shall set me free. I'd laugh out loud, knowing she's always guiding me.

When I left home, I became a legit hustler, quickly learning to stand on my own two feet. I made my money fast and figured out how to survive adulting on my own accord. Always seeing my parents struggle with finances, I lacked the financial skill and knowledge to have a healthy relationship with money. Note to parents: please teach your kids how to manage their money, as it's so important and such a gift to them.

My lack of financial knowledge would be one of my biggest learning curves later in life; in fact, I still don't live within a budget. But I've gotten much better at understanding the energy money brings and how to appreciate it, receive it, and let it go again, trusting it will come back. It's all about your mindset and the relationship you have with money.

Over the years, I've made alliances with women who would become my sister tribe; we've seen each other through break-ups, make-ups and everything life threw at us. By the grace of God, they've been there by my side from the beginning of the beginning. All of us carried some residual trauma from our childhoods, and we saw ourselves in each other, and that's the energy that brought us together and bonds us for life. Due to the nature of this first story, I want to take a moment and thank my sisters for being so brave in allowing me to use their names. I know people judge, and this story has the potential to be judged by people who can't relate to or understand it. I've chosen to reveal this otherwise intimate part of my/our lives because if anyone's going to tell this story in its truth, then let it be me.

As women and individuals whose stars continue to rise, I don't ever want anyone to have the power to hold my/our story over our heads. We own our journey, we're proud of where we've come from to get to where we are, and we've earned every moment of the life we're living today. When I look at us, I see strong, fierce, loving, beautiful, compassionate women, each with something special to contribute to this world and who never gave up on themselves or each other.

At some point over the past two decades, I have lived with every single one of these sisters, and not only as roommates. One time we took over a six plex and all lived in the same building. Those were some of the best times of our lives. Not many people can say they've gone through the things we've experienced together. And for that, and a plethora of other reasons, I honour you, my glorious sisters. Ride or die, I will always have your backs!

I remember telling them way back when, that one day, I was going to write our story, and although this is just a slice of it, a promise is a promise, my sisters.

So, beloveds, I implore you to read with gentle eyes and an open mind, without judgement and remembering that we all have a story and that every story matters.

And with that said, the first stop on our journey was in the subculture and erotic world of strip clubs and exotic dancing, where we met as young warriors, rebellious and free. There was nothing typical or usual about us, so not surprisingly, we did things our way.

My performer name was "Sade"—the smoothest of operators.

When I say we danced to the beat of our own drum, I mean it. No apologies issued, and I say that in the nicest way possible. We all understand that dancing isn't a life goal... Well, maybe it is for some—no judgement.

But I never looked at us as strippers, per se. Yes, we

took off our clothes for money, but I like to think of us as entertainers who worked in a strip club. We were smart about it and weren't taking off our clothes in vain. We had mastered the art of seduction and getting men to pay us to sit while remaining fully dressed and drinking champagne, which was the goal of every shift to find that sucker, ha ha!

You'd be surprised the reasons men come to strip clubs. Yes, most are there for the drinks and naked women, but a lot of men were more interested in just having someone to talk to and listen to them because for whatever reasons they aren't getting the attention at home. If I can offer this little bit of tea from my experience, I'd say check for your men. Make sure they're getting the attention they need, because like it or not, right or wrong, if you're not giving it to them, somebody else will. Sorry to be the one to have to say that, but I'm here for every woman, and women should know the tea.

And by the way, it's never your fault. Even if you're the hottest bitch on the block who's doing everything right, men can and will be dogs. No matter how good you treat them, there's still a chance that he's going to do whatever he wants, so there's that too. But a good man will possess that wherewithal to respect boundaries and his relationship, and those men exist, they're just not easy to find. (#unicorngoals)

When it came to the places we worked, it was always the best. We were an asset to anywhere we went, and the bosses and doormen always adored and protected us. We were invaluable and in high demand by clients, beautiful to look at with enough attitude and smarts to keep things interesting. Bottom line, we made the club money and that's why we enjoyed certain preferential treatment.

We didn't fit into a box or society's norms, and we had no interest in conforming to anyone's expectations. That mentality and extra edge served us well because against all odds we managed to maintain our integrity in a world that didn't hold integrity in very high esteem.

When I look back on those days, I want to give myself a big hug. Knowing how damaged my self-worth was at the time makes it easier to understand how I even got there in the first place. We were all a little damaged in some way, but we used that to fight our way back to life, and to me, that is so commendable in my eyes.

News of my dancing broke my mom's heart, and of course that broke my heart. In fact, she didn't speak to me for a little while, as it was too difficult for her to process, but eventually she made some sort of peace with it, but she never liked or supported it.

Also, she didn't know about things that had happened to me that contributed to my choices because I had kept it from her. I knew telling her would destroy her, and I couldn't bear that thought, so I kept my abuse and trauma a secret all my life. A heavy burden to carry.

Those experiences contributed to my skewed self-worth and self-image, and speaking only for myself, in some twisted reality the clubs were maybe the best thing that could have happened to me. In a weird way, it became my safe place. I knew I was damaged, but I also knew at least I wasn't damaged out there in those streets where God knows what would have happened to me. In the clubs is where I really started to heal, grow, get to know myself, and find renewed confidence. Crazy but true.

In fact, my sister Sophie was the first person to introduce me to numerology. One night downstairs in the changing room, she started dropping knowledge about the significance of numbers. That conversation opened my mind to a new way of thinking and gave me different information to start seeing life another way. The first book about it I read was called *The Life You Were Born to Live* by Dan Millman.

It was the first of many turning points. We weren't just girls on a pole. We were special, and we knew were destined for something else. I think it's remarkable that my personal work started in the changing room of a strip club while smoking a joint, doing our makeup, and reaching for higher goals.

So aside from breaking my mom's heart, which was horrible, how could I regret any of it? Meeting those women changed my life. They are my "framily" and that experience shaped the woman I am today. We are living proof that you can get yourself out of the clubs and turn your life around, which was exactly what we did.

Our truth was, we didn't hate ourselves; we were just doing the best we knew how with the tools we had.

But thankfully, much to do with the natural order of things, this passage of time and life experience, which lasted a few years, eventually came tumbling down. After doing what we went in to do, each for our own reasons, the day would come, a time for change. It's different for every entertainer or dancer, but fair to say most of us know when it's time to get out, although the idea of getting out and staying out is easier said than done.

In our case, there was strength in numbers, a timing and a synergy that came with the collective decision for our sisterhood, so we were lucky in that sense because we had the support of each other.

Finally ready to grow beyond our personal demons and the seductive lure of the stainless steel pole, smoky locker rooms, shady clients, foggy afternoons, and drunken late nights, it was time for us to join the "real" world, to live among the "commoners" and find regular-people jobs.

MASTER OF SINGLE

All foreign concepts to us twenty-something fancy-free young warriors now attempting to become respectable young women in the eyes of the world.

And so began the process of transitioning out of the business to integrate into mainstream society. Words can't describe the pain and determination it takes to transition from club life to a J-O-B and a biweekly pay cheque. Who knew?

Many moons and chapters of our lives later, our paths have set us in different directions, but we will forever be bonded under the umbrella of sisters who once danced to live and now live to dance. I love my girls beautiful and free—Stephanie, Sophie, Patricia, and Marie Eve—I will forever be proud of us and applaud our courage to have recognized the potential beyond our damaged selves to want and to go for better. Brava!

I've seen it with my own eyes. So many girls try to get out and fail time and time again because the allure of the money is often greater than the motivation to get out. If you don't have someone pushing and supporting you, it's much more difficult to do it alone. It's a fool's errand, and we were no fools. I can only hope and pray that those who have the courage to forge their own pathway out find the same opportunity in sisterhood to help them get out and stay out. Exotic dancing, if you choose to do it, is a place you land when you're running from something (most of the time), and if you're lucky, it's for a time, but not a long time.

But to each their own path, no judgement, Godspeed.

The hardest part of leaving was taking that first step out. We'd become accustomed to a certain lifestyle and money; it was the only life we knew. There were bad nights but many nights where we made hundreds of dollars (sometimes thousands) and worked four to five nights a week, so you do the math. Back then, money to us was something that we didn't even think about; it was spent as easily as it was made, and repeat. Post-dancing, insert reality check.

Thankfully, we were fortunate to have people on the other/brighter side of life, willing to help us get our footing in the "real world." At the time, Stephanie was friends with the owner of a sushi restaurant that was tucked away in a two-story building on Saint Catherine Street in Westmount. It was the hottest and best sushi joint in town. He was kind enough to give us jobs for which we were grateful. And, just like that, we went from showing our sushi to serving sushi. Yes, I said what I said, and you're welcome… ha ha!

The change of pace, job, and money was all kinds of brutal. Like I said, we'd been making hard, fast cash, so to go from that to working in a sushi restaurant, grinding and hustling for minimum wage… I had to ask someone how to spell it. I mean, trauma much.

My first position was working in the kitchen, making the house signature salads. That lasted for a hot minute but wasn't for me. Eventually I found my sweet spot behind the bar, bartending, where I developed a skill set that would go on to serve me well.

For the first couple of months of redesigning our lives, we held on for dear life. We were so poor; I mean, everything had become a concession. We had to rethink our total way of living and moving through the world. I don't think I was as prepared for the struggle as I thought I was.

It was a stark wake-up call how little we'd thought about the cost of things, including rent. Suddenly bills started piling up, and leisure and lux had all but disappeared.

MASTER OF SINGLE

At one point it was so bad Stephanie and I shared a loaf of bread because neither of us had enough money left at the end of the month to buy our own. That's just one example of why I say it's easier said than done to stay out once you get out. It's an uphill battle, and it takes a village and fortitude to change.

Fast forward a few months, a couple of our friends joined our new normal, becoming part of the restaurant's dream team. Not all of them were ex-dancers. That was how we rolled. If one of us got an opportunity, we shared it with the entire tribe.

Things were going as well as could be expected, given the circumstances, when one fateful night change came knocking at my bar. It was a weekend not unlike any other; the owner of the restaurant was sitting at my bar, chatting with some of the clients.

On this night, however, the conversation was different and caught my attention with both ears. He kept going on and on about this party he was attending later that evening, boasting about the star-studded guest list, from Hollywood stars to supermodels, needless to say, I was jaw-dropped with every word that spilled out of his mouth.

What is this party? I asked myself. More importantly, why wasn't I invited? As it turned out, it was a very exclusive, invitation-only, private event being thrown by one of our city's most influential and powerful people who was known for his insane, next-level parties. At that point in my life, my lived experiences were limited; they included dancing, a couple of rave parties, a little travel but not much, an ex-boyfriend, and smoking some weed. I really didn't have a grip on the who's who of the city, and in that moment I didn't care. All I knew was that it sounded like a dream party, and Lord knows I was thirsty for a little break from my new normal nightmare and real-life hustle. I wanted to feel important and rub elbows with the rich and famous who's who of Hollywood... I mean, who wouldn't want to be part of that? You feel me?

He sat there almost bragging about this superposh party that nobody could get into. I wasn't one to sit on the sidelines when I wanted something, and nine times out of ten, I'd get it. So I started plotting my plan to figure my way in. Come hell or high water, I was going to be there, and they were going to love me.

That's when I approached my girl Elizabeth, not an ex-dancer but a stunningly drop-dead gorgeous brunette with a slamming body and face to match. She was one of the top servers on the floor. I pulled her aside, quickly briefed her, and asked if she wanted to figure out a way to get in with me. With a resounding "Hell yes," we partnered up to party it up.

Mission party-gate accepted.

By now I had also told Stephanie about the party, but she'd gotten invited on the downlow via invitation of someone on the list. Unfortunately, she couldn't get us in because she was going as a "plus one" and didn't have any leverage to help us. But she supported our mission because she wanted us there.

We asked a few people for help, hoping someone could get us on a list, but to no avail. Every rejection only fuelled us more and further heightened our determination. We went into tunnel vision, balls to the wall, nothing to lose, and a sick party to gain.

After we finished our shift, we hopped into one of our cars and started driving around the city like freaks out at night, asking and looking for anyone who could help. I'm not kidding when I tell you the first, if not the second, stop was a place called Shed Café on Saint Laurent Street, an iconic bar back in its heyday. It was also where Liz once worked.

MASTER
OF SINGLE

"Let me run in and see the manager. Maybe he knows someone," she said.

I sat there waiting with the car running idle, fidgeting as I anticipated our next move. Liz rushed back and jumped into the car, smiling from ear to ear with her eyes as wide as her whole face.

"What? What? What happened?" I exclaimed with the utmost urgency. "Tell me!"

Like a magician with a rabbit and a hat, she pulled out two—count 'em, one, two—invitations to the main event! I mean... Whoa! What the actual fuck? It was a party miracle wrapped up in one sweet little moment. I screamed in disbelief! We both started squealing like schoolgirls who'd just been kissed by a boy for the first time.

We had to stop ourselves long enough for her to explain that the manager just so happened to have two extra tickets from two girls who didn't want to go. I literally couldn't believe my ears. All I could think was, *Suckers!* Their loss was our massive gain. Period. Thank you. Next.

We were halfway there.

I can't remember the name Liz got, but I'll never forget mine. For all intents and purposes, on that night I stepped into the persona of Miss Meyer. It was crazy exciting, but we weren't out of the woods yet. This game of smoke and mirrors we were playing had to work; I wouldn't breathe easy until we had both feet firmly planted inside that party.

After a few more minutes of uncontrolled screaming and dancing in our seats, we collected ourselves and wiped our happy tears. Now we had to get ready, and time was of the essence... The details after that are fuzzy at best. My next clear memory is of us looking superhot and our hearts beating out of our chests the whole time during the thirty-minute drive it took to get there.

That's when I started worrying. What if they ask us for ID? We were imposters after all, attempting to infiltrate the security of one of the city's most anticipated events and posing as the girls on the invitations. I started to panic at the thought of getting busted, but Liz calmed me down. "If they ask, we'll just play the game and distract them by being pretty and smiling... basically charm our way in. Worst case, we'll tell them that we didn't know we had to bring ID. Then cross our fingers and hope it works out." *Okay*, I thought, *yeah, good plan*.

As we got closer, we approached a gated entrance and crossed through a cast-iron gate that took us off the paved road and onto a winding dirt road leading us through what seemed like a magical forest and up to the most incredible-looking home situated in the middle of a national park. My eyes had never seen anything so beautiful or rich. I loved everything about it; it was stunning! It looked like the work of the great artist Gaudí, with a nod to *Architectural Digest*.

It was lit, and we were coming in hot.

There was so much security around the entrance that my nerves were playing tricks on me. One of the security guys ushered us through to the next checkpoint. I rolled down the window and handed him our invites. We sat there smiling and batting our eyes adoringly, hoping to deter him from asking for ID. We were so extra in our attempt to overcompensate and way too eager to get in, which I'm sure translated to looking crazy, but we were so close. I could hear the music calling my name... "Meyer, Meyer, come to the dance floor." LOL!

The security guy checked the list and leaned into the driver's side window. A few more seconds passed; he gave one last look at each of us and to our motherfucking delight, he waved us through.

OMG, we were in! We wanted to scream but didn't.

MASTER OF SINGLE

That would have been weird. It took everything to contain our joy that was bursting to come out, but we maintained our cool until we were officially inside. I'm sure the fact that we were both beautiful and looked like we belonged in that world and at that party worked to our advantage. Fake it till you make it is a real thing. We might have faked our way in, but we were exactly where we were meant to be.

Words couldn't describe the feeling I had as we walked through the front door and stepped into the vast open-concept kitchen space, which happened to be bigger than my entire apartment. We continued through into the main room where the magic and the party were all the way happening. I wanted to cry I was so happy.

I'd never seen anything close to that level of lux. The house was legit to die for, and I felt richer and more special just by being under that roof; that's how easily impressed my younger, inexperienced, unmastered self was. I didn't realize that even the rich would gasp at not only the opulence but also the way he brought it all together. Not all rich people have good taste and know how to have a good time, but this host, whoever he was, clearly had both.

The room we occupied looked like a tropical paradise with sauna temperatures and a huge indoor pool surrounded by large stones and beautiful lighting. Massive wood artifacts, probably from his many travels around the globe, decorated the rest of the space. There was a state-of-the-art, fully equipped DJ booth off to the side, people were playing tam-tams, and sick house music filled the space with a magical energy. Couches and different lounge areas dotted the room for our leisure comfort.

Beautiful people were sprawled out everywhere—smoking, laughing, and singing—while more beauties danced in bikinis around the pool. I mean, party of the year, and we were there. Hallelujah!

NICOLE JONES

On one side of the room were massive floor-to-ceiling glass patio doors that overlooked the outdoor grounds, which included a carrousel—yes, a full-sized horse carousel—like the ones you see at amusement parks. I noticed individual cabanas and even a private lake on which a gondola sat quietly in the glow of the moonlight. You know you're rich when you have a lake and your own gondola. Just saying. It was so next level in every way, and all I could do was take it all in. We had arrived. I wasn't sure where the hell I was, but I knew I had arrived.

I grabbed Liz and headed to the bar where I ordered two vodka cranberries, doubles please, bartender. Once settled in, I started to scan the room for the celebs I'd heard were supposed to be in attendance. I did see one or two, but it wasn't as exciting as I thought it would be. I was feeling like a superstar VIP myself sitting on top of the world, even just for a night, and felt just as important as any other star in that room. Suddenly they looked like regular people among the crowd of beautiful cools. For all I knew, they were looking at us and saying, "Who's that girl?" And rightfully so. We were the virtual unknowns in the room, and we were no shrinking violets. We came to party, be seen, and they noticed.

At some point we were presented with party favours offered by one of the guests who was generously passing them around. As the goodies were being handed out, I inquired what they were exactly? I was told it was ecstasy. I had heard about these designer drugs, but at the time they were foreign to my recreational habits. I wasn't very experienced other than knowing my different strains of cannabis. But I was more curious than anything else. I didn't want to turn away any opportunity to elevate my experience.

I decided to try it, and with that it was down the hatch with no looking back. Maybe thirty or forty minutes into it,

MASTER OF SINGLE

I could sense tingling throughout my body and my vision altered into a morphed state. Straight lines became compromised, and lighting was enhanced with warm hues, music filled my body like it was part of my bloodstream, and my heartbeat held perfect rhythm to the beat of the drums. Crazy!

Fast forward an hour later, forget about it! I was feeling no pain, and for the first time, I was legit flying higher than I'd ever been before. This ecstasy, or as I referred to it as "unleash the beast in you," released my inner dancing queen, and I was feeling myself (not literally, although...), but it was a wildly exhilarating experience. It stimulated high levels of serotonin, resulting in a feeling of euphoria. I was off in a world all my own, a world governed by the music and however my body flowed.

I took my spot in the middle of the room and danced for hours and hours, non-stop, giving everyone watching a show and a half, sexy to death and without apology. You're welcome, party.

It was crazy to me how everything became so heightened and intensified by that little pill. I don't remember much about the moment to moment, but I do remember that when I started dancing, it was dark outside, and the next thing I knew, I was still dancing but now the sun was coming up.

As I danced my way into the next day, still feeling no pain, suddenly I was tapped back into reality... yes, a literal tap on my back.

At first I thought I was just so high that I was imagining things, but then I felt another tap. This time I turned and came face-to-face with a security guard who was just standing there looking right at me. I didn't know what to think or what he wanted. Was my dancing getting me in trouble? What was going on?

He leaned in and said, "The owner would like to meet you." Me, high AF, trying to focus enough to contain myself and stop dancing long enough to listen, was damn near impossible.

Confused and caught off guard by his request—not to mention feeling like I was going to implode because of the ecstasy, I replied, "I'm sorry, who? What? Owner who?"

Clearly unable to form a coherent sentence.

I'm sure he knew people were high at this party, but I'm also sure my level of amateur preceded me because he looked at me as if I were crazy. He paused with a look of concern and slight annoyance on his face and then repeated it again, this time in a matter-of-fact voice that slightly scared me. "The owner of the house, who's hosting the party, would like to meet you."

This time I caught it quick, and it stopped me where I danced. For lack of anything smoother to say, in my ecstasy-induced state, I stupidly replied, "Ohhhh, the *owner* owner." A feeble attempt at trying to redeem myself and playing it off like I didn't hear him correctly the first time. Trying to fake it, and not doing a very good job, pretending that I knew who he was talking about the whole time. But the truth was, at that point, I honestly had no idea who the owner was.

Back at the restaurant, my boss had mentioned his name, but like I said, I was young and inexperienced. Unless I'd danced for him at the club—which I never did—I wouldn't know him or any of the top echelon players in the city, but that was about to change.

Mr. Security Man gestured for me to follow him; I was a nervous wreck and could barely see straight let alone hold a conversation with the owner! It was all too much to handle. Out of options, I took a deep breath, nodded, smiled, and followed him. I thought about running but didn't know where I'd go. There was no place to hide even if I tried to make a dash towards the lake—which I did consider. In my current state, I figured I'd probably drown before someone would have the chance to save me. So yeah, not my best plan.

As I followed Mr. Security Man, doing my best to sober up, that's when a dose of reality hit me. Scrambling to get a grip, I started playing out the conversation in my mind, first figuring out who I was again! Would I say Miss Meyer or Nicole? *Oh no*, I thought, *this is a disaster waiting to happen, and my perfect night is about to go down in a blaze of burning doo-doo.*

By now, my high and my paranoia had become one. It felt like the longest walk of my entire life, like a single stowaway walking the plank. I prayed that by the time we arrived wherever he was taking me, I would know what to say. But nope, that didn't happen either.

Before I knew it, I was standing in front of the owner and our host.

I can't imagine what I must have looked like, standing there in front of him, a hot, sweaty mess from dancing all night and so high it felt like both my eyes were in the same hole. Do you know how hard it is to act straight when you're flying? Or to think clear thoughts and make a good impression when you don't even know who you are in that moment? It was one of my greatest and most challenging acting roles to date. And the Oscar goes to…

My mouth was dry, my hands were clammy, and my legs were shaking. I was trying to keep it together and avoided looking directly at him. When I did finally make eye contact, I saw his kind eyes looking back at me. That seemed to calm me down—at least enough to stop shaking.

NICOLE JONES

He extended his hand and introduced himself. I reached my hand to meet his, still unsure what name to say, so I opened my mouth and let whatever name came out, land. "Hi, I'm Nicole," I said faintly as I cleared my throat, hoping he heard me just enough to keep the conversation moving.

He replied, "Nice to meet you, Nicole. Are you having fun?"

Using the remaining minuscule amount of saliva in my mouth to answer back, I said, "Yes, I'm having a great time. Thank you so much." It was the truth; I was having the time of my life. So good that I almost forgot who and where I was.

We stood there a few minutes more, him looking at me and smiling, and me still trying to avoid making eye contact without seeming rude. I finally said awkwardly, "This is a really great party." As if he didn't know. He gave a little chuckle, but I wasn't sure if it was at me or with me. Either way, I was mortified and felt like I was melting in my shoes.

Of course he knew it was great; it was his party, duh! Way to make an uncomfortable situation even more uncomfortable.

All I could think was that he was on to me because he knew everyone on his guest list and was probably questioning who I was and how I got in. That's what I'd be thinking if I were him. But after sweating it out for what seemed like an eternity, he released me by generously saying, "Good. I'm glad you're enjoying yourself. If you need anything, let me know, okay?"

"Okay, yes." I nodded. Eager to get out of his presence as quickly as possible, afraid he'd ask me more questions, I closed the conversation with, "Thank you again. I'm going to go back and dance now. Is that okay?" He nodded and smiled. I waved shyly and then regretted waving (so cheesy), but it was worth the embarrassment for the best party of my life and a night I'll never regret.

Like a trooper, I made my way back to the dance floor, grabbing another double vodka cranberry on the way and popping another pill to help shake things off. Not sure that was the best idea, but if I learned anything from that night, it was that my bad ideas were also my best ideas, and if it wasn't broken, why try to fix it?

I was more determined than ever to squeeze every drop out of my night.

After that second pill, I lost all sense of time but gained all the feels. I was on such a cloud that all the security in the world couldn't pull me down. I danced until I couldn't feel my legs anymore. I didn't want it to end. Of course all good things eventually do come to an end... but wow, what a party and a story for the books. Case in point.

Once sobered up (hours later), Liz and I made our way home where I crashed my life away for the next forty-eight hours, sleeping like I was in an induced coma. It took another forty-eight hours after that to be fully back in my body and reality, but my reality would never be the same again.

As if the experience of the party wasn't enough, the residual effects were long lasting. With a new world of possibilities etched in my mind and a feeling that I couldn't quite put my finger on, something was telling me that the best was yet to come.

The next week, post-party pandemonium and now mostly recovered, I was at home in the middle of the afternoon having just stepped out of the shower when the phone rang; it was the host's secretary on the other end.

"Hi, Nicole," she said. "I'm calling to invite you to dinner on behalf of (insert name of one of Hollywood's most adored iconic actors who has a known thing for black women) on Thursday. Are you able to attend?"

Huh? Dumbfounded, I stood silent in the middle of my living room in my bathrobe.

Was I being punked?

"Hello? Are you still there?" she asked.

"Yes, I'm here," I replied.

"Are you able to make it to dinner?"

"Hmmm… I'm sorry, but is this a joke?"

"No, Miss, this is not a joke; it's an invitation. Are you able to make it to dinner on Thursday?"

Hesitantly I answered, "Yeah, I guess I'm able to attend, but I'm confused. Are you positive you have the right person?" This was so out of left field that it had to be a bizarre case of mistaken identity.

"Great!" she exclaimed. "And yes, Miss, I'm sure I have the right person. I'll call you again soon with more details."

"Okay, thanks… I think." She chuckled at my uncertainty, said thank you, and hung up the phone.

Whatever was conspiring in the universe, it was surreal. I mean, come on… are you kidding me? Things like this don't happen to girls like me. Or maybe just maybe, sometimes they do. But it still begged the question, how did this happen?

Have you ever felt like you were in a twilight zone with more questions than answers? That was the feeling I had.

Still in shock, I did what anyone in my position would do. I immediately called my girlfriends and told them to get their asses over ASAP—911 stat!

Feeling outside of my body, like everything was happening to me without my permission, I kept moving forward. If this was indeed true, it was going to require the perfect outfit and all-hands-on-deck to help me get there.

MASTER OF SINGLE

My wardrobe back then was a struggle. I loved fashion, but I didn't have much of it. The bulk of my things were lower-end brands, not so much high-end fashionable designer digs. But thankfully I had good personal style and a great body that made inexpensive look expensive.

Finally my friends arrived, riddling me with questions that I had no answers to. I was just as confused as them, if not more. I kept asking myself how that person even knew who I was and why the host's secretary was calling on the star's behalf. I had only met the owner briefly, and I'd gotten in under false pretenses. I'd introduced myself as Nicole, but I never gave a last name. I could only draw one conclusion: these were some seriously rich people with CIA covert Illuminati kind of power. LOL.

I started to put out feelers around the city among the people I knew and who knew people. Through the grapevine on the DL (down low), I managed to piece some parts of the puzzle together. I found out that this megastar who'd invited me to dinner had been at the party and, unbeknownst to me, had spotted me, but I hadn't noticed him. Sorry 'bout it.

And as the story goes, he reached out to the owner, who was a friend of his, and asked him to find and contact me on his behalf. Drop the mic. Wow, wow, and triple wow.

Two days later, another phone call came from the same secretary with the location where we'd be having dinner, which on its face was another mind fuck. Of all the places in the city, we were going to the sushi restaurant where Liz, Stephanie, and I worked. Go figure. But at that point nothing surprised me anymore. It was all so weird and crazy; there wasn't any sense to make of it, so I didn't try and just kept moving with it.

Until the day I was dressed, in a cab, and physically on my way to the restaurant, part of me still didn't believe it was happening. When the elevator door opened to the restaurant's top floor, I stepped out in my outfit of choice, which was a high-low-dress situation with a short, black mini velvet spaghetti strap number and long white sheer overlay with dragons on it.

Full disclosure, it was a dress I'd bought to wear when I was dancing and was also the fanciest thing I had, so fuck it. I wore it, and I owned it.

I stepped out of the elevator, feeling so nervous. Immediately all eyes were on me as if the staff knew more than I did. The manager came up to me and said they were in the private room, waiting for me. But wait! What did he mean, "they"? How many people were at this dinner? More questions I didn't have answers to… Great!

Before I could ask, we were walking towards the room. He opened the door, and I swear, there were at a least ten people, all strangers to me, sitting around the oval dining table talking. Among them was my future ex-fiancé, but on that night, he was accompanied by his then girlfriend. How crazy is that?

As I entered the room, everyone looked up and stopped talking. I noticed one empty seat—the hot seat beside Mr. Hollywood. I was greeted by the nicest guy with the most charming French-Canadian accent. He welcomed me and made a general introduction, basically yelling out, "Hey everyone, this is Nicole." I recognized him from the party. I'd been dancing close to where he'd been sitting, and I vaguely remembered him smiling at me. Everyone said a collective hello, and I waved back shyly.

He brought me over to the empty seat and introduced me to the man of the hour, which I guess made me the woman of the hour. I'm not an easily starstruck person, but this was impressive. I know many a person who would give their right arm to have the chance to meet, let alone have dinner with, this beloved megastar.

MASTER OF SINGLE

As I took my seat, he turned to thank me for coming and said I looked nice.

"Sure, you're welcome. Thank you for the invitation and the compliment," I answered back, literally screaming *WTF* in my head. So many thoughts were swirling around, but I didn't have time to decipher anything.

I sat there, trying not to look like an amateur, and then suddenly the charming guy who'd welcomed me, out of nowhere said, "Nicole, you work here, right?"

"Yes," I answered.

"Okay, good. Why don't you choose the menu?"

Choose the menu! What? "Hmmm… sure, if that's you want," I said in my most confident voice, pushing through the lump in my throat.

This was an extra tall order, and I'd need help, so I excused myself and went to find my girl Stephanie, who was working with the chef and would be the perfect person to help organize a great service. It also gave me a minute to release my mixed bag of emotions over this all-too-surreal situation.

We created the menu together, ordering the best of everything, and then with one last hug, she sent me back into the twilight zone—a very nice twilight zone, but still a twilight zone.

I re-entered the room, reclaimed my seat, and awkwardly looked over at my "date." Neither of us had much to say, so thank goodness the food started arriving shortly thereafter. What I didn't know was that outside the conference room, a storm was brewing.

The owner of the restaurant was pacing and fuming, doing laps around his own place. Apparently, he'd been asked not to enter the conference room, essentially banning him from the room for the sake of their privacy.

Obviously, that didn't sit well with him, leaving him livid that he couldn't enter a room in his own restaurant. I get it, he was angry, but hey, the client's always right. Right?

Meanwhile, inside the secret room, I sat unsure of what to say or how to bridge a conversation with Mr. Hollywood. It didn't help that he wasn't very talkative either and wasn't giving me much to work with. I remember smiling a lot and keeping my mouth full so I wouldn't have to speak. Keep in mind that I still wasn't sure why I was even there. And then—wait for it—just when things couldn't get any weirder, they did.

In the middle of dinner, a phone rang. The man with the charming accent answered his phone. I overheard parts of his end of the conversation: "Yes, she's here. She's very nice, yes, yes, yes... okay, hold on." He handed me the phone and said, "Someone wants to talk to you."

Talk to me? Who in the world could be calling on his phone to talk to me? I didn't even know this man with the accent. *Twilight Zone* 3.0. I reluctantly took the phone and inquisitively said, "Hello."

"Hi, Nicole, how's everything going? I'm sorry I couldn't be there. Is everyone treating you nicely?" Yup, you guessed it—it was the owner of the house, calling from Japan to check in on me. But why? And WTF!

The surreal moments just kept coming, but what more could possibly happen? Were we going to take a rocket ship to the moon to have dessert? It was that level of crazy happening in my head.

"Yes, thank you, everyone's very nice," I replied.

"Good," he said. "So, listen, do you want to come to Vegas this weekend? You can invite your girlfriends if you'd like."

Pause for yet another WTF moment. I went silent, which was becoming a common practice when talking with him.

MASTER OF SINGLE

"Hello, are you there?" he asked.

"Yes, I'm here."

I was doing my best to process the request when he asked again, "Would you like to come to Vegas this weekend?"

I turned to my right, and there was Mr. Hollywood looking at me while I was on the phone considering going to Vegas with his friend, whose party I'd just crashed. Totally normal scenario, said no one ever.

To this day, I marvel at the series of events that make up my life. Like I said, things like this don't happen to girls like me... until they do.

After a moment of reflection, I answered, "I'm on schedule to work this weekend." He laughed in the same way he laughed when I told him he threw a great party, like I was amusing him or something. But now I was starting to think he was laughing at me more than with me. He asked again, this time I could hear the smile in his voice, and with that, it felt like the only answer was yes, so I said, "Yes, I would love to, thank you so much."

He seemed pleased. "Great! Someone will call you with details. Have fun tonight, and I'll see you soon." And that was that.

I looked over at Mr. Megastar and then at everyone else around the table, feeling more speechless than ever and needing air badly, so I excused myself again.

Hollywood was cool with it. "Yeah sure, no problem," he said in his smooth and even-keeled voice.

Smiling to keep myself from freaking out, I got up and exited gracefully. I needed to get out of that room like a desert needs water. I also needed to get my head straight and my girls together to let them know about Vegas.

I quickly gathered them into a hurried huddle, trying to

contain myself to only speak the words that needed to be spoken. After I delivered the news, they looked at me with enthusiastic eyes and a resounding "Holy shit, yes!" We group hugged and gave a little squeal of excitement before breaking and going back to our respective posts. But before it could be official, we'd have to cover our shifts and get permission to take the weekend off.

After doing our due diligence, we went to the owner of the restaurant, eager to get his permission. I spoke on behalf of the group and said, "We just got invited to go to Vegas for the weekend. We've covered our shifts. May we take the weekend off, please?" All four of us looked at him with puppy dog eyes, almost on bended knee.

Remember, he was already fuming because of the room situation. I was aware of what had happened, but there was nothing any of us could have done to change it. Instead of taking the high road, he decided he'd take his frustrations out on us. Looking right at us, he said, "No."

I couldn't believe he denied us. It was clearly out of spite and jealousy, and I wasn't going to allow us to miss an opportunity like this because of his ego. I knew some of the girls were scared about upsetting him; he was a friend, after all, who had given us a hand up when we needed it, and we appreciated it. But we didn't owe him anything except to be good at our jobs, which we were.

Our jobs weren't providing us with the means to be living in the lap of luxury. We were working our asses off and barely making ends meet. We could always get another job, but who were we to turn down an experience of a lifetime? I couldn't justify it, so nope, not on my watch. I looked at the girls, and there were no words necessary. The look in my eyes said it all: I got this. I turned back to him and his mad-looking face and simply said, "Then we quit."

It was such a ballsy move, and I couldn't believe the

MASTER OF SINGLE

bravery I had to make such a hard decision on behalf of the group, but he left me no other choice. It was him or us, and I chose us for us, and that was that. In one fell swoop he lost his assistant sous-chef, head server, bartender, and would-be manager. We stood strong in our conviction, even though we could see the blood rushing to his face, livid that we had just quit.

And with that, I went back to the table and the girls went back to finish their shifts, and we weren't even mad. We agreed to disagree and quit as a result. On that night, we held the power and the cards. He should have just let us go to Vegas for the weekend. Ego's a bitch and will bite you in the ass every time.

After that heavy and dramatic moment, finally the night started winding down, and I was feeling more relaxed. I didn't care anymore how or why all this was happening; I was just enjoying the fact that it was happening. More things had happened to me in one night than in my busiest and best year.

Back then I wasn't as evolved or rooted in my spirituality and core beliefs as I am today. I hadn't yet developed the wherewithal to simply understand how to receive blessings and life gifts without questioning the why to death. However, I was evolved enough to know a damn good opportunity when it called from Japan.

As for my dinner date, I wasn't sure what to make of him or his invitation. I mean, it was super flattering, but he didn't come across as very social or conversational, which made it hard to read him. I never got a clear indication of what he might have wanted from me; it was kind of like pulling teeth trying to get to the root of the issue. Nonetheless, I was polite and hospitable to the best of my ability; after all, this was a major moment that would give me a great story to tell for years to come, so thanks for that!

We closed out the night, said our goodbyes, exchanged numbers as per his request, and went our separate ways.

As promised, in the days that followed, I received a call from the secretary, who shared the flight information and details about the next steps to Vegas. By now I should know to expect the unexpected, but trust me, it never gets old. She went over the itinerary for myself and my three girlfriends who'd be joining us. The plan was to meet at a certain time at Star Link Aviation, where we'd be flying with him on his private jet and staying in his personal home once there.

WTF? Private jet? I'd dreamed of flying on a PJ but never imagined I'd be living my dream with my best girls by my side. It felt so fancy, and we weren't mad at it.

I was starting to see how making the decision to get out of the clubs was the best move we could have ever made. It seemed to open the doors to endless opportunities, and although we knew we'd done the right thing for ourselves by leaving, moments like that confirmed it, proving if you want a different result, you must make different choices.

As per scheduled, we met at the airport, they loaded our bags onto the private jet as we made our way on board and were greeted by the pilot and crew. Sitting to the left and facing us was our new friend and host. He smiled as he stood to greet us, and I felt like I was meeting him for the first time, seeing as I was such a hot mess at his party. I didn't even remember what he looked like, besides his kind eyes, which I never forgot. They felt familiar the minute I saw them again.

I reintroduced myself as a formality and out of respect, this time with much more ease and confidence. Then I introduced him to my friends. He seated us accordingly, with me sitting adjacent from him. You know when you feel like you're in good hands? That was the all-encompassing feeling with this person. It was so exciting. Even though we were living through the riches of his life, I allowed myself to feel, even for a borrowed moment, the power of possibilities as I daydreamed my wildest rich-bitch dreams.

I mean, it's not every day you find yourself on a private jet, drinking Bloody Caesars with your girls on your way to live it up in Vegas.

As we took flight with sheer delight, we were in heaven literally 35,000 feet above the clouds. It was better than my highest high. The five-hour flight to Vegas was fun upon fun upon fun. We all got along so well; we laughed, talked, we joked and got to know each other better.

And we never spoke of "party-gate."

Following his initial party, I had done a little recon on our host, and it seemed like I was the last to know who this powerhouse was, but I quickly caught up, discovering that he was a successful self-made business mogul, creator, and innovative thinker. The founder and visionary behind the world's most iconic entertainment company. He also was revered for his path to success as a self-made millionaire, a life and success story that didn't come easy. An extraordinary rags-to-riches story, but what was most impressive was his humility, quiet demeanour, and generosity.

Even though he wasn't the most strikingly handsome man in a conventional way, his magnetic energy made him more handsome than most, and that was hard to deny.

I also sensed that maybe he recognized something special in me too just by how he was being so kind and curious about me.

Finally we arrived in Las Vegas, baby! The desert air was thick and dry, and the heat was about to get turned up even hotter with our arrival. We were an untamed bunch, and with our host leading the way, anything was possible, nothing was off-limits, and by now I knew to expect the unexpected.

The red-carpet treatment continued as we stepped off the jet into an SUV that took us to his amazing home off the strip in a quiet Vegas suburb. I remember walking into a beautiful wide-open and colourful space filled with cool artwork, a pool table off to one side, an open-concept kitchen, and all kinds of rooms and secret caches. It was the second house of his that I'd been in, and clearly his good taste preceded him.

Outside in the private backyard was a massive in-ground pool, which was so inviting that the girls and I didn't think twice before seizing the moment and jumping in fully dressed. It was a blast, and what a way to start our trip. It also solidified to our host that he had a crazy and wild crew, ready-to-have-fun and I think he quite liked it.

Also staying at the house was a friend of his, who immediately upon our arrival volunteered his services as our cabana boy, serving us drinks, giving us massages, and whatever else pleased our fancy. He was cool and a nice, fun addition to the crew.

After changing out of our wet clothes and into our swimsuits, we lounged around the pool, drinking for a while; eventually we made pizza to help absorb some of the alcohol from drinking all day.

Then came time to assign the rooms, and I was given the option of staying with him or my friends. I chose my friends only because I wasn't mentally or emotionally prepared for anything else. I didn't want to make it an awkward or uncomfortable situation, but when it came to any sort of physicality, the idea unearthed anxious emotions within me. Provoking uneasy feelings of inadequacy like I was out of my league. I thought, no way could I be good enough for him.

But this weekend was not the time or place to be dealing with those feelings, and so I played it safe and kept it moving.

Not surprisingly, he was supercool about it only proving once again his kind and caring nature.

The plan for that night was dinner, and then in true Vegas style with his crew of lady luck by his side, we hit the casinos.

Oh my, Vegas! We dined at the uberchic Bellagio Hotel and Casino, Picasso restaurant, which suited its name as it boasted original Picasso artwork on the walls. It was a five-star dining experience, and the first time I tried caviar and foie gras while sipping champagne, and I loved it—maybe a little too much. Who knew I had such a refined palate? Excuse me.

The remainder of the trip was just spectacular, and our host was generous beyond measure, spending all his time with us, present and always in good humour. It felt like we'd all known each other for years.

Once at the casino, he offered to bankroll us girls one thousand dollars each, with the condition that we split the winnings fifty-fifty. So fair, so fun! Meanwhile, he asked me to stay back with him, bringing me into the VIP areas where he gambled more money than I'd ever seen in my entire life and all my friends' lives combined—like it was nothing. But in my simple mind I was thinking, *Damn, that's a car, a home, or enough to pay for an education.* But hey, who was I to say anything? Despite my inability to comprehend winning/losing so much money, nonetheless, it was impressive to watch him play. But I wasn't expecting it to be such an emotional experience.

NICOLE JONES

Remembering this story and season, reminds me that it was also the first time I'd ever been in awe of a man in my life, including my adoptive father, who sadly didn't deserve or earn my love or respect—period. That's why I won't give him too much energy, except to say that in public he was well liked and put on a good front, active in different local organizations, but as a father figure—he failed miserably. He was abusive, drank too much and ruled with an iron fist.

Yes, he worked hard to keep a roof over our heads and supported my mom's dream of helping kids in need, but I always felt like he resented his life by following her dream.

On a human level, I could see right through him that he wasn't a good person and his misguided actions played a huge part in my adult issues later in life.

He and I were two different beasts. I was light, and he was dark. I always felt like I had to protect, and grew up thinking we all deserved better than him as the patriarch, but it was what it was.

It's been said that girls go on to marry a man like their father, and sons look for a woman like their mother, but growing up, I knew early on to not let him set the tone for me in terms of what a good man was, he didn't deserve that honour.

It's sad but true that throughout my younger/formative years, with some exceptions, most men in my life had either used, abused, and confused me, including him. When my mother died, it became toxic and self-destructive for me to continue maintaining a relationship with him, ultimately cutting all ties. When he passed three years later, I didn't even know or attend the funeral. When I heard the news, as terrible as it sounds, it felt like a weight had been lifted from my shoulders and my healing could finally begin. And I did heal through doing the work and extending forgiveness, not for him but for me.

MASTER
OF SINGLE

And that's all I'm going to say because it's not about him, I just wanted to give some context as well as to share knowing that I'm not the only girl who didn't have a respectable, healthy male role model or father figure growing up.

To let those girls know that you don't need to have had the father of the year to go on to choose a good man. You're not a victim of your experiences, it's just part of your story and most importantly your past does not have to show up in your future.

Like I said, I was an old soul and wise beyond my years.

Meanwhile, back in Vegas, I didn't have any expectations besides having a great time while making new memories, and I'm happy I didn't because I don't think our collective connection would have been as natural or as special had it been calculated.

Now I bet you're wondering how it all plays out… Well, beloveds, this is the one story where you'll just have to continue to wonder. Not often but sometimes when it's extra special: what happens in Vegas must stay in Vegas.

But don't worry, there's much more to come (literally)—from here on, I'm spilling all the sexy single tea.

But I will say this—and you can draw whatever conclusion you'd like—I chose the experience over my fear, and that weekend I blossomed from an unmastered, insecure girl to feeling like a real woman for the first time in my life.

As the trip wound down much to our dismay, our cool crew had one last blaze of glory. Then before we knew it, we were back on the jet headed home. You've got to love that private jet life and single-girl twenties. But even more, you got to love those once-in-a-lifetime experiences that bond a sisterhood and shape who you are. Amen!

On the way home, we all started to grapple with the reality of what we were going back to—no job and challenging times ahead—but there were no regrets. I was a lot of things after that trip, least of all worried for any of us.

We brought that same inspired energy home, knowing that we weren't meant to live the nine-to-five grind, revealing our true essence that we were more creatives than corporates but still all business. Wasting no time before putting on our creative caps, we started designing our future the way we wanted to live.

Tapping into our inner artist a few of us went on to create the first all-female event production company in Montreal called NESS Productions, with each letter representing our names.

Liz had her own plans to pursue, so she wasn't part of the company, but we supported each other's new ventures. For us this wasn't just a company, it was who we became;

Nicole, Marie **E**ve, **S**tephanie, **S**ophie = NESS Productions.

It was the beginning of the rest of our lives, and what a ride it was. We led the way in event production, throwing elaborate and amazing themed parties that brought a new attitude to going out.

Our other sister Patricia, who wasn't with us in Vegas, joined us later to become the company's official photographer, and incredibly enough, she's been documenting our lives in photographs ever since—twenty-plus years and counting. How awesome is that!

We called our launch party the Virgin Party, and we dominated the city, no apologies given.

It took place at Union Café in Old Montreal, a beautiful venue, but in true NESS style, we totally revamped it,

MASTER OF SINGLE

adding white flowing drapes everywhere. We had a cellist, sick DJ, magicians, and circus performers. Everybody in the city wanted to be there. Funny how things happen... I went from faking my way into the party of the year to throwing the hottest party. Full circle much.

But the real kicker was the return cameo from Mr. Hollywood, who was in town shooting a movie and surprisingly reached out to me again. Of course, I invited him to our launch, not thinking he would accept. But if I'd learned anything from our host, it was that you must go for what you want in this life, because nobody is just going to hand it to you. So I asked. Nobody was more shocked than me when he said, "Yeah, maybe I'll pass by."

And then he did! Imagine my surprise when he rolled up—no security, nothing, just his driver waiting in the car outside. He walked through the front door, moving through the crowd, eventually stopping to ask somebody for me, like he was an average Joe. Yeah, not so much.

But I must say, I quite respected his humbleness. Even in the wake of a mob of adoring fans, he was cool as a popsicle on a hot day. I remember one of my partners rushing towards me and screaming, "Oh my God, he's here!" The crowd went wild; they couldn't believe this mega superstar was at our event, and quite frankly, neither could we.

The party was already a huge success. The crowd and vibe were awe inspiring, but him showing up pushed it over the edge of next-level amazing! I mean, the cellist was great, but this went beyond validating us and solidifying our place in the industry.

Give us an inch, and we'll take over the damn city.

Girl power one hundred. Crown on. Drop mic.

When I finally made my way over to him to thank him for coming, he was modest and kind. He complimented the event and asked me if it was successful to our vision. In one sentence he'd said more than he did the entire time at dinner a few weeks earlier. Mind you, at that dinner there was so much going on I'm sure I wasn't as engaging as I could have been either. I own my part in that whole awkward situation. But on this night, I was just happy to see him and grateful that he showed up to support our event.

As for our lovely Vegas host, who unfortunately was out of town that night, we all stayed connected, becoming like a family over the years. Who says you can't choose your family? I've done it three times already. Proving love always wins.

The many good times and years that followed, he lovingly referred to us as "the girls." Whenever there was a party or fun vacation, he'd be sure "the girls" were included and by his side, and we happily showed up every time to have a great time.

We represented him to the finest capital *T*, and he exposed us to experiences and parts of the world I didn't even know existed and levels of luxury I only saw in movies. Bouncing from villa to mansion and catamaran to yacht, styling on the private jet and hitting up the hottest parties (mostly his) around the globe, there was no better time to be young, single, and me.

Fast forward twenty years later, he's still one of the most beloved and adored people in my life. Although our lives have changed, I'm not crashing parties or quitting jobs to avoid missing the next big event. In his own way, he's always been a huge supporter of my journey. He believed in me—he told me so—and that meant the world to me. I always kept his words close to my chest; they were rare and special accolades that often motivated me to keep going, knowing I didn't want to let him down.

MASTER OF SINGLE

I'm not sure to what extent he knows how much of a role he played in shifting my life in a new direction and helping me to see it with fresh eyes. I never really sat him down to tell him. But I hope that I've shown him with my actions and how I've lived my life with integrity, honour, and constantly going after my dreams.

If I had to give a message to my younger self, I'd tell her what happened to you was not your fault. That you are special and have so much to offer. To learn to trust the universe sooner. That you did the right thing, crashing the party and quitting that job. You're doing great. Trust the process, because honey, your life has so many blessings in store for you, you couldn't even imagine. And no matter what, never doubt that you are light and love.

You matter, and what you have to offer matters too.

The end... Every end is a new beginning... Chapter two... I see you.

Chapter Two

I Do But I Can't

OKAY, SO YOU'RE single or single again… here's the tea. Don't take more time than you need getting over someone who doesn't recognize your worth. Nobody deserves that much of your power.

That's why this chapter is about taking your power back and being the star of your own life.

I know all too well that the struggle of a broken heart or dashed dream is real, but let's remember that single is your relationship status, not your identity, and it can also mean being in a relationship with yourself. I'm going to repeat that as often as needed to keep reminding you; if you're in relationship with yourself, you are never alone.

It's remarkable to me how developing that side has brought me to discover this place of serenity like living in a constant state of meditation, knowing I'm good with me.

The kind of relationship you have with yourself is not a precursor to your future romantic relationships, but it is indicative of the type of relationship you're likely to find yourself in.

This includes lovers and friendships.

Relationships are not guaranteed; it's the chance we take in love to put ourselves out there, but that doesn't always mean you've given your heart to the right person. Knowingly or not, we mirror back to the world what we believe we deserve. If you think you deserve less than your worth, then that's what will show up in your life in terms of relationships, personal goals, friends, and dreams.

On the other hand, knowing your value and owning it without apology is your right, and may no relationship or person take that away from you. This is not to be mistaken for arrogance; it's often the way we assume our power that defines that thin line. I want each of you to think about what it would look like if you made yourself the star of your life. What would change and what would you be doing? How would it feel and how would you be of service?

Envision it, then write the script, cast the players, and give yourself the leading role.

Be specific. Make your intentions crystalized, then surrender it, knowing the universe is there to catch it and meet you where you are. It's true that you get out of life what you put into it, so go for it and dream big.

My goal in saying this is to give you a new paradigm to put things into a different perspective. Whether you use it or not is up to you. But better to have the tools and not need it than to need it and not have it, right?

That said, the casting process for your lifetime movie can be a tedious one. Ask any actor and they'll tell you that the worst part before the best part, which is landing the role, is the audition process.

I've auditioned up to five times before getting the part, which only goes to show that even those casting sometimes don't know what they're looking for until it's standing right in front of them. So, stay open to giving people a chance. When it comes to love, trust that the role will be cast when the right person walks into the room, and you will know it before they even say their first line.

Equally, however, be prepared to see a lot of noes before finally finding one yes.

But what happens when your dreams don't work out and everything you've imagined for yourself falls through? Whether it be in love, personal, or professional? That can be a devastating thing to contend with.

When I turned thirty, I was going through it—from a life-shattering break-up, incredible heartache, and feeling like a hot mess—it was not my most shining milestone moment. For a lot of women, turning thirty is a huge transition in their lives. When things are going well and you have a plan and vision for your life, it can be great.

But if that plan doesn't work out and you find yourself directionless and are single, that's when it can be scary as hell, as you'll soon read.

The good thing about getting older is the wisdom we gain through lived experiences, but that doesn't always make it easier. No matter how much we know, a broken heart still hurts, and bouncing back from shattered dreams doesn't have as much spring in it as it once did.

Regardless of how much time passes after a painful break-up, the reality of being single again especially at a certain age can be a real mind fuck, when you realize "Damn. I'm single and not in a good way."

It's possible that without warning, this can trigger a landslide of feelings that you never even knew were there, leaving you to deal with a mixed bag of often messy emotions. I'm here to remind you that if you ever find yourself in that situation, you're going to be okay. You're only human, and sometimes we fall into the deep end, but it forces us to swim back to shore and save ourselves, and that's where you can start to rebuild.

As self-proclaimed master of single, I know that mastering one's single life isn't a perfect science, and thank goodness it isn't. The lessons presented to us on our single journey if we choose to accept them can pay in dividends going forward.

However, it's not always easy getting back to a good positive place, particularly after a difficult break-up. It takes work and it can suck, just plain old suck, before it gets better.

But hey, what sucks up must come down, or at least that's what he said. Ha ha!

Heartache, feeling lonely, and being concerned about your love life and future are real things, and no matter how good you are with yourself, sometimes even that isn't enough to trump the waves of sadness that come with a broken heart or disillusioned dream.

Beloved, beware—these feelings can catch you off guard and be triggered by occasions like Valentine's Day or your birthday. Maybe you're invited to a wedding and are the only person in your group without a "plus one." Or the big trigger, New Year's Eve, and standing alone without anyone to kiss among a sea of people in love. It can also be something as simple as walking by that favourite restaurant you and your ex once loved that opens a floodgate of emotions you weren't expecting. There's not always a rhyme or reason, which is why we call them triggers.

MASTER OF SINGLE

This is a good time to remember it's not what happens but how we deal with it that matters—another nugget of Mama's wisdom, one that's served me well on my journey.

Those icky feelings or emotions may include sadness, pity, confusion, loss of confidence, loneliness, anger, resentment, or all the above. But here's the secret—being honest and brave enough to sit with those emotions, hate them, love them, learn, and grow from them is the gift you give yourself. Being real about what you're feeling will only help shift you out of the dark place back to the light.

It's so important to face those scary emotions head-on to rebuild your self-confidence, self-worth, and give yourself the best chance of success.

Knowing full well in those moments of free fall, finding peace of mind can be easier said than done, but do your best to remember this: whatever you're experiencing is just one of the many moments in the many changing seasons of your life.

Much like when you feel nauseated and there's nothing you can do but be still and let it pass, rest assured that what you're experiencing is normal, and it shall pass.

I can hear you thinking *Is it really that simple to stop the noise in our head that clouds our better judgement and dampens our spirit and ability to make good decisions?* The answer is yes, it is that simple. This is your power of choice, so choose to connect to your power and use that power wisely.

Another thing to be aware of is something called "monkey mind," a lesson I learned from one of my greatest teachers, Eliane aka Ely aka Ms. Ely, a brilliant artist with an incredibly developed soul awareness and spirit about her. She taught me that the monkey mind is not reality. It's when we get stuck in our head or feelings, and emotions are jumping all over the place but nothing is grounded or clear. It's a toxic mindset that can have you spinning out of body and acting out of character, even thinking or doing crazy things.

Here's an example: Say you're broken-hearted and already feeling fragile with your self-worth at an all-time low. You start questioning everything about your life and have a sudden spurt of irrational behaviour i.e., the monkey mind.

Suddenly you pick a fight with a friend for no reason or hook up with a guy for the wrong reasons. Even worse, imagine cutting off your beautiful locks out of spite, thinking that if you cut your hair, you'll cut away the pain and have a fresh start. Wrong! Then you regret it every day of every month until it grows back. It's one thing to want a fresh start; it's another to do it because you're not thinking clearly.

Another common mistake is masking your painful emotions with food, work, alcohol, or drugs to the extent that you dig a hole so deep you lose yourself. No shame—I'll be the first to say that—I'm guilty of most of the above.

If nobody ever told you, you are better than any of those dead-end options, but there are times in those moments of panic that we just can't pull ourselves out to see beyond the struggle.

But here's the good news—you are stronger than you think.

Any problem or, as they say in Jamaica, any situation whether good, bad, ugly, or a mix of it all is meant to help us grow, enlighten us, and give us the opportunity to learn from. If we don't ever fall, how will we learn to get back up? If we don't experience sadness, how will we know true happiness?

Amid these temporary moments of alarm, remember that breath is your friend.

MASTER
OF SINGLE

I like to call this part of the process our "single growing pains," which loosely translated means you're growing through it and you're doing great.

It may not feel like it at first, but in my experience, moving through while purging and letting go of the toxic emotions that no longer served me has also saved me and ultimately freed me to become stronger.

When you find yourself ruled by your emotions, I strongly suggest consulting someone you trust before making any major or rash decisions. It may not stop you from acting the fool, but it might at least give you a chance to rethink doing something you may regret later.

A dear friend, a wise man, and a Nobel Prize winner, once said to me, "Whatever you do, do not freak out." It's a lesson I took to heart, and I learned how not to freak out when freaking out is knocking at my door. If you can't do that, at least remember this: if you wake up with breath in your body and will in your heart, then you are #tooblessedtostress.

Find one thing that you're grateful for and stay with that moment. Say it out loud: I'm thankful for my health, for cute puppies, a sunny day, my family, friends, cupcakes with sprinkles, my job, or whatever you're grateful for. Crystalize it, which means to really see, feel, and believe it. Eventually you'll feel your energy shift. It's a mild physical transformation, but before you know it, you'll feel more connected to yourself.

Calling on the power of prayer always helps to lift my spirits and give me strength. Aligned with my spiritual core, depth of positivity and faith have gotten me through my darkest days, but it's important to know what works for you.

Maybe it's meditation or yoga or a boxing class to help

relieve the frustrations or blasting your favourite song and dancing like nobody or everyone's watching. Doesn't matter. Whatever it is, if it will help make you feel better and shifts your energy, do that.

I would be remiss not to add the best proven medicine in difficult times, hands down, has been the support of my girlfriends. Always there with an empathic ear, a bottle of wine, and unwavering love and support. It's important to let our friends be there for us.

Another effective tool I discovered is a technique called tapping. It has helped me immensely during trying times, especially in rebalancing and recentring my energy. The technique of tapping, or EFT (Emotional Freedom Techniques), is a combination of ancient Chinese acupuncture and modern thinking, and it works by altering your brain energy, body, and overall system at the same time. It's kind of like shaking up your insides to recalibrate your energy.

When I'm feeling frazzled or in a downwards emotional spiral or stressed out, tapping helps bring me back to being in my body and almost instantly relieves my anxiety. It's special and quite cool, and the best part is that you can literally do it anywhere. Oh, and it's free. Boom. Healing in the palm of your hands, now that's personal power at its best. If you'd like to learn more, check out thetappingsolution.com.

However, there are bound to be times when all the tapping, yoga, or other calming techniques in the world won't take away the pain, and that's okay too. It's okay to not be okay. It's healthy to admit you're not doing well rather than hold it in and suffer in silence, which can lead to all kinds of pent-up issues and emotional blocks.

Again, let that shit out, kind of like when you were little and had the sniffles. Your mom would make you blow your nose or cough up the phlegm to get it out of your body. Same endgame, different circumstances.

If all else fails, there is one final outlet you can turn to. It's not my favourite suggestion, but if you need it, there's always something called the pity party. This is a window of time in which you're free to lose all sense of reality, a no-judgement zone that allows you time to feel all the feels about whatever's going on. Go ahead and eat a whole bag of cookies while wearing that tear-stained T-shirt or the same PJs you've been living in for the past forty-eight hours while sitting in dim lighting, curtains closed, curled up on your couch. If that's what it's going to take to move you forward, fine, but on one condition—that you know this is a small and short-lived window.

Depending on the level of the heartache, a pity party can last anywhere from fifteen minutes to an entire night and sometimes bleed into the next day.

Under dire circumstances, it could be a whole weekend situation, but that should really be the cut-off point. Any more than three days and you start to fall into victim mode, and that's never a good look. Remember, nobody deserves that much of your power. Ever!

Besides, what are you, a masochist?

Even though it's technically your "party," never overstay your welcome.

Important! During this lapse of time, avoid at all costs stalking your ex's social media accounts, because let's face it, you're bound to find something that will push you over the edge. Whatever you do, do not pull out the photo albums and reminisce about your last best relationship when you were happy and in love. In fact, get rid of all memories that may come back to bite you in your ass. And for God's sake, please spare yourself the trip down the blame lane riddled with could have, would have, should have. Never *should* on yourself. Abort immediately!

Remind yourself that you are worth more than what you weren't getting in your last relationship. More importantly—let me repeat this again—it's not your loss if someone didn't recognize your worth. You have everything you need to be strong and complete on your own.

Don't you feel better and stronger already? I know I do.

Here's another tip: When hitting the restart button and finally stepping back out there, when you get dressed, do so with intention and mean it. Slip into your favourite jeans, tee, and a hot pair of heels, or that gorgeous dress you bought and never had any place to wear it, and put it on proudly. We're calling this your rebirth moment. My rule of thumb when it comes to dressing up is that you can never be too overdressed; worst-case scenario, you'll be the best-dressed person in the room, and nobody can be mad at that.

Drape yourself in what makes you feel beautiful and powerful, because when we look good, we feel good, and when we operate from a place of feeling good, life is good.

And that includes the things that people don't see. Taking that extra time to wear undergarments that make you feel good is like a secret weapon; the little things matter, and your joy is in your hands.

Remember, the love is in the intention; the reward is in the feeling.

Finally, when I'm feeling down, shifting my focus off myself and doing something to help someone else always helps change my energy in a positive way. Paying it forward with a simple action or gesture gets me out of my head and back into my heart. It's a beautiful thing.

And now for this next story, which I'll preface with it was one of the tougher stories to write and relive.

MASTER OF SINGLE

So here goes everything…

That's what friends are for is the best way to introduce this chapter, a journey through my perfectly imperfect lens, a human being with faults, cracks, dents, even a couple of fractures, but not broken. The life tools and knowledge I've acquired over the years are also the glue that has held me together in moments of unravel. But there have been times when the glue wouldn't stick and my toolbox was empty. This story represents that moment on my sometimes-rocky journey to becoming master of single.

In truth, I feel a little nauseated, revisiting this story. After it happened, I quickly took the lesson and the hidden blessings and promptly put the rest out of my mind. Writing about it brings me back to a time I'm not proud of when I felt scared, sad, heartbroken, and totally lost.

Why include it? Because I practice what I preach in that facing uncomfortable emotions can be our greatest teacher, and I am stronger than I think.

This story was a time of great transition, growth, and learning through the good and bad. Besides, if I didn't include the hard stories, then you're not getting the whole truth, and you deserve the truth.

Once upon a time, I was vulnerable, and the suitor in this story was tenacious, creating the perfect storm. Remember that superstar dinner in chapter one where among the guests around the table sat my future ex-fiancé? Well, voilà! That's the precursor to this next story.

My bestie Stephanie introduced us and was good friends with both of us. From her purest heart she played matchmaker, thinking we'd make a good couple. As it turned out, she was right. He and I became fast friends.

The downfall was that we both came into the relationship with a lot of personal baggage, which is why I stress the importance of doing your personal work before committing to another person. You don't want to bring your past trauma into a new beginning.

One after-hours party later at club Stereo, we were having a great night, laughing, dancing, and just enjoying each other's company. At some point in the conversation, our eyes met, but this time it was different, and something beyond friendship clicked. Neither of us questioned it; we just went for it, and the rest is history… or, in this case, chapter two.

That night, we went back to his place, had sex, and I never looked back.

It was passionate, and a great night that felt right. I felt happy and safe with him and fell fast and hard in love.

From the beginning, I admired him. He represented everything I imagined my man should be at that time. He was half Italian, and Lord knows I loved me some Italian men, but he was more than that. He was assertive, adventurous, funny, kind, and successful in his own right. He was a leader, provider, and lover who treated me like his queen. At one time, he was the man I imagined would be my happily-ever-after. I could even envision what our children would look like.

Fast forward five years later and, of course, I said yes when he asked me to marry him.

Unfortunately, over the course of those years, our relationship had changed, and although I knew we weren't in the best place when he proposed, I was so in love, and that was all that mattered.

So you can imagine how heart-shattering it was when it all came crashing down. When I say I know heartbreak, trust me, I know heartbreak. From the beginning, the relationship was all consuming and heavily co-dependent, and by the time we were seven years in, we were beyond repair. As much as I wished and wanted him to be my fairy-tale ending, our broken just couldn't be fixed. When I finally found the courage to leave him, which was a battle of its own, I barely had a leg to stand on.

Let me explain what happened. Throughout the relationship, I was the co-pilot to his life, but I want to be clear that I don't blame him for what happened. It takes two to rumble, and I take my responsibility as an equal player in the demise of our relationship. That said, just by way of his strong personality, he did drive most of the relationship, and I spent a lot of time fighting to be heard because I wasn't equipped emotionally or spiritually to express myself.

When we first met, I was still quite impressionable and getting to know myself. At the time, the girls were a few months into working on NESS Productions, but the unrealistic pressure he put on me and the company created a lot of tension in our relationship.

In the beginning, we were doing it all, performing, creating decor, booking gigs, and transforming clubs into themed events. Like any new business, we weren't making a lot of money at first, and it consumed a lot of our time. Nothing about that worked for him, and we argued relentlessly until eventually I gave in and walked away from my own company.

It was devastating not just for me but for the girls and the company too.

At that point I hadn't acquired many possessions or financial security, and what I did have he replaced with his bigger and better versions. I remember coming home one day to find some of my clothing in the garbage outside our front door. I was confused, so when I got inside, I asked him, "Babe, are those my clothes in the garbage?"

"Yeah," he replied. "I threw them out. There's new stuff upstairs on the bed." I didn't quite understand his motive. Why would he do something like that? It was very hurtful.

Under different circumstances, any girl would love to come home to new designer outfits laid out on her bed by the man she loves. But these were not those circumstances. His actions made me feel a certain kind of way. Already struggling with my own self-worth, that only compounded it, making me feel like I wasn't good enough, which was a major trigger for me.

I still hadn't found my voice in the relationship, and when I felt certain emotional triggers that brought up hurtful emotions, I would shut down and not say anything, much like I did that time.

I'll never forget him saying, "You don't think I'm going to wear Armani (high end) and you're going to wear Le Château (low end)?" I'm sure he thought he was saying something logical and was being generous, but his actions hurt me to the core. I just stood there, suffering in silence and unable to express my frustration. The fear of speaking my truth kept me silent. I just went with it, which is what I did for most of our relationship.

I wouldn't say he was wealthy, but we lived quite well; he was the provider and held the financial control. I played the part of the lady of the house, taking care of everything and everyone, hosting people, and almost every day someone would come over. Only years later I was able to look back and see the signs of dysfunction that I ignored because of my blind love.

He put a ring on it, and it was a whopper of a ring at that. A stunning two-and-a-half carat diamond ring with the most gorgeous pressure setting and set on a wide rounded platinum band, designed by him just for me. He loved showing it off, maybe even more than I enjoyed

MASTER OF SINGLE

wearing it. It was a killer ring, unique and special, just like me. I loved it, and I loved him for caring enough to design it for me. He gets props for his impeccable taste; he always loved the finer things, and I did learn a lot from him even if some of the lessons came the hard way. He opened my eyes to understanding my personal style and showing me a high-end living as a lifestyle, so yeah, it wasn't all bad.

I loved saying the word "fiancé." I'll always remember those times fondly. It was the first and the last time I ever had the honour of calling anyone my fiancé. It makes me kind of sad to think about it, but hey, what's a girl to do besides be grateful for the experience and having known true love?

I came to enjoy the spoils and lifestyle that his money provided for us. When we first met, I was bartending, but I barely worked. He wasn't fond of me working in certain environments, and I didn't argue. I picked my battles; besides, the alternative wasn't bad. We spent a lot of time travelling; we lived in a beautiful home, wore nice clothes, ate the finest foods, and had lots of fun overall.

I'd succumb to giving him a lot of my power because at the time I felt the life he was offering was better than any life I could have imagined on my own. Looking back, I can see how I let myself feel inferior, and that had nothing to do with him; that was all me. Lesson got.

There's no question in my mind that despite our dysfunction, we shared a special love, and to our credit, I believe we loved each other the best way we knew how. I can't fault either of us for what we didn't know, and I won't speak for him, but I can say with clear certainty that he was the love of my life. Unfortunately, our two broken halves couldn't quite make a complete whole, and that would be our downfall.

At some point, we became known for being the party couple, hosting friends in our beautiful home that we'd transformed from his single, ground-level bachelor pad to a super fly, two-story home designed to fit our social lifestyle. By all accounts, it was the ultimate party house with two bedrooms upstairs and partying downstairs.

On the lower level there was a state-of-the-art surround sound system, a high-tech custom-made DJ booth, a massive flat-screen television, blackout curtains, and yes, a dance floor accompanied by a disco ball hanging in the middle of the room. He even had a urinal installed off the main bathroom, which was a hit with his guy friends, not so much with me when it came to cleaning it. Gross.

Even before me, he loved partying and being the person to show people a good time, whether it was hosting, cooking, entertaining, or travelling. He relished in introducing people to new flavours, music, fashion, and art, et cetera.

But when drugs were introduced into the mix, it became a slippery slope for our already fragile relationship. The first time I ever tried cocaine was with him. Again, my choice and not his fault. It was also when I discovered I had an addictive personality, which meant, to my detriment, I liked it.

Most gatherings culminated with our guests partying the night away, sometimes into the next day. A total disaster from the start.

I quickly learned how to handle my alcohol and substance intake like a professional partier, and that was a huge red flag. We became so co-dependent that when we got high, we'd feed off each other, which propelled us to become masters of debauchery. When our guests would leave, our private party would begin. We'd engage in hours and hours of intense sex and drug-induced passion.

It's common for guys to not be able to "get it up" when

they do blow (street name for cocaine), but he had no problem getting activated, and I was right there by his side, ready, able, and willing to satisfy the moment. Which often surprised both of us how my little 125 lb. frame verses his strong 225 lb. body was able to sustain, but I did, line for line and fuck for fuck.

It was impressive in all the wrong ways.

It's incredibly difficult, if not impossible, to maintain any sort of healthy and balanced relationship when you're always recovering from the night before. By the time we'd get back to somewhat "normal" function, the weekend would always come too fast, and the cycle would repeat itself again. It was a vicious loop that was quickly taking its toll.

To the outside world, we projected a life that looked fun and exciting, and a lot of it was, but privately, we were a hot mess. A mess I was too embarrassed to admit to and too afraid to let go of. As time pressed on, I felt myself wanting things to change. I was no longer able to live in the dysfunction, but we were in so deep it was hard to undo.

The real turning point for me occurred while visiting my mom. She didn't know what was going on in my relationship, but moms always know when something's off with their kid. She looked at me and said, "I don't recognize you anymore." I felt my heart drop.

She could see me, which made me see myself, and my reality scared me.

That's when I started to work on myself to understand certain behaviours and patterns, hoping that if I changed, it would motivate him to change as well. Wishful thinking and a huge lesson for me in that you can't get someone to change a problem they don't see.

The more I evolved and grew as a person, wanting to carve out my own identity, he'd find ways to stunt my growth. I didn't want to believe it at first. I mean, if he loved me, shouldn't he want me to be happy and grow to become a better person? Shouldn't the person you love inspire you to be your best self? He would do subtle and not-so-subtle things; for example, if I began to show strength or personal growth in any area of my life, he would barely acknowledge it, or he'd push it to the side with a nonchalant "Yeah, cool."

He struggled to be supportive and truly happy for me. I looked to him for encouragement, and what I got was discouragement. His indifference flattened my confidence and changed the way I looked at him and myself. Painful.

By that time, I knew three things: one, I had a lot of growing to do; two, if our relationship was going to have any chance of surviving, we both would have to want to change and evolve together; and three, if the first two didn't happen, I couldn't marry him. It was a heartbreaking reality, but it was the reality we were in. I so badly wanted to believe our love would somehow make it through.

I think the idea of change scared him because he was a man set in his ways. Maybe he thought I'd outgrow him and our relationship, which he was probably right about, or that he'd end up losing control of me—right again. And I think in his mind maybe that meant also losing me too. But the truth was, I loved him so much and so deeply all I wanted was to give us a fighting chance to change for the better, together as a couple.

He had all the power in his hands to keep me and us together, but he just couldn't get out of his own way to give himself the chance to consider the idea of change. He was unable to meet me where I was, and I could no longer stay where he was. That's the moment my truth became clear, and once you know the truth, you can't pretend that you don't. Well, you can, but it's excruciating. In the end, my evolution became our relationship's kryptonite, but in the same breath, it was also my saviour.

Our broken dynamic went on for quite a while with no real hope for change. Eventually the day came when my spirit couldn't take it anymore, and I felt like I couldn't breathe one more toxic breath. I knew that if I was going to have a chance at becoming my authentic self, free to see just how great I could be and grow to become the person I was meant to be, I would have to leave him and the life we'd created together. By the end, things had become unbearable. Neither of us was happy. I wanted to tell him "I do love you, but I can't go on like this." I just didn't know how to get out, and he didn't know how to let me go.

He'd tell me that he didn't want us to break up, but inside I couldn't help but wonder if maybe it was his ego speaking, because his actions didn't show it. He wasn't a person who handled losing well or looking weak very well. I felt the thought of losing me after everything he had "invested" (his words, not mine) in me was more than his ego could take both personally and publicly.

So there we were, caught in this gridlock… that's how co-dependent we were. No longer able to live together but not sure how to live without each other. We argued non-stop, saying things we could never take back. But despite it all, he still wouldn't let me go, and he didn't make it easy for me to leave.

I was scared and felt stuck; I had no money, I was embarrassed to reach out to anyone, and I was terrified to lose the man I'd loved for seven years.

Things took another sharp downwards turn when he started to use my vulnerabilities against me, threatening me with anything he knew would hurt me. In retaliation, I would mirror his vile behaviour back to him, accusing him of being just like his father, which I knew was his hot button and very hurtful due to the volatile nature of their relationship.

I was in survival mode, but I hated myself for stooping so low with the sole intention to hurt him back. This situation was bringing out the worst in me. We were in full-on Wars of the Roses, and trust and believe that if I go to war, I'm fighting to win, so if you come for me, I'm coming right back for you. There's a warrior living inside me, and back then it would come out when I felt attacked or I needed to defend myself, but it wasn't pretty.

I was fighting a hopeless battle. I would later learn how to harness that energy to become a more peaceful warrior and learned to fight to be understood, not to win.

I continued to try to reason with him, but he resisted any logic or understanding, unwilling to see the toxicity of our relationship and how it was destroying us. What I know now that I didn't know then is that if I'm not happy with myself, I can't make anyone else happy. And in that moment, I knew I wasn't happy. That was my first honest aha moment with myself, realizing I had real work to do to begin to understand my own happiness. By that point, I wasn't worried about being single, I just wanted to be happy.

Like the flick of a switch, my work became clear, and the rest is the journey that set sail many an argument and lesson learned. But while some things were becoming clear, other things were starting to spiral even further down a path of uncertainty. One too many volatile arguments and sleepless nights in the guest room, knowing in my heart it was over and that my exit would be a difficult and painful one.

MASTER OF SINGLE

The final straw was an explosive last and vicious argument. Knowing I was one foot out the door and quickly building the courage to take the second step, he realized that he was out of cards to play, so he went for the jugular. He came at me in the most cruel and spiteful way by turning my adoption against me. It was the most hurtful thing anyone has ever said to me.

He knew very well that my mom was my hero and that she had raised me to understand that family isn't just who brings you into the world but who shows you love.

And if you ever come for my mom or my adoption, then you better prepare to die.

Depending on your experience, being adopted can really mess you up as an adult, leaving lasting scars on your self-worth, identity, and overall spirit. I was fortunate to have a mother who guided me through it and never made me feel anything but loved. Because of her support, I was able to rise above and become a well-adjusted adult, and I'm very proud of that. He knew that was the one place you just don't go.

In his verbal diarrhea rant, he proclaimed that my being adopted is what messed us up, that all our issues stemmed from that and not from his controlling ways or our co-dependent toxic relationship. He went on to say that if I fixed my issues about being adopted, we wouldn't have any problems. Are you fucking kidding me? Ha!

I fully admit that being adopted affected me and governed the way I did certain things in my life, but even if his comment had some semblance of truth or merit, which it didn't, his intention to use it to cut me to my core was unbelievably ugly, unforgivable, and the ultimate deal breaker. Shame on him.

There was no way he could come back from that and no way I could ever unhear it. I didn't care anymore about the idea of losing "us." All I wanted was to figure my way out. So when I saw my opportunity, even though it wasn't pretty, I took it.

It would be a tricky exit left because we were always together, and during this turbulent time, he was keeping even closer tabs on me. One afternoon while he was picking up a friend at the airport, I knew it was my chance to leave. I didn't have an exact plan; in fact, I didn't have any plan at all. I just knew I had to seize the small window of opportunity to get out.

I immediately called the first person I trusted and who knew of our hardships—my sister Stephanie who, like I said, was a friend to both of us, but on that day she showed up for me, her sister, who was drowning. That's what sisters do; they come to the rescue like an angel from the heavens. No questions, no judgement, she was just there when I needed her the most.

She arrived at our house to meet a frantic version of myself, rattling off a quick overview of what was going on. Knowing I had a limited amount of time, I gathered a few things, threw them in a couple of garbage bags, grabbed my doggie Asia (a caramel-coloured butterfly Chihuahua mixed breed). Other than that, I left most of my possessions behind, but none of that seemed to matter. All I wanted was to get out with my spirit still somewhat intact.

In case you're wondering… yes, I did leave the ring behind because it was the right thing to do.

I thought about keeping it. It was a gorgeous ring, but I knew he'd never leave me alone if I left with it. Losing me was enough, at least let him keep his ring.

Besides, all I wanted was a clean break.

We loaded her minivan as quickly as we could and drove off. And to this day, I never looked back, except to see how

MASTER
OF SINGLE

far I've come. My head was spinning. I was scared, anxious, and terrified of what he'd do when he realized I was gone, but I was also grateful to be free. I loved him, and I felt badly about leaving in such an abrupt and shady way, but given my options, it was the lesser of two evils.

I prayed that one day he would be able to forgive me, but in my heart, I didn't regret my choice to leave.

It took him years to even acknowledge me after that. Ouch.

If I could say anything to him today, it would be that I forgive us, and I wish him the love that he deserves.

Fast forward a few days. I'm couch surfing from friend to friend, no clue where to start my rebuilding process. It was the first time I would be on my own in a long time after being solely dependent on him and his support.

Then one day, post-break-up and halfway to a depression, the heavens sent me a gift—enter Judy. I'll never forget that fateful day; I was sitting on the corner of Guy and Sherbrooke Streets, bawling my eyes out with my head hanging low and tears cascading into my coffee. My phone rang, and it was Judy. Barely able to breathe, let alone speak through the sobs, I answered. Somehow I managed to say enough for her to drop her life and come to pick me up. The amazing thing (besides everything about her) was that at the time we were new friends, still getting to know each other. But despite the newness of our friendship, she opened her heart and ultimately her home, inviting me to live with her until I figured out my next step.

How incredibly generous of her.

On that day, we went from new friends to roommates to fast-progressing best friends to sisters living in her cozy and charming one-bedroom apartment. It's no wonder that I hold my sisterhoods so close to my heart; my sisters are my pillars of strength. They raise me up to make me a better, stronger woman, and I will love them forever, forgive them always, and judge them never.

Fast forward years later, today Judy and I share godmother responsibilities to our respective doggies and cousins Princess Dior and little big man Wolfgang.

Living together was great from the get-go; we got along like two peas in a pod. She cared for me, nursing me back to strength and mental health. She provided me with a safe and stable place to collect my thoughts, giving me a much-needed sense of security that allowed me the time to take a breath and start to get clear about my life.

As great as that was, I was far from being emotionally okay, but that would have to wait. I didn't have time to sit in my pity party. My first order of business was to get on my feet, and to do that my broke ass needed a J-O-B to start to secure them bags (i.e. money). I ended up turning to my fallback, good ol' bartending. The saving grace of it all was that because I was willing to put in the effort to help myself, the universe met me where I was and provided me with what I needed to keep moving forward. The universe is wise and all-knowing, which is why I say it's one of our greatest allies.

I found work quickly and landed a job at an ubertrendy number-one Montreal hotspot of the moment, Ristorante Cavalli in the heart of downtown.

As I struggled to push through my heartbreak, working hard to keep my focus on building my new path and bank account, I felt empty on the inside, like I was just moving to keep moving so as to not feel the pain I was in. But one can only shove pain down for so long. Then one day all those matters of the heart I'd been avoiding came bubbling up like a tsunami of emotions. All directed at myself, my ex, our failed relationship, and the disgruntlement of it all.

MASTER
OF SINGLE

In the weeks that followed, I went through all the stages of a broken heart and scorned lover. I became angrier, bitter, and more resentful. I begrudged all the years and time I'd wasted, and I was pissed about having to start my life over at thirty years old. By now I thought I would have been married with a couple of kids running around the house.

But when my new reality came rushing in, I wasn't ready for it. I'd never experienced pain like that over losing a man I thought would be my forever person. Even though I knew why we couldn't be together, it didn't make it hurt any less.

I was afraid I would never find love again or that too much damage had been done and I would struggle to trust men. Would I ever have children? I questioned if maybe I'd made a mistake because inside, I still loved him. In this place of fear, I began to doubt my decision. Did I rush to judgement? In the same breath, I was so angry with him.

As the dust settled, I could sense that something had changed and hardened inside me. I looked at men differently. I had developed a type of armour towards them that I didn't have before. I vowed to myself to never let a man control me again or lose myself to a relationship.

Unfortunately, the next man at the heart of the second part of this story was in the eye of my emotional storm. He just didn't know it, and neither did I for that matter. Flashback to my earlier bartending days, I had a customer who quite fancied me. He was an older man, a successful exec-power-suit-lawyer type. He was handsome in a classic way and quite charming with his quiet nature and demeanour. When I stopped bartending, as per my then fiancé's request, I ultimately lost contact with all my customers.

Post-break-up and upon my return behind the bar, he and I became reunited and quickly picked up where we'd left off, professionally speaking. I remembered that he liked my dirty martinis, shaken not stirred, but as good as they were, it wasn't just about the tiny. He'd tell me that I was beautiful, exciting, fit, and sexy. He'd look at me with starry eyes as he complimented me, and he'd also say how he loved my quick wit and killer smile. All true things. Can't blame the man for having a keen eye and good taste.

There was something about our bartender/customer relationship that made me feel empowered, or maybe I was just looking for anything to validate me to myself, and I had him wrapped around my little finger.

It was a dark time; my mind was a mess, and it felt like a throwback to my dancing days when I saw men as objects to be used. His attempts to get closer to me were persistent, with every visit ending with an invitation to dinner. In the past, I'd always refused because I was in a relationship, and I'm not the type of girl to ever step out on my man. I take great pride in being able to say that I've never cheated on a boyfriend or my then fiancé. I also knew that he was married. In my world, married men (or guys in relationships) have always been off-limits. Period. It's just not in my moral DNA to go after another woman's man. If another woman came after my man, I'd cut a bitch down to the white meat. Come to think about it, I have, and she deserved it. Note: Don't ever come for my man. Shots fired.

But the lesson I was about to learn would be one that would test not only my morals but also my relationship with myself. To hide my pain and manage my emotions, I boasted a strong facade of being fine, leading with my tough-girl persona, but it was all a front. The truth was, I was a hot mess express coming through, and like a runaway train, I was about to hit a wall. So the next time he asked me out, not surprisingly, I found myself accepting.

MASTER OF SINGLE

Admittedly, I was not in a state of mind to be considering anyone else's feelings but my own, and I was acting purely from a self-serving place. I'm not proud of my actions or my decision; it's mortifying remembering how desperate I felt. Allowing my emotions to be so uncouth that they swayed my moral compass so far to the left that I could justify accepting a date with a married man, I knew it was below me.

From this place of disillusionment, combined with the resentful energy coursing through my veins from my break-up, I was so lost that I couldn't tell my ass from my elbow or my karma from dharma.

All I saw were dollar signs when I looked at him, and in my warped thinking, I was plotting ways to use his infatuation with me to my advantage. I guess you can take the girl out of the club, but there's always a little club left in the girl. I figured with the right combination of charm and suggestive flirting, I could get anything out of him.

Further justifying my crazy plan, I told myself that if I was going to break my hard rule of accepting a date with a married man, then he was going to make it worth my while and a dinner wasn't going to cut it.

Now hold on and pump your brakes. I know it sounds bad, like I'm about to pimp myself out, but it wasn't like that. Although I was dancing my own moral line, I knew in my heart that I wouldn't allow myself to cross it, and for me that line was anything physical.

Remember at the beginning of this chapter I wrote about feeling so desperate that it can lead you to make bad decisions? Well, clearly, I know of what I speak. There was no tapping or yoga or any breathing through it; not even the advice of my dearest friend could have effected change in my mind. I was on a mission, one for whatever reason I had to see through.

NICOLE JONES

Whatever happened, it would be my lesson to lose.

On the night of the big date, as I was getting ready, Judy was leaning on the side of the bathroom doorframe. She listened, mortified, as I explained how I was basically going to seduce this man into giving me money for my time. She tried masking the horror on her face and in her body language, looking at me the way you would a ten-car pileup. You don't want to stare, but it's so compelling you can't look away, and you just pray that nobody got hurt. God bless her heart, she really tried to talk me down off the cliff, but my mind was set; there was no turning back.

I put on my pretty pink strapless, ruffled dress, beat face on point (slang for makeup done).

I slipped on my kitty heels, and I was out the door, on my way to meet my death… I mean my date.

Our meeting place was a lounge/bar in Old Montreal, and for the entire cab ride there I felt nauseated. I had to keep taking deep breaths to not lose my nerve. I was the first to arrive, which gave me a chance to down a couple of cocktails that helped calm my nerves and gain the liquid courage I needed to focus and get my head in the game.

He finally arrived, happy to see me, and I was just tipsy enough to look like I was happy to see him too. We had a couple more drinks and chatted a bit. By now the mix of charged emotions and alcohol had me feeling no pain. Before I knew it, I was wasted, slurring my words and barely able to speak or make eye contact. And then came the moment of no return. Ready or not, I opened my mouth and spilled my tea.

Turning to him, I slurred some semblance of a sentence: "Ifffff you whant my time, you gonna to payy." Not surprisingly, he looked at me confused and slightly embarrassed for me. So of course I continued. "My time is waluable. Youuuu like me; if you wwwant me, you payy." Oh my God, what a disaster.

Sitting there looking a hot drunken mess and all out of sorts, an unravelled shell of my former self, remarkably I remember having a moment of clarity. *What the fuck am I doing?* In an instant, my delusional bubble burst like a balloon, and my brain exploded.

He could see that I wasn't in a good space. For goodness' sake, a blind person could see I wasn't in a good place. Before I could speak again, he gently and politely took my hand, pulled me in a little closer to stop me from spinning, and very softly said, "I do like you, Nicole, but I don't think this is what you really want. I'm sorry, but I can't do what you're asking." As slurred as my proposition was, it was clear enough for him to catch and veto the message.

Mortified much.

That was the moment my world went dark and everything came crashing down. All the pain from my past to my present, and a few too many drinks, set me into a downwards spiral that sank me so fast I couldn't have saved myself if I tried. I don't remember much after that, except bursting into tears, pulling my hand away from his, and running out of that lobby like Cinderella leaving the ball at the stroke of midnight. But this was no Cinderella/Prince Charming moment; it was more like the ultimate walk of shame but without the sex.

I hailed the first cab I saw, my head spinning, and tears poured down my face. By the time I got back to Judy's place, I was literally a sobbing mess in my pretty pink dress. I barely made it to the washroom where I stayed hugging that bowl for dear life. Through it all, in true best-friend form, she was there waiting because she knew what she knew. Without me having to say a word, which in my condition wasn't even an option, she was there to catch me from falling any further.

I managed to make it back to the couch, and that was the extent of my abilities. The last thing I remember was taking off my kitty heels and using what little strength I had left to thank her before passing out half sitting up, half lying down, and in the dress I'd never wear again.

The next morning, despite a horrible hangover, bruised ego, and egg on my face (small price to pay), I woke up with an unexplainable feeling of gratitude. I was most grateful for his rejection of my ludicrous advances, sparing me a decision I would have regretted forever.

I could feel space and breath flowing again, and with it came a clarity I hadn't had the day before. It was the beginning of me getting back into my body, like having a breakdown to have the breakthrough.

Throughout this tumultuous whirlwind of losing myself, I miraculously found myself.

I returned to bartending, never to cross paths with said customer again. I guess he knew to give me space, which suited me just fine. We did see each other years later when we were in the same restaurant, but this time we were both having dinner independently. From a distance, through the crowd, we acknowledged each other and exchanged a polite nod and half smile, never to speak of that night again.

The lesson I took from that experience is one I humbly pass on to you: it's okay to lose your way, but it's not okay to sell yourself short. It was a firm reminder that I am stronger and more capable than I gave myself credit for. If that's what it took to shock me back into my body, then so be it. I concluded that I am not the sum of my bad decisions, and just like everything else, these feelings of being scared and alone, insecure, and weak, would pass. And they did, because look at me now, bitches. LOL!

Shortly thereafter, post-married-man-gate, I started counting my blessings and not my problems, looking at the glass as half full. Most importantly, I dived into doing my work. Little did I know back then that it would be the beginning of my journey to mastering myself and my single life.

I'm so happy I got through writing this chapter. Hallelujah! It was touch-and-go for a while.

I wasn't expecting it to be so difficult or emotional, but reliving it feels better than I thought it would, if only to remember how far I've come and then release it back into the universe where it belongs.

Amen.

Chapter Three

BEING SINGLE

THE GOOD NEWS is... congratulations, you're single! The other good news is that there is no bad news... yay! Welcome to the land of freedom and butterfly wings where all things are possible. I wanted to add a chapter that wasn't about a guy but instead about the relationship with yourself. Mastering your single life from this moment on is officially the new "in a relationship"—one with yourself.

Before going any further, I'd like to acknowledge the tremendous respect I have for all the single parents out there. I tip my hat to every single (wink, wink) one of you. Nuff respect!

I'm mentioning this because it's important to recognize that there's a difference between being single with no kids and being a single parent.

After the break-up with my fiancé, I never had another relationship where having kids was an option in my eyes.

NICOLE JONES

There were men who would have liked to have a child with me, but it was something I took seriously. I never wanted to have a child with someone for the sake of having a child, and none of them inspired me to go down that path.

It's a subject, particularly at this age, that I've had to make peace with, and thankfully for my sanity and my soul, I have.

I love children, especially other people's kids. My maternal nature comes naturally and is wholehearted. But I have faith that in my lifetime, through a divine way that is not mine to see, that somehow I will embody the role of being a mother.

Greatly due to the way I was raised, I believe there is more than one definition of motherhood. I trust in God's plan for me in that if I haven't been given the blessing to birth a child, perhaps that blessing in the traditional way was not meant for me, and that's okay. There are so many children out there who deserve and need a loving home, and I hope to be able to give that to a child one day. For me, that would be the greatest victory ever. Godspeed.

I'm grateful that I had ten years dedicated to mentoring a young girl. She filled a space in my heart and soul that allowed me to pay forward what I knew to help her grow into the beautiful woman she's become.

As well, having my soul sisters and brothers, who have birthed some of the most amazing children and brightest lights this world has ever seen. It's an honour and a pleasure to watch them grow up and be part of their lives. Being loved and surrounded by them is a blessing.

At the top of the list of amazing kids are my beyond-measure brilliant godsons (both officially and unofficially) they are the beats of my heart and light in my eyes. These three beautiful boys, smart, loving, hilarious, witty, kind, critical thinkers who have taught me so much, and when they speak, I listen.

It's a long story, but the short version is our firstborn, beautiful Sebastiano, is my original but unofficial godson. Officially, I am the godmother to our sweet centre Leonardo, and lastly but certainly not last, my free-spirited Lodovico is my precious and third unofficial godson. In simple terms, collectively, they are my godsons and that's all that matters.

We share a unique and unbreakable bond, and I take my responsibility as godmother as serious as serious can be. Committed, when it comes to them, is my middle name.

They mean everything to me and give me all the motivation in the world to keep going to succeed. All I want is to spoil them with my love, always be there, and help them grow into the incredible young men they are becoming. It's my honour.

I realize it's not the same thing as being a mother; sadly I only see them when I travel to Ibiza to visit or they come to Canada. I'm not there for the sleepless nights and other multitude of parenting responsibilities while juggling everything and the kitchen sink that most single parents contend with.

Which is why I acknowledge that being a single parent is one of the most commendable things a person can rise to the occasion to do. I can only imagine the added pressure it puts on someone when there's a child or children to consider. And finding that balance to make space and time for your personal or romantic life.

I don't even let guys meet Dior on the first date, so I can only imagine the struggle.

I'm saying all this because I understand that some of my ideas about being single and moving through single life might appear to be way out there given your responsibilities as a single parent. I totally acknowledge that.

However, the beauty and similarity we do share is that mastering your single life isn't about finding a person to love; that's the bonus. Mastering your single life at its core is about accepting, loving, owning, and living a fulfilled happy life on your own accord. Not worrying about who may or may not be waiting on the other side. It's about honouring the best relationship any of us will ever know, the one with ourselves and, in some cases, with our kids.

That said, single parents take note. You might have to modify some of what you read (in case you haven't already noticed, LOL) to fit your lifestyle. Take what works for you and leave the deal breakers behind for the next single to pick up.

And I'll leave you with this: First to the single moms… my wish for you is to know and remember that you are divine feminine power, a fierce warrior and giver of life, the greatest gift of all. No matter what your circumstances or how many kids you have, you deserve to be happy. Whether with or without a partner, your life is valuable and you merit love, passion, and happiness, the same as the rest of us fabulous singles!

To the divine masculine, single dads… the world needs more stand-up men like you who are willing to step up and show up for their kids. And you too deserve the unconditional love of someone who will appreciate your strength and conviction and raise you to be an even better man.

Our journeys may look different, but the endgame stays the same.

Love yourself first, and the rest will follow.

MASTER OF SINGLE

Okay, moving on and getting back to all that juicy freedom I spoke about at the beginning of the chapter. Let's explore this idea further and examine the beauty in what I refer to as the single freedom factor (adjust where applicable).

I define this freedom as the ability to wake up and design your day according to your own wants, needs, and selfish desires or guilty pleasures. I say guilty pleasures, but there really shouldn't be any guilt about it. There is tremendous power attached to so much freedom that is solely reserved for singles only. We hold the power to our freedom.

This single superpower brings with it a certain kind of indulgence, adventure, and flexibility of mind, body, space, and time. Never leave home without it, and use your power wisely.

Now, it's common as a single person in waiting to think that the grass is greener on the other side. The idea that once you find your person, life becomes this magical wonderland where people frolic through the flowers and the sun shines on your love alone while rainbows dance constantly in the sky. But it's equally as important as a singleton to keep our own lawn fertilized, mowed, and healthy, and don't forget curb appeal. Why? Because often people in relationships, particularly those in unhealthy ones, are looking at your well-lived single life and manicured lawn, thinking that looks damn good too. Facts.

Which reminds me of another "momism." Growing up, I admired people with money, and my mom's response to my always wanting what we couldn't afford was to tell me, "Be careful who you admire. You don't know their life. Always admire yourself before anyone else."

Of course she was right. Just because something looks good on the outside doesn't mean it will be good on the inside. Admire thyself first, and never compare yourself to anyone else.

I encourage everyone to embrace your single time and take your opportunity to tap into and get to know you—no excuses, no distractions. This inner personal work we are so privileged to have the opportunity to do for ourselves will help build a sense of connection to yourself that nobody can take from you. It's incredibly empowering to know that you are whole and complete with yourself, on your own and anyone who comes into your life will be a welcome addition.

This is work every person, single or otherwise, should seek to embody.

Speaking of connection, I started a new morning routine that helps me connect to myself before the rest of the world. Before even putting my feet on the ground, I lie still in awareness with my eyes closed, connecting my body and breath to the morning energy. I slowly open my eyes to the light of the day, then turn to Dior and give her a kiss good morning.

From this place of awareness, I take three deep cleansing connective breaths to get my energy flowing and centre myself.

With a gentle Om sound that awakens my voice, I say one thing out loud (you can say as many as you want) that I'm grateful for.

I crystalize my intention for the day, and from that space of connectiveness, I slowly get up, leading with an open and grateful heart and a yes/and attitude.

It's a ten-minute practice that sets the tone for the rest of my day.

Because of it, I feel more grounded, I don't annoy as easily, I'm more open, smile easier, and I have more

MASTER OF SINGLE

patience for myself and others. It sets me and others up to succeed.

Let's pivot into this next section.

When was the last time you had fun? I'm talking about present, in the moment, laughing out loud, totally into whatever you're doing kind of fun? If it takes more than a minute to recall, it's been too long, but that's okay. The great thing is that it's never too late to get back to having fun. Over the years, I've proudly mastered having fun in all its purity and applying it to my controlled, chaotic big-kid life.

When in doubt, find the fun, because if you're not having fun in life, then what are you doing? You're done. These pearls of wisdom are complements of my precious godsons who over the years have reminded me that no matter what, "Madrina, we must always have fun." Smart boys, my loves!

Alright, this feels like a weird segue from my godsons to this next topic, and I say that to take the awkwardness out of this transition. After you put the kids to bed, please join me as we enter into grown-up territory and shift the focus onto one of my other favourite kinds of fun. Yes, people, I'm talking about the single sexual fun factor. Woohoo!

The single sexual fun factor is an important component in a single's life. The desire for sex doesn't stop just because you're not in a relationship, am I right? Our sexual pleasure isn't something to take for granted; instead, we should welcome the idea with open arms and legs, if you dare.

I suppose this is as good a time as any to disclose that I love sex and I love to fuck, and yes there is a different between fucking, having sex, and making love. I'll explain... having sex is the action, and pardon *moi*, but fucking is just a heightened way of saying the same thing, as opposed to the tenderness of making love. Unless I'm in love with you, then chances are we are fucking, and there's nothing wrong or bad about it. Sorry, not sorry.

I enjoy embracing my sexuality. I have a tremendous respect for my vessel, aka my body/aka my temple, and (nine times out of ten) I'm particular about who I choose to share it with. And whomever I decide to give access to my temple will be a very lucky man.

For those with body-image issues, let me say this: it's not about having the perfect body. There are times I don't love everything about my physical appearance, but even in those times, I still love my temple. Don't waste time judging yourself when someone will appreciate and enjoy having you.

One of my go-to, picture-perfect examples of a woman who's comfortable in her body and isn't afraid to go for it when it comes to sex is the divine and delicious character Samantha Jones in *Sex and the City*. Tied with Carrie Bradshaw as my show favourites.

Samantha's devilishly bold ways of putting herself out there is a prime example of a woman who uses her single power to please her sexual desires to the ultimate degree. Granted, she's got balls and is a fictional character who operates from an extreme spectrum of sex and lots of it. And yes, her tactics might leave a lot to be desired, depending on whom you're asking, but either way you cut it, her no-nonsense approach to her personal pleasure is matter-of-fact and highly successful. Most of all, she's having fun and let's face it, it's really her crazy sexual antics that make the show great. That and Carrie's fashion but really sex sells because we can all relate and it's fun!

I've tried a few, and surprisingly, her tactics are mostly applicable in the real world minus minor adjustments for the common person... then again, maybe not? Word has it that common isn't so common anymore.

The point is, where there's a will to have sex, there's a way to have sex.

There are a few simple sexual guidelines I follow as a single woman, including one that might seem like a hassle to stay on top of, but please pay attention. This is important. As a single woman who's out there and has done the heavy lifting on this one, I stand firm in this first suggestion as part of mindful living towards a single's sex life. I'm speaking about self-maintenance, personal hygiene, and overall upkeep. Now stay with me here; I can feel you getting nervous. I can't stress the importance of this enough for everyone but even more for singles who are out there making connections and first impressions.

Now, being mid-pandemic, the narrative has slightly changed the conversation, but nonetheless, it's important because people are still having sex. With that said, I would be remiss to not mention staying informed and up to date on public health and safety measures is essential to keeping yourself safe.

And having a plan for sex will give you that sense of control, freedom, and allow you to relax into it with your person of choice. It might be something as simple as both parties agreeing to get tested and exchange results before engaging sexually.

Hopefully this whole situation will be behind us sooner than later, but in the meanwhile, be smart about it.

Wow, nothing like talking about a global virus to kill the mood. LOL.

Okay, getting back to what I was saying, and please just hear me out. Even though you might not be having as much sex these days, this suggestion isn't only meant for that reason. It's also about keeping yourself together for yourself.

Taking care of ourselves is not a punishment, and it shouldn't be reserved solely for those special occasions or the person who might be getting into your pants to enjoy your treasures—preferably without the unsightly or untamed "treasure hunt," if you get my drift. The time you invest in taking care of yourself is an investment in yourself. I don't care if you're having sex once a day, once a week, once a month, or once a year (please don't let it be once a year), it still stands true in its importance.

Whether your thing is to wax, shave, pluck, peel, thread, or something else, if your original landing strip has turned into a field where cows can now graze, this can be a problem—unless you're dating a farmer or are intentionally throwing back to the seventies. And guys, if you're reading this, no woman should be flossing her teeth when she's down there trying to please you and do the damn thing. For God's sake, it's already enough of a job. Just saying, it matters to us too, and it's not cute.

The idea of self-maintenance is not limited to shaving or waxing. You can also factor in pedicures, manicures, haircuts, treatments, facials, exercise, and eating well as the new upkeep.

These are the things you can do to keep yourself feeling top-shelf. Don't let being single deprive you of that personal victory. Act, live, and move through your life, putting in the same time and effort you would if you were in a relationship with a partner because—surprise—you are in a relationship—with yourself.

Now listen. I'm not suggesting you become the town tramp who's shaving it up and laying it down everywhere you go… unless that's your thing, then more power to you. Who am I to judge?

MASTER OF SINGLE

Being ready on "go" is a real thing for singles who are out there in the land of sexual possibilities.

I'll give you an example. Let's say you're out one night and you meet a potential suitor. Flirting ensues, pheromones become heightened, and the sexual chemistry is clear. If given the choice, wouldn't you prefer to feel secure knowing that if things did escalate to the next level, you'd be ready and able to engage? Come on, nobody wants to be in that situation when a hot piece of sex is standing in front of you, undressing you with their eyes, and you're thinking about your hairy legs, crazy pits, or worse—a grown-out, messy bush! Oh Lord. Listen, if you're fine with going full on, bush out, unpolished hangnails, ashy feet, and grown-out roots, I'm not going to stop you. Go for it!

Just know that every non-action has a reaction, and that's all I'm going to say about that. The choice is yours, but don't say I never warned you.

Of course there are exceptions to every rule. This isn't about being perfect or together all the time. In fact, being perfectly imperfect is one of my favourite things to be and absolutely has its time and place when it comes to self-care. We all need our off days to not care about what's happening down there, or anywhere, and that time for me is usually during my pause for period. I dread having my period; it's my monthly nightmare. The first twenty-four hours are hell, my back's as tender as a soft peach, and my stomach feels like it's imploding from the inside out. I'm crampy, cranky, and irritable; it's not my best look and certainly not when I feel my sexiest. Who can relate?

It wouldn't matter if Michael B. Jordan wanted to get some (as difficult as it would be to resist, he's so damn h-o-t), when it comes to my period… sorry, not sorry, my goodies are off the block and off the clock. And it's not that I haven't tried it—I once heard that it helped to relieve period cramps, but the whole thing is just too much of a bloody mess and what a nightmare to clean up afterwards. And no, I don't believe in giving blow jobs while I'm out of commission. If my man can't go a few days without sex or a blow job until I'm feeling better, then Houston, we got a problem.

I know that was a little TMI, but it comes with the package and a natural part of life, but don't worry, it's almost over. Ha ha. All this to say it isn't about being perfect. It's about caring enough about yourself to take the time to do right by you and to know when and how to choose your battles and make your appointments wisely.

And scene.

Speaking of self-care, when it comes to dating, I'm a big believer in dating myself. A lot of my friends, both single and coupled, are often busy with work, are in relationships, married with kids, and aren't always available to join me when I feel like going out. That doesn't prevent me from living my life and taking myself out. When I see a woman eating or having a cocktail at the bar with herself, I think, *Respect to her for owning it*.

A woman out alone also makes her more accessible for men to approach. It shouldn't be the reason men approach you, but if it helps them feel more comfortable, then so be it.

Note to men: If you find yourself in a situation with a group of women and one catches your eye, a good icebreaker and polite thing to do would be to send a round of drinks or shots over. Include everyone at the table or you'll risk coming off looking cheap. It also gives you a non-creepy reason to go over, and cheers, it also makes for a good first impression on her girlfriends. First impressions matter to the girlfriends. You're welcome, guys.

MASTER OF SINGLE

If you think it sounds ridiculous to date yourself or it makes you laugh nervously because you can't imagine yourself at a bar alone, I'm officially passing my torch on to you and giving you this as your single homework assignment. Take yourself out—that is, when things reopen—and put yourself out there in a safe and responsible way.

And now, without further ado, here we "guy" again...

Chapter Four

BLIND FAITH

MY ENCOUNTERS WITH men as a single woman have been a lot of things but least of all boring. Like many of you, I've gone through different stages of dating at various times in my life. Sometimes I was a serial dater, and other times I was happy just chilling with myself and flexing my single-girl muscle proudly. Then there were those times when my habitual routines became redundant and I found myself wanting to shake things up. That's when I like a good pivot.

Note the importance throughout this book of being able to pivot quickly. As quickly as a cat can pounce, a woman should be able to pivot, even in heels.

So let's pivot into this next single-girl story…

It started with a call from my friend/accountant telling me about one of her single friends/clients who was looking to meet and make a connection with someone nice and of a certain age. That was my first hint that something was up. What did she mean by "of a certain age?" At the time, I didn't catch that small print.

She continued to sing his praises as a kind, successful, charming, sophisticated businessman, strongly suggesting that we should meet. I don't know about you, but I'm not a blind date or setup kind of girl, however, in the spirit of shaking things up, I said why not and gave her the green light to connect us.

Besides my blind faith in her, I'm not sure what possessed me to accept a date sight unseen, but for some reason, at that time, it felt right, so I didn't kill it with questions. In hindsight, I realize that my heart and mind were open to new things. And not wanting to taint the experience with physical prejudgements, I didn't even ask to see a picture of him. Lesson: always ask to see a picture.

With my permission, our mutual friend did her due diligence and connected us. He called me, and we had a brief conversation. Based on that, I felt safe and comfortable enough to keep moving forward. He gave me the option to choose the restaurant, and I chose the best, a place called Da Emma, a fine-dining, family-run Italian eatery in the old port. Everyone's favourite part about this place is that the owner and head chef Mama Emma is in the kitchen, cooking up the real-deal, most authentic and delicious Italian dishes. It's also a place where I'd worked before, so I was comfortable knowing I had friends there.

Here's a tip: when on a blind-faith date, go somewhere where you know at least one person if possible. That way, if things go south, you have someone on the inside to go to.

Alternatively, if you can't do that, then have a friend call thirty minutes into the date to "check in." This "unexpected" interruption can also double as your emergency call and reason to leave if need be.

MASTER OF SINGLE

My attire for the date was specific and mindfully put together. The look was strong, classy, stylish, and confident—all things me. I rocked a vintage, high-waisted black distressed leather knee-length skirt and a thin cotton beige body-con scoop-neck blouse (tucked in to emphasize the high-waist look).

My legs were looking sexy in sheer lace-embroidered pantyhose paired with five inches of patent leather stacked booties with gold hardware by Nine West. The hair was flowing and my makeup was on point. The look reflected my personal style—elegant with a touch of attitude and a nod to sexy but not floozy; I wanted to leave something to the imagination. Most importantly, the look commanded respect.

I arrived at the restaurant on time, and upon my arrival is when I started to panic just a bit. This was really happening; my first-ever blind date; it was becoming very real. *Crazy* was the thought I had running through my mind as I was about to meet and have dinner with a total stranger. A man I'd only spoken to for minutes on the phone. My stomach started to do back flips with nervous energy. My heart was in my throat, and all I could think was, *Please, Lord, let him have all his teeth and not smell bad.* At that point, I was hoping for the bare minimum. The juxtaposition of the nausea and excitement aroused my adrenaline but terrified me at the same time.

As I entered and approached the hostess's stand to give the name of the reservation, she replied, "Oh yes, the gentleman is already here." My initial thought was, *He's early or eager.*

I wasn't sure which was better or worse.

I followed her in, and as we turned the corner, I quickly yet subtly scanned the room with my peripheral vision, hoping to spot him first. That's when I saw one lone man sitting at a table off to the side. We made eye contact, so there was no turning back.

First impression: he was well dressed for his age.

Remember off the top I mentioned that I didn't catch it when my friend said "of a certain age?"

Well, when I saw him, it made sense. He stood up to greet me in his pastel, cashmere V-neck sweater, smiling from ear to ear, seemingly happy with what he saw. Unfortunately, my reaction was slightly different.

I'm by no means an ageist; in fact, I appreciate an older man, but looking at him, it was plain to see that he was at least twenty years my senior. Not to be rude, but he had age spots.

I like a mature man, but this was pushing it, and might I say, very disturbing.

So much for having an open mind.

Still, I was proud of myself for pushing beyond my comfort zone, but that was about all I could take away from the situation.

There we sat, two single people, strangers really, who shared a common friend who did our taxes and set us up, and now we were having dinner together. Awkward to say the least, but the actor inside me said that the show must go on!

To save face and the evening, I pushed through the lack of physical attraction to give room for his other potential qualities to come through. Including his seemingly good manners.

I was pleasantly surprised when he allowed me to choose the wine. I chose a most delicious bottle, Gaja from the Piedmont region in Italy. I proceeded to order my favourite dishes on the menu: burrata and tomato with basil to start and a serious piece of lamb on the bone to

MASTER OF SINGLE

finish. What can I say? Every now and then a girl needs some meat on a bone, and clearly it was the only bone I was going to get that night.

I had resigned myself to accept the situation for what it was in that it wouldn't result in a romantic connection. Which was fine. He seemed cool enough for me to stay and simply enjoy his company over a nice dinner and good wine. I considered my seeing the date through as my Good Samaritan action for the week.

The banter was surface at first. We kept topics light, talking about fashion, travel, and careers. Much to my delight and after a couple of glasses of wine, the night started to warm up, and so did the conversation. We didn't get too personal or deep, which again was fine by me—that is, until he did get personal but not in a good way. His out-of-left-field unsolicited sharing of his personal life threw me for an unexpected loop. That's when the night went from blind date to a freaky Fridate.

There I sat, thoroughly enjoying my scrumptious lamb dinner, starting to relax into the evening, when legit out of nowhere, he flips the script, like Dr. Jekyll and Mr. Hyde. In the middle of a perfectly neutral conversation about pastels versus patterns, he boomerangs to start talking about his ex-wife and their nasty divorce. I almost choked on my lamb. If there was ever a time to pivot out, this was it!

WTF? His whole disposition changed. His voice dropped into his lower register, and he had disdain in his tone as he continued with this crazy story of who, what, where, and when.

But the only question I had was "What the hell is going on?" It was very uncomfortable, and I couldn't muster up a reaction beyond shock. Maybe it was the wine that opened him up, but all I wanted to do was put the cork back in to shut him up. Clearly not everything is better with wine.

Every word flying out of his mouth felt like a verbal assault on my face as he recounted his tales and berated his ex-wife. I didn't think it could get any worse, and then, lucky me, it did.

He added another layer to this bizarre situation by divulging his infidelities and the mistress he was seeing during the last years of his marriage! I mean, come on... Who does that?

I was speechless, and I'm rarely speechless. To save myself, I checked out and stopped listening. I didn't drive my ass all the way out for him to ruin my delicious lamb dinner, no sir.

Eventually his mouth stopped moving. Incredibly enough, he leans in as if to look to me for a reaction, acknowledgement, comfort, or consolation. I was gobsmacked in crazy land. I blankly stared back at him with my mouth full of lamb. I couldn't imagine what he wanted me to say. And what I wanted to say, he wouldn't have wanted to hear. But instead of lowering myself to his level, I reserved my opinion. It wasn't worth the breath it would take to tell him what a jerk he was and that it sounded like he deserved what he got.

There was zero sympathy given. All I could think was that this guy was way too old to still be such a jerk. So I had a choice. I could let his poor behaviour and asshole tendencies affect me and make a terrible scene by storming out, which he would have absolutely deserved. But I'm a lady (in public anyway), and I wouldn't have done that to myself. So I took a breath, collected my thoughts, and very graciously looked at him. I then clenched my teeth, forced a smile, stood up, and excused myself from the table. But not before saying in my best nice/mean voice that while I was gone to the ladies' room, he should get the bill. It was my subtle, not so subtle way of saying the evening was over. I don't do crazy.

MASTER OF SINGLE

Hard pivot left.

Note: No matter what the circumstances, always exit gracefully and never let them see you sweat. You're too cool to be thirsty, as defined by the *Urban Dictionary* and the *Housewives of Atlanta* as "too eager to get something or desperate." I am neither.

Thankfully, he knew how to take the hint. When I returned to the table, the bill had been settled.

I didn't walk out with him; rather, it was a cold goodbye at the table, ending with a half-hearted, limp handshake. Certainly no goodnight kiss—hell, no—and clearly no chance for a second date. Despite how amazing the food was, the evening left a bad taste in my mouth and had me wondering if age didn't mature a man, then what would?

I hung back to have a last glass of wine at the bar, purge my experience to the bartender, and decompress from my epic fail of an evening. In the end, I concluded that I wouldn't let the experience jade me from the idea that there are still good men out there... somewhere just waiting to be discovered.

But most upsetting was the waste of a great outfit.

Would I blind date again? Hell to the no, no, naw.

Next time, please send complete résumé, letters of reference, contact numbers, and a full-length photo.

I'm slightly kidding but also slightly not. I was blind, but now I see.

The next day, I chalked it up to a bad dream—a nightmare, really. I shook it off and then called my friend to ask just how well she thought she knew me. She laughed. I didn't, but we're good, although for unrelated reasons, she isn't my accountant anymore.

I did learn a lot about myself though. I can have the patience of a saint and my instincts are always right and one hundred percent. I'm not the blind date setup kind of girl. Furthermore, it drove home the point that when it comes to maturity, or lack thereof, age doesn't matter. Sad.

What does matter is taking from every experience something positive that helps you grow. I suppose in this situation one could argue that I got a nice dinner out of it. To which I would say, "I can do bad all by my damn self, thank you very much."

Not in this lifetime is any dinner or wine that good to put up with any man's baggage full of bullshit.

The moral is, buy your own dinner, ask to see a photo, know your worth and what your boundaries are, and never be afraid to walk away gracefully.

Thank you. Next.

Chapter Five

BEST FRIEND OR BUST

WHEN IT COMES to friends, I've said it a million times and I'll say it a million more—I'm so blessed to have a fierce tribe that runs deep and over many decades strong. I proudly nurture friendships that go back twenty-plus years, some even stemming back to the age of five. And although we might not see each other, I love them, and thanks to social media, we're still connected, which I think says a lot about a person's character.

As I've gotten older, my friends have become my framily, a term I use throughout the book to frame the friendships that have always played a huge part in my life, whether single, coupled, or it's complicated; framily has always been the anchor that keeps me grounded.

My tribe is a diverse and extremely loving, creative group of beautiful souls and talented individuals. Each in their own way elevates me with their love and light, and I do my best to offer them the same in return. People can be quick to bestow the title of "friend" for lack of having a better title to give, but I'm very specific when it comes to calling someone my friend. In my opinion, the title of friend is earned, not given.

To qualify us as friends, there needs to be something behind it—a shared moment or an experience that qualifies some sort of history—and we should probably know each other's last names. If you introduce me as a "friend" and you don't know my last name, that's a problem, and in my opinion, that constitutes more of an acquaintanceship than a friendship, which is okay too.

And if we don't know each other's last names (which I admit even with friends, can sometimes happen), let us at least have had a conversation where we shared a story and learned something about each other over a cocktail. That's the minimum to being my friend.

It's important to me to distinguish the different levels of friendships so that I know who deserves my attention and time; both of which are valuable. Here's the breakdown, my framily are my MIPs (most important people). These alliances have been earned over time; they're the ones I put my back into and would defend first and ask questions later.

Then you have the VIPs (very important people). I also have their backs by letting them know that if I heard someone talking smack about them, I'd tell them.

There's a little-known category I made up and affectionately call PILs (people I like), which makes up the sum of those I consider friends. This group is composed of people I care about, see occasionally, but don't necessarily know very well.

After that we fall into the murky water of friend versus acquaintances on the cusp of "what was your name again?"

MASTER OF SINGLE

These are individuals I might see around the way and exchange pleasantries with, but I don't necessarily remember their names (first or last) or even where we know each other from. We've all experienced that moment when someone says hello to you by name and you draw a complete blank as to theirs. So awkward. If this happens, please don't be offended if I ask you to remind me of your name. As awkward as it might be in the moment, I'd rather ask than stand there pretending like I know. Of course there will be people who just won't make the cut and that's ok it's important to know who they are too.

Then there's the distinction between male and female friendships. Growing up, I was a tomboy hanging out with the boys. I played sports and never cried over a scraped knee. I learned early how to maintain healthy platonic male friendships, but the older (and prettier) I got, the trickier it became.

Especially when both parties are single, there's always that potential of crossing the line from platonic to problematic if things were to turn intimate. And once you cross that line, it's difficult to come back from it.

I have a few very special male relationships in my life, from my gay boys to my straight men. I treasure them all greatly because they're clear, respectful, kind, and uncomplicated. Most of the guy friends in my life are in relationships, but I'm also friends with or know their significant others as well. It's great and important to have couples that are not jealous of opposite-sex friendships, and if you're that opposite-sex friend, it's your job to make sure that you respect both parties in the relationship equally.

As a single girl, I think it's tremendously important to have healthy platonic relationships with men in your life. The energy and presence of a man who's not your lover or significant other is an important and valued energy to have around, particularly for single women. Guys bring a different perspective to the table, and that balance of feminine/masculine divine energy is important to staying connected to all parts of ourselves. I look at it like, my male friendships keep me connected to Mars, and I keep them connected to Venus. Cute.

However, those male platonic relationships, especially with your single guy friends, are sometimes more difficult to sustain. Especially if one catches feelings for the other, it can become awkward quick. If the feelings are not reciprocated, then it can put the relationship in a vulnerable place, forcing one or the other to decide between the friendship and your heart.

If I could turn back time…

This next story makes me happy and sad in the same breath. I feel happy because it's the story of one of my dearest, most treasured relationships with a man I've cared about as a friend for over a decade. On the other hand, it makes me sad because things got messy, framily was fractured, and inevitably someone got hurt.

He was such a nice guy—a little rough and tough on the outside, meaning his demeanour wasn't super approachable, but I could see right through the mask he wore. The side of him not many people got to see was a shy, funny, kind, sweet, and generous being, and when he was around me, his tough-guy persona fell a little bit more every time.

We met while I was bartending and working at a bistro/café called Rosalie; it was always a good time when he'd come by.

We'd talk about everything and respected each other's personal lives and sometimes would get together for a friendly lunch. At the time we were both in relationships, me with my fiancé and he with a woman he'd had a child with, a beautiful daughter whom he loved. He was an amazing dad too.

Our connection wasn't sexual. We joked, laughed, and brought out the silly in each other. We were both Capricorns with birthdays only days apart and shared similar morals and values, especially when it came to loyalty, family, and friendships.

Unfortunately, this was a problematic friendship for my ex. He didn't care to understand our platonic dynamic. I stood my ground for a while and fought for our friendship and my right to have him as part of my life; after all, I'd known him before I met my fiancé. But eventually fighting with my ex over my friendship became such a burden that I ended up distancing myself from him for the sake of my relationship.

It made me angry that my fiancé didn't trust me enough or even try to get to know him, which was such a double standard because he had girlfriends before I came along that he was still hanging out with. I accepted this, but he couldn't offer me the same grace or trust in return.

Typical egotistical behaviour. So I bit the bullet and stepped out of my friendship to stop the arguing. But in my mind, the friendship was only suspended until further notice. My friend could see that I was struggling with the situation and was cool enough to take a step back without giving me a hard time about it.

Fast forward to the end of the fiancé fiasco and ultimately the end of our relationship. It wasn't terribly long before my friend and I reconnected; thankfully, this was after my emotional, mental, and spiritual breakdown to breakthrough (i.e., the married-man debacle). By the time we saw each other again, I was much more stable, back on my feet, and happy to have my friend back in my life.

Like expected, we picked up where we last left off, suspension lifted. This time, however, it was a different ball game. We had both become single, which was an interesting turn of events that wasn't lost on me. I was happy to have him back in my life but very aware of the slippery slope that came with it. As two attractive single people who shared a close relationship, one must stay vigilant.

Even though it was platonic, the potential for danger was just one bad decision away.

Our friendship continued to grow, and we became closer over the years. He was always a gentleman, picking me up when we'd go out to eat, and I never so much as saw a bill.

He was a man of pride and moved through the world leading, chin high and chest front like a lion and protector, and that's the way he liked it.

I was also there for him as a friend he could count on. This one time, he was going through some serious financial challenges when his business crashed, turning his world upside down. It was a traumatic time for him. Among other things, his pride took a hit, and being a man or great self-respect, it wasn't easy for him to be vulnerable or ask for help. And when he did, he was sorely disappointed to see that the many people he had helped over the years and who were now doing very well financially had turned their backs and all but disappeared on him.

That's why it's so important to know who your real friends are.

I was just barely getting financial traction back in my life. I couldn't really afford to do much at the time, but I

MASTER
OF SINGLE

could see he was hurting. I wanted to do something nice for him to lift his spirits because he'd always been so good to me, and it was hard to watch him suffer. So one day I invited him to lunch. It was a small gesture with a huge impact. He accepted my invitation reluctantly, but he accepted. He was extremely humbled, having rarely been on the receiving end of someone else picking up the bill, but he felt safe being vulnerable with me. I was so happy to do this for him, and we enjoyed a lovely afternoon of Mexican food and cocktails.

Fast forward again a couple of years and lots of hard work later. I'm now working in television as a reporter for CTV Montreal, and with my contract coming to an end, not sure of what to do next, I decided to create my next move. The problem was, there was a lack of opportunity to keep growing in my own city, but I was motivated and wanted to explore new options, perhaps even a bigger market. And with that, I set my sights on a move to Toronto.

It's no secret that I've always had a love/hate relationship with Toronto, and it's not personal to the city. It comes down to a personal preference thing. It's a city I've always felt lacked in soul, and soul is my fuel and what inspires me. In Montreal, the soul and artistry are a huge part of the makeup of our city, and we feed off that as artists. Toronto, on the other hand, is a bustling, business-driven financial city and is much more controlled in the way people think, move, and exchange energy. Different cities for different folks and different strokes.

But timing was everything, and I was ready to put my personal feelings and preconceived notions aside and go with an open heart and mind to explore what was potentially waiting for me on the other side.

Around the same time, I started realizing that I was just one of a long line of Montrealers or professional people who were moving to Toronto, aka the Tdot, in hopes of further pursuing their professional goals. You've heard the saying: "If it makes sense, then it makes dollars." Sometimes you follow the dollars and make sense of it later. I gave myself one year to try my hand at this new market and adventure that was Toronto.

I was fortunate to have my dear friend Charles from Montreal connect me with his friend Anthony in Toronto, who was a Montreal expat and supercool guy who generously offered me a place to stay.

Living with him was great. He was welcoming, easygoing, and spoke plainly, as if to warn me, telling me to prepare myself. He repeated a couple of times that Toronto was vastly different from Montreal. The people weren't as easygoing or as open-minded as I might be used to. He went on to say that the vibe was much more conservative and not as spontaneous or artistically driven; just as I'd suspected. I received and accepted the information, but my overly excited nature had me thinking things would be different for me. I was determined to be the change I wanted to see.

But what a difference twenty-four hours makes. I'll never forget it; I remember waking up on that first morning, ready to meet and embrace my new city, feeling so positive and inspired. It was a beautiful summer day. I felt strong, beautiful, shiny, bright, and I wanted my outfit to express on the outside how I was feeling on the inside. I rocked a beautiful long black deep V-neck bohemian linen wrap-style dress with an open back. It was fun, original, and showed my personal style. Most importantly, it made me feel beautiful, and that was the energy I wanted to share and lead with throughout my day.

I stepped outside, feeling good from my head to my shoes. I walked up the block to the main street and turned the corner. In less than an instant (if that's even possible) my joy went from a high to a dreadful case of self-awareness.

I noticed immediately that people were giving me shady, disapproving glares, looking at me as if to say "Who does that girl think she is?" That was the vibe I was getting, and I know that vibe because I've given that look before. After that experience, I'll never give it again. Being on the receiving side of such bizarre energy really threw me off my game; it was very disturbing and not a good feeling.

One thing about Toronto people is that they're not subtle or shy. They blandly stared at me, snickering and whispering to each other. I even caught a couple of people chuckling, like I was the butt of some awful joke or something. I wanted to check all of them, but I felt so vulnerable that part of me didn't want to believe it was really happening. It was all so extra, and I couldn't even pivot out of it, and you know how I love a good pivot. The whole situation made me feel uncomfortable, unwelcome, and surprisingly insecure, none of which I was, making it that much more mind-blowing.

Being original and having personal style has always been part of who I am. So to have that feel like it was being mocked or ridiculed, I just couldn't process it.

I tried to shake it off, telling myself that I was just being paranoid or was experiencing new city jitters and kept pushing through with my day. But it didn't get better. Everywhere I went, I felt as if I were sticking out like a sore thumb. I couldn't believe that I was allowing other people's reactions to affect the way I was feeling about myself. My posture had collapsed, and my head that I held so high now hung down. I could barely make eye contact with people in passing. It was one of the most off-putting situations, and still to this day when I think back on it, all I was doing was being myself.

NICOLE JONES

With much difficulty, I managed to get through what I thought was going to be a positive, productive first day getting to know my new city, but it turned out to be a slap in my fashionable, positive, full-of-faith face.

By the time I got back to the apartment, I was in tears. I didn't want to cry, and I couldn't even figure out what the problem was. I sat there waiting to exhale in a city that had me feeling like I had to shrink down to fit in, and that was a painful reality. The whole situation messed me up. I had to figure out quickly what to do to get myself back on track and fix the problem 911, because it was beginning to feel like the start of a very long year.

A couple of months later, I moved out of Anthony's place and in with my dear girlfriend Nancy (also a Montreal native), who offered a different perspective on my experience. She was a boss lady during the day, running a successful business called Olivier's & Co, a fine culinary store.

But at night she was all about having fun, and for me at the time, fun was a much-needed addition to my experience. Her condo was in a trendy posh community, and I hoped that this move would inject new life and the opportunity to see the city with fresh eyes. We had a blast together (sometimes too much fun), and she was a huge supporter in wanting me to succeed, introducing me to everyone she knew. Eventually I was hired by Sutherland Models, a top modelling agency. It was exciting, and although it wasn't in the field of television that I was pursuing, I was just happy to be part of something.

But as one problem was solved, another would pop up. The agency had requested that I get new photos done to start building my modelling book, insisting that I use their photographer. The only issue was it wouldn't be cheap. Not having worked since arriving in Toronto, which

MASTER
OF SINGLE

compared to Montreal, was a very expensive city to live in, I'd already cashed in my RRSPs just to afford the move, so money was very tight. Paying to get photos done was not at the top of my budget priorities.

This whole time, I'd stayed connected to my friend back home. He was aware of my hardships, and by this time, he'd recovered from his own financial issues. He could tell I was struggling, and like a true friend, he came to visit me, bringing a much-needed piece of home with him.

We went to dinner his first night in town, and it was amazing to reconnect with him. It made me feel that everything was going to be okay, even just for one night. During dinner, we discussed my situation with the agency, and he graciously offered to give me the money to get my photos done, which was incredibly kind of him to want to help.

But the mixed bag of emotions in seeing him, already feeling overwhelmed and a little homesick, drove me to drink more than I normally do. I don't know what I was thinking, but I drank cognac, something I'd never drunk before, and boy oh boy did it hit me.

I was drinking to celebrate his being there but more to forget that I was there. He, on the other hand, was sober. He wasn't a big drinker, which was a good thing because I was drunk enough for the both of us.

By the time we left the restaurant, I was beginning to unravel, and then the unthinkable happened. I became so horny. I felt this insatiable surge of intense sexual energy come to pass. I wanted to be touched, feel loved, and I craved the body heat and weight of a man on top of me. The unthinkable part was that I ended up making a pass at him, one of my best platonic male friends, and it wasn't even cute. I was way too drunk and way too messy to be taken seriously. When I threw myself all over him, he had to pull the Matrix move a couple of times to avoid my desperate attempts to lean in for a kiss. He knew very well that I would regret it the next day.

But drunk Nicole is also very persistent, and eventually he gave in. We went back to his hotel room. I was doing surprisingly well, considering I couldn't see straight, but all that was overshadowed by my ravenous need for sex. What a mess. We started to fool around, and I could tell he was reluctant, but I didn't care. I was on a mission to get laid, and unfortunately, he was the casualty. My impulsive nature and desperate, sinful side were no match for him.

There we were, in bed, with me mostly naked on top, straddling him, and him partially naked, but before anything could really happen, my world flipped upside down and came to a screeching halt with the onset of nausea and a spinning head.

In one swoop I jumped off him and bolted to the bathroom like a sprinter reaching for the finish line; it was so embarrassing. To make things worse, his hotel room was one of those modern, trendy type rooms with a glass wall separating bedroom and bathroom. Just my luck. Damn you, Toronto, and your trendy ways. I never appreciated how important one's privacy was until I was behind a glass wall, lying naked on the bathroom floor, and hugging the bowl. I wanted to disappear, but I could barely sit up, and of course I wouldn't let him help me. I was already so mortified. Not my finest hour.

At some point he fell asleep, and eventually I peeled myself off the floor and painfully made my way to the bed. I curled up in the fetal position, passed out, and woke up still in the same position, except that he had put a blanket on me. How sweet and humiliating at the same time.

The next morning, there was a note from him that read, "I had to leave to catch my flight. It was good seeing you. I hope you feel better." I wanted to die all over again. What had I done? And with one of my best friends. I just hoped that my antics hadn't affected our friendship.

It was a worst-case scenario, and all I could do was hope for the best. I reached out to him to apologize for my behaviour. He laughed, clearly at me. Putting my ego aside, I gave him his moment; I think I had it coming. At least if I was going to nosedive, thankfully it happened with someone who cared about me.

That's what I loved about him—he never judged me, even when I judged myself. In some weird way, that situation brought us even closer together. Nothing like a drunken shit show to bond a friendship.

You might be wondering why we didn't just couple up. There was an obvious connection between us, and once you've seen someone at their lowest and still like them, one could make the argument that there might be something more to be explored. But as much as we cared about each other, I knew that we were very different people with vastly different lifestyles.

As friends, our differences and lifestyles didn't affect us, but I could see the potential issues arising in a romantic relationship, and I knew that if we tried and failed, it would break my heart to lose him as a friend.

I was relieved to know that our friendship was strong enough to withstand a bump in the road like what happened in Toronto, but I wasn't willing to push it by throwing us off a cliff to see if we'd land on our feet.

But wait… the story doesn't end there… It turned out that he'd developed genuine feelings for me at some point down the line of our ten-year friendship. The only problem was, I was sure I didn't feel the same. I tried to laugh it off, telling him he was crazy and let's not ruin a good thing, but he dug his heels in deeper.

Things became awkward and weird. He became pushy about it, and eventually I couldn't handle it anymore. It had changed the dynamic of our friendship, which broke my heart, but there was nothing I could do about it.

He wouldn't accept my position, and so I had no choice. I started to put distance between us until ultimately our relationship was no more. It was a sad turn of events, a worst-case scenario and the loss of a dear friendship. I never thought it would happen to us, but it did.

By the end of my year in Toronto, I hadn't gotten the results or work experience I had hoped for. Modelling was fine but didn't pay enough. I ended up taking a second job in a nightclub doing bottle service, which was like torture to my soul; I didn't move my life to push bottles in a Toronto nightclub. All in all, it was a huge lesson and life experience that ultimately brought me back home with my pride having taken a little bit of a hit.

But coming home, I was even more determined to succeed, knowing I wasn't alone in wanting to thrive in doing what I loved in my own city. So with nothing to lose, I created a show idea that would hopefully inspire artists to want to stay in Montreal. My idea was to create a platform where artists could showcase themselves and get the visibility they needed to let people know they existed. I pitched the idea to CTV Montreal, which may I just say, as soulful as our city is, that doesn't necessarily translate to the corporate world. Being a young black woman presenting this off-the-beaten-path idea to a bunch of older white men—sorry 'bout it—for whom soul didn't seem to matter much. They'd been doing the same thing the same way for decades, so getting them to see my vision was a huge challenge.

After some hesitancy, a lot of convincing, and with the help of my mentor George, who held a high and respectable position with the network and who believed in me, they eventually approved my idea for air.

They gave me a one-minute spot within the newscast to put forth my vision for a segment I affectionately called *City Lites*. I know it doesn't sound like a lot of time, but one minute in the six-o'clock news is prime time, baby, and nobody else was doing what I was doing.

The opportunity wasn't lost on me. Determined to succeed and make it work, I did.

I hosted and produced my segment that ran for three successful years, boasting some of the city's top players and artists as guests and affecting positive change on the city and individual lives.

I nurtured that platform like it was my baby, giving every guest the chance to shine, and that felt so good in my soul. And after a successful run that could have easily continued, life redirected me, presenting me with a once-in-a-lifetime opportunity that would fill another part of my soul, one that I couldn't refuse.

And with that, I resigned from my position and moved to New York to pursue my acting dreams.

My leaving was bittersweet, and the biggest surprise was the support I received from the network, who at first doubted me and now were sad to see me go. With my leaving, they decided not to carry on with *City Lites*, citing it was mine to lose and nobody could replace me.

In the end, this roller-coaster called life has never disappointed, always giving me a ride for my money, nor has it ever let me down. Even in my darkest, most uncertain times, it's shown me that no matter how far I fall, I can always rise to become a stronger, even better version of myself.

My best advice to anyone doubting themselves, feeling

stuck, or not knowing what to do, I would say be brave and take chances. Even if you can't see the entire picture, start where you are because the most important first step is to believe in yourself.

Things won't always work out, but sometimes they do, and you'll never know unless you go for it.

CHAPTER Six

COMING IN HAWT

WELCOME TO CHAPTER six, my single lovers, a midway point yet just the beginning of my great single-girl adventures. If you've been drinking the Kool-Aid so far... ha ha, I'm kidding! Hopefully you're starting to see that single bright light at the end of the tunnel.

Let's recap what we've discovered so far. We've learned how to laugh at ourselves, to love and be loved, and how to grow through it all. We've partied like it was 1999... got knocked down only to rise and live stronger, and most importantly, we survived to tell about it.

Part of being successfully single is the ability to fuel your own life. Ideally, it would be amazing to have a partner who supports you with words of encouragement, someone who's there to pick you up when you fall and push you past your fears to go for your dreams.

But having that someone in your corner isn't everyone's

reality, which is why it's so fundamentally important that you learn to be in your own corner and have your own back.

When I set out to write this book and change the narrative of what it means to be single, I did it with conviction because I had something to say and share. Not expecting that it would spark my own inner superpower, reminding me of the undeniable force that lives within.

If I leave you with one thing (hopefully more than one), it would be to remind you all just how powerful you are.

The love I have for myself is without a doubt the most honest love I've ever known. When you're down and there's no one around, it can feel like a long way up, but every time you pull yourself back up, you stand a little longer, stronger, and taller. A partner can bring great things to your life, but the things you do for yourself to take care of you will serve you forever. And all those around you will prosper from your happiness too. Happy single, happy life.

One of the great parts about creating the life you want to live is that you have the power to choose to paint the world with as many different brushstrokes as you please. I'm so happy to not just be one thing. I've faithfully followed my dreams wherever my heart led me, knowing wherever I landed was where I was meant to be in that season of my life.

One of the most underrated aspects of being single is the time allowance that it brings to spend with friends and family. You also have more time to get involved with your community and volunteer your time, stepping outside yourself to help others.

Before moving on, let's have a moment of self-reflection and give ourselves some much-deserved love. This is a practise I do on a daily basis, even giving myself hugs when I need it. So, on the count of one, let's all wrap

MASTER
OF SINGLE

our arms around ourselves in a loving embrace and say, "I love me." Ready, set... ONE! Good for you; best hug ever!

Listen, relationships are great and fun and also come with a sacrifice that once you're in a relationship, your time naturally becomes split. Having to take into consideration someone else's feelings, thoughts, schedule, likes, and dislikes, which I guess is the point, but you'll never meet someone worthier of your time or sacrifice than you. That's why for this chapter... pack your bags. We're going on vacation!

Travel is certainly not limited to single people, but travelling alone offers a whole new set of opportunity and adventure.

One of the many amazing things when you travel alone is that nobody knows your name until you tell them. It comes with an anonymity that's as freeing and beautiful as can be. Not knowing who you might meet or who will have the pleasure of meeting you, are exciting and mysterious prospects.

As a matter of fact, this chapter was written while sitting on the beach in Jamaica; it was my birthday gift to myself. I wanted to go somewhere alone, change the vibe, get reinspired, and just focus on writing for a week. Not to mention that having a birthday in January, one of the coldest most blistering months, was the perfect time to get away and take a break from our brutal Canadian winter.

Travelling alone teaches you a lot about yourself and shows you how good or not you are at being with yourself. It pushes you out of your comfort zone, which I think is healthy to do every now and then, and that applies to most areas of life. Ideally, it's great to travel with a curious and open mind and to be intrigued by new things. I love meeting the locals and picking up a few words in a new language to better communicate and engage with them.

But make no mistake about it, and you heard it here first: the most universal common language I've found in all my travels isn't English, French, or even Spanish. It's unequivocally body language.

Yass, girl, I said it and I'll say it again. The most universal language we share is body language. It speaks clearly, doesn't mince words, and will take you far in communicating what you're feeling. Think about it. Other than verbal communication, what else really connects us?

There's music and body language, and we knowingly or unknowingly are communicating through both mediums all the time.

Women, we are great body language communicators! We like to bat our eyes, flirt with the flipping of our hair, and we know how to walk with a little extra swish in our step that will get attention. We are seductresses, even when we're not trying to be, and we're releasing pheromones that drive men crazy.

Men, on the other hand, not so much. Their repertoire of body language is much more limited to grabbing their balls, puffing their chest, flashing their money, and making grunting noises like they're savages in the jungle. It's primal like a mating call. And I hate to love it and love to hate it.

I remember when I discovered just how powerful this theory was. I was in beautiful Brazil where the primary spoken language is Portuguese. Every morning I'd go to this corner café stand to get coffee and a chlorophyll acai smoothie. I was obsessed with this drink, and it was my favourite way to start my day.

In fact, I loved it so much that I wanted to make a business out of it and import it back to Canada to share with everyone.

However, nobody who worked there spoke a lick of

MASTER
OF SINGLE

English, so the language barrier was preventing me from communicating my wishes.

One thing I learned early on was that they weren't going to work to understand me as a foreigner, so if they wouldn't meet me where I was, I would have to find a way to meet them where they were.

Determined to get the recipe, that night I went home, took out my dictionary and binder, and translated word for word everything I wanted to say from English to Portuguese.

One way or another I was going to get that recipe. Quitters never win, and winners never quit.

The next morning, feeling confident, I walked over to the juice stand, binder and dictionary in hand. I placed my things on the counter and smiled kindly at the man behind the counter, who was looking at me like "What does this foreigner want with her books up in my business?"

I took a deep breath and did my best to express and communicate what I had practised all night, but it wasn't translating literally, but with every word, he seemed to become more confused. So I decided to abort and resort to plan B, body language, which by the way, wasn't even a plan until it became the only plan.

With a perpetual smile on my face, there I was, using my body to communicate what I wanted. This seemed to please the man behind the stand. He started to pay closer attention to understand what I was trying so desperately to communicate. Pointing to the drink first, then using my arms like an airplane, rubbing my belly the way you do when you love something, and pointing to myself as a Canadian, hoping he'd be able to connect the gestures to make a complete thought. I must have looked nuts, but I was trying hard and I think he appreciated my effort, which appeared to be very entertaining because he called the other employees over to watch me too. Everyone was staring at me, laughing, but I didn't care. I would have probably laughed at me too. It was like an amusing mix of body language, *Portuguese for Dummies*, and charades.

You know the saying, don't give up before the miracle happens? Well, I didn't and it paid off.

Before I knew it, he was waving me to follow him to the back kitchen. Thinking about it now, it might not have been the best idea to follow a strange man in a foreign country into a back room. But in that moment, I trusted the process, feeling like something must have landed, and I was curious about what he wanted to show me.

No more than ten minutes later, I walked out, having not only seen him make my smoothie, but he gave me the original packaging so I knew exactly what it was!

As happy and excited as I was, thinking Canada's going to love this, my acai importation dreams were cut short. I found out that it contained certain ingredients not approved by the Canadian Food Inspection Agency, essentially making the drink impossible to import.

What did I take away from that experience aside from how effective body language can be? I learned that I'm also okay making a fool of myself and being uncomfortable. In fact, I'm even okay with other people laughing at me. In the end, I believed in what I was doing, and that's all that mattered.

And with that said, this is a great time for another pivot. Have you ever noticed how much sexier you feel on vacation? Maybe it's something in the water or your sun-kissed skin that brings out your natural glow and beauty. Or blame it on that third island cocktail that's got you feeling yourself. Whatever it is, vacation brings out the best in us. One of the reasons we get away is to leave all the noise and stresses of life behind and embrace something new, fresh, and exciting.

Which is why we tend to pack our favourite pieces to wear because they make us feel beautiful, and that's what vacations are for, to get away and feel like the best version of yourself.

I have an admission to make. My name is Nicole and I'm an overpacker. What else can I say but that I love having options? I'll pay the overweight fee just to have what I want with me because I just never know how my inner fashionista is going to feel on any given vacay day.

I do low-key envy those who can pack a backpack and be gone for a week. I find those people fascinating! Clearly, we're not cut from the same travel cloth, but hey, to each their own.

Let's not skip over the idea of meeting a potential someone special as part of your single travel experience. The possibility of hooking up with a beautiful single stranger from a faraway land with whom you share a mutual connection with can lead to unadulterated moments of passion. Vacation is the perfect backdrop for an *Eat, Pray, Love* moment, emphasis on the love part.

But here's where it gets good. Love doesn't necessarily mean meeting someone and falling *in* love. Consider the idea of loving the one you're with while you're with them.

You can love meeting a stranger who makes you want to scream their name and unleashes the sexual beast in you that wants to come out to play.

I know firsthand how amazing, exciting, and exhilarating it can be to allow yourself to be connected to your head, heart, and hips. An idea I learned in acting class.

The other part of it is trusting your instincts to be able

to recognize a good opportunity when it presents itself. These are all possibilities when it comes to travelling single.

On the flip side and in the same breath, I'm the first to say vacationer goddess beware! As much as I evoke using your power of freedom to have fun, I can't emphasize enough the importance of doing it wisely. Being a free spirit is not to be mistaken with putting yourself in dangerous situations. I'm extremely vigilant when it comes to my safety, especially when I'm travelling alone.

It goes without saying, but it's worth saying anyway, that one should always beware of the creepy strangers. They are the opposite of the beautiful strangers, and they are in every country.

Do not panic. This can be easily vetoed simply by being in tune with yourself and your surroundings; trusting your judgement is key to protecting your person. If something or someone doesn't look or feel right, then it's not. Period point blank. Being far away from home is not the time to second-guess your instincts, so without being paranoid, just stay vigilant but still allow yourself to have fun.

Throughout my many travels, I've been blessed to meet people who have contributed greatness to my life, joy to my heart, pleasure to my libido, and peace to my soul.

I've made connections with men who have become my friends and my lovers. So consider this as my travel pay-it-forward moment to inspire you to do yourself a solid and get on a plane, train, or automobile. Cross a border, hit the road, and stamp a passport, but for God's sake, please take yourself on a vacation! And love every single minute of it.

The few handpicked, lucky, beautiful strangers I've met and engaged with along the way have served me well. This next story is about one of those connections... so as we say yes to travel and yes to life, let us tip our hat to staying open to all the possibilities.

This next great adventure takes place in my absolute favourite spot in the world, Ibiza, Spain! It's a destination I've been travelling to since 2000, give or take a summer or two.

Otherwise, it's my happy place and my annual vacation. It's also where the other half of my heart lives—my beloved extended family, including my soul sister Elisabetta, and brother Ray, who together brought into this world my precious godsons.

When I think about how amazing our boys are (their sons/my godsons/our boys), it's no wonder they're so amazing; they are a product of equally amazing and special parents.

The matriarch Mama Betta is like the salt of the earth. She's a different hybrid of woman and not to be compared or mistaken with anyone else. Once you meet her, you know you've been in the presence of someone special. I will forever be grateful to her for having had babies for both of us to love. Like I mentioned, technically they are her sons, but she shares them with me. So yeah, they're our boys.

The other part of them is the gift of their father and patriarch, Papa Ray. An incredibly talented artist, actor, and quite a brilliant and stupendous man of conviction, great pride, and who has all my respect.

This family, after my own family, are the most important on the planet to me, and having the honour of godmother bestowed upon me has been the greatest blessing and the next best thing to having my own kids.

I'm so fortunate to have them in my life.

On its face, Ibiza is an island distinct and magical in

energy and vibrations. The earth itself contains high levels of rose quartz in the soil, which is known to heal and bring balance to our mind and body energy.

This small yet not so small island, population approximately 135,000, doesn't disappoint and delivers on all fronts; it also doesn't keep time. Whether you see your fair share of late nights followed by early mornings, nobody's keeping track of time in Ibiza. Unless you're a businessperson who's rushing to get to a meeting, well then you're probably on the wrong island to begin with.

For the most part, time is a non-factor and work is a distant second to having fun.

Its reputation precedes it as a renowned party destination, but it's so much more than just that. To love Ibiza is to know Ibiza and its gorgeous beaches, secluded health spas, incredible villas, and stunning sunsets that overlook the mighty and majestic Balearic Sea.

It's riddled with passionate souls who roam freely, spreading and receiving love, and is dotted with hidden treasures and charming little nooks to eat the delicious fresh catch of the day.

One of my favourite spots to connect to myself is in the presence of Es Vedrà, a small, uninhabited island that sits tall in the sea approximately 1.5 miles offshore. It's a magical enclave surrounded by decades of myths and legends. One legend has it that it's the third most magnetic place on earth after the North Pole and the Bermuda Triangle. I don't care about truth or legend, all I know is what I care about, that the energy that emanates from it is all-powerful and consuming in the most impressive way.

If you travel to Ibiza alone, chances are you won't be by yourself for long. People are kind and welcoming, and friendships are easily made. My best advice is that upon arrival, you surrender the need to rush, be impatient, control, or plan too much.

The clock that governs Ibiza has no beginning or end, no day or night, and no absolute direction. The energy of the sun, the twinkle of the stars, and light of the moon are all you need to guide you. Trust the island, tap into its magical energy, and it will provide you with everything you need to have an unforgettable life experience.

I know that may sound whimsical and weird to some, but you'll better understand once you've experienced it for yourself.

Happy travels!

Another aspect of beauty on the island are the different types of people that come from all over the world to congregate. It's where I developed an affinity for bohemian nomad men. They are lovers by nature with an easygoing spirit about them and simple at their core.

There are two types of men that I am typically attracted to: nomads are one and Italian men are the other, and not necessarily in that order. Mind you I love my beautiful black men and most exotic men too, as long as you possess some sort of vibe about you. I will give any man a chance to prove his worth.

I like my men to be taller than me at least by a couple of inches and handsome in my eyes but not prettier than me, as I like to be the pretty one in the relationship. They should be strong but able to be soft when needed.

He should also be rational, smart, curious, spiritually tapped in, supportive, sweet on the inside, approachable on the outside, and with enough edge to give him personality and character.

And he's got to have a sense of humour, because if

we're not having fun, then what the hell are we doing? We're done.

The courting man in this story satisfied my Italian desires when he showed up by way of a visit to my family's house one afternoon. He was a family friend, which gave him instant credibility, because without question, I trusted their judgement and when it comes to me, they are extraprotective of my well-being. If he was anything less than a good guy, they wouldn't let him near me.

I remember sitting outside on the veranda, and when he walked through the gate, I was intrigued upon first sight. He was so good-looking—almost too good-looking—but I liked the confidence he exuded and his easygoing laid-back vibe. He looked fresh and cool in his linen top, designer shorts, and sandals. Almost like a hybrid of the types of men I like in one gorgeous specimen.

He spoke with the most charming Italian accent, which gets me every time, and I would soon discover a slew of other great qualities about him. His dark brown curly locks framed his face just so, and his stout physique told me that he could probably hold my weight standing upright. And those eyes... ocean-blue, crystal-clear beautiful, intoxicating, mesmerizing, and too dreamy for words. Once I connected with his eyes, it was game over, as if I'd gone deep-sea fishing and he was the catch on the other end.

I was so enthralled with him that I didn't even stop to notice if the feeling of attraction was mutual. But after collecting myself from acting like a fanatical teenager, taking a breath and a step back, it became clear that he was into me too. I might not have had his mesmerizing eyes, which I'm sure allowed him to get away with murder—but I wasn't showing up empty-handed. I brought what I brought to the table too, and I was happy that he noticed.

MASTER OF SINGLE

Smart guy. Thank you very much.

After a few drinks and some harmless flirting, my naughty side set my mind to wander and wonder how amazing it would be to be staring into those eyes while riding his masterpiece. Hmmm… I mean, I'm only human, and we were in Ibiza where the only bad thoughts are the ones you don't think. Ibiza's a place that inspires you to seize and enjoy the moment however it presents itself, and there was certainly something presenting itself. When it came to him, my motto was "fewer questions, more action."

We hung out with the family for a while longer until the sun began to set; that's when he proposed we go out. I didn't hesitate for a second before blurting out a resounding, "Yes, sure, great idea, love to!" I quickly caught myself, adjusted my thirsty ways, and reeled in my overtly excited high-pitched enthusiasm. But I couldn't help it; it was exciting to be going out in Ibiza with this beautiful stranger with all kinds of potential. I mean, come on, you'd be excited too. Who wouldn't be?

Remember, though, that too excited can come across as desperate, but too lackadaisical can be mistaken for being aloof, so I had to find that balance in my body language that said "I might want to fuck you, but I also want to get to know you." It was an interesting balance to strike when it came to him.

Before sending me on my way, my sister, who's always looking out for my best interests, took me to the side for a quick 411 download, letting me know that he was a nice guy from a good family and that I was in safe hands. But to beware of his playboy/party-boy reputation.

I was happy to have the heads-up, and honestly, I wasn't surprised.

Not only was he drop-dead gorgeous, but he was also young, at least eight to ten years my junior. Not to mention he also had the financial means that afforded him a very nice lifestyle. Absolutely he should be a playboy; in fact, it would've been weird if he wasn't. He was doing exactly what any hot guy in his position at his age and with his means should've been doing. Bravo, good for him and great for me.

I'd rather him be honest about being a playboy than run around cheating on girlfriends, so the only thing that mattered to me was that he was single and potentially be DTF (down to fuck). Those were the only criteria on my mind, and I think one of those answers was becoming obvious, so I asked the other question, and the answer was no, he didn't have a girlfriend.

Good talk.

He didn't know it yet, but this playboy had just met his match.

We said our goodbyes to the fam, and off we went into the Ibizan night.

Right off the bat I noticed that everywhere we went he knew the right people, and everyone—I mean everyone—knew him. Every place was quick to receive, seat, and serve him in true baller style, down to his favourite table and bottles waiting for him. This made his influence and VIP status on the island clear to see, and you know I love a good VIP status. Food for thought: Why do mediocre when best is an option?

As the evening pressed on, so did we. After a quick stop back at my family's house to change and pack an overnight bag, we were off to write part two of an already boundless and fantastical night. We were having such a blast; our chemistry was hot and only getting hotter. We set a literal blaze everywhere we went, and I say this next thing with a lot of humility, but the combination of our hotness was a lot to handle. His mesmerizing eyes and good looks, paired with my sexy, exotic chocolate... If I wasn't me, I'd be turned on by us. That's how delicious we looked together—yay!

Okay, be honest, have you ever noticed a couple that looked so hot together that you secretly imagined how amazing their sex life might be? I certainly have, and surely I'm not alone in this.

Our eventual transition from the club to the bedroom couldn't have come soon enough. With the break of dawn peeking through after a night of partying and heavy sexual buildup, I was feeling legit, lit.

I couldn't wait to have the weight of his body on top of me and those eyes of his looking right through me as he unleashed his beast. The minute our naked bodies collided... forget about it. We were on fire, and it was fucking amazing! Full pun intended.

His sexual style was a perfect match to mine. Attentive but dominating, I let him take control and liked it. It was a fusion of sensual, seductive, and savage energy. He made me feel special with his tenderness and mindful awareness of my comfort and pleasure... and more pleasure. Eventually, somewhere between saying "more" and calling out our safe word—LOL—exhausted, we finally crashed with every part of ourselves gratified. Now that's the way to go to bed.

Speaking of crashing after a night of partying in Ibiza, I want to let all would-be newbies to the island know that it's a common occurrence, especially for first-timers, to miss your flight off the island. There are many reasons why this might happen. Perhaps you're still partying in the clubs when you should be at the airport, or you're recovering from the night before and completely sleep through your alarm. Other times you just can't bring yourself to leave, or like in this case, you're still in bed with your lover.

Whatever the reason, don't sweat it; it's like an unspoken initiation that you miss your first flight home on your first visit to Ibiza.

But I'll tell you this. I've never met a single person who regretted missing their flight.

So. You're welcome.

I did end up missing my flight off the island days later, but it wasn't an accident. We both knew we didn't want what we had started to end. It was an easy decision for him to stay, as he really had no responsibilities to be concerned about.

As for me, I was working in television, and at the time, I was my own boss, which allowed me to have a lot of latitude with my schedule. But the saving grace that allowed me to extend week after week after week was because I'd done my due diligence prior to leaving.

Not knowing I was going to meet him, obviously, when I was making my original travel plans, something inside me was telling me to bank as many segments as possible just in case I decided to stay longer.

So I took the cue and worked my ass off to bank as much as possible, and it paid off.

That's why it's good to always follow your instincts. I was so happy to know that I didn't have to rush back just for work. Banking those segments was the best decision I'd made in a long time. If the network had content to air, it didn't matter whether I was there or not because the show still went on. Yup, not just pretty.

Initially I was planning on staying a month, but it ended up being closer to three.

MASTER OF SINGLE

Thankfully, my family gave me their blessings and allowed him to occupy most of my time, but they were just happy for my happiness. And not much could have burst our bubble.

This beautiful stranger turned beautiful friend turned beautiful lover treated me like his queen. He was so sweet to me. There was really no downside. I loved every second of his attention and affection, which in the beginning took a minute to adjust to because I was used to taking care of myself. I've always been a person who was better at giving than receiving, but he made it easy for me to just let go and receive. Because of how he was with me, it was an easy and equal pleasure to reciprocate and make him feel like my king. Call us crazy kids or blame it on Ibiza, but whatever it was, we were living, loving, partying our asses off, and making no apologies for it. Good times indeed.

As I remember that enchanted time, I'm also reminded that all good things eventually do come to an end. But like I always say, with every end is a new beginning…

With the summer winding down, we approached our final days of this unbelievable ride. The funny thing was that I had no expectations after we went our separate ways. Which even surprised me that I could be so matter-of-fact about accepting it ending. The whole experience was incredibly fulfilling that I wasn't thinking about the future; it wasn't mine to see, and the gift of the present was enough for me.

I hadn't created any illusions of grandeur in my mind that this relationship would carry into our "real" lives. I felt quite realistic about our Ibiza fairy-tale romance and accepted it for what it was, knowing I might never see this incredibly special person again, or at least for a long time.

The truth was fact. We lived oceans apart with borders between us. That was the reality, and I was okay with it. I could have easily self-sabotaged our ending by getting caught up in the emotion of the thing, but instead I focused on the experience. What a shame it would have been to taint our final moments with negative, troubled thoughts or heavy unrested emotions, so I didn't. But it takes two to let go, and little did I know that he wasn't as ready to let me go as I was to let him go.

One of his traditions after spending the summer in Ibiza was to end the season with his family back in his hometown of Sicily, Italy. On the eve of my departure and our last hurrah, he surprised me by doing something I didn't see coming a million light-years away.

As I lay there on the bed, listening to him tell me about his plans and starting to think about my own life back home, he blew my mind when out of nowhere and in his ever-so-slick way, he invited me to join him on his trip back home. I'm sure I must have looked like a deer in the headlights with my eyes bulging out of my head, questioning if I'd heard him correctly.

This was huge! An Italian man, or any man for that matter, typically doesn't bring a girl home unless he really cares about her. I was in total shock in the best way possible and probably a little nervous at the thought of meeting his family.

In my mind, I was already preparing to say goodbye and release him back into the world.

Just when I thought our fairy tale had struck midnight, clearly we were going into overtime.

I started thinking I knew that I had one final segment banked to air, and I could use that to extend my trip one last time. It would be a tight return home, but I knew I could make it work.

Then my thoughts were interrupted by him asking me

MASTER
OF SINGLE

again, (insert sexy Italian accent) "*Amore*, you want to come to Sicily with me?" This time without hesitation, I said, "Yes, of course. I would love to." But I prefaced with the importance of me leaving on time, that if I stayed any longer than expected, it would put my job in jeopardy, so without a shadow of a doubt I would have to get back to shoot the next week's segment.

He agreed, and that was that. We finalized the details and booked our flights. To celebrate, we got naked and devoured each other one last time in our Ibiza bubble… Oops, we did it again, and we loved every delicious minute of it.

Remember when I wrote about travelling being one of the greatest freedoms and gifts you can give yourself, especially as a single? Well, I had this story in mind. Although your story is bound to be different from mine, the point remains the same. There's an extraordinary experience out there waiting with your name on if you just give yourself the chance to let it find you, wherever that may be.

About Sicily… before we knew it, we were in the sky and off to meet his family, who were the kindest, sweetest, most welcoming people ever. A true Italian, family-first, tight-knit, lots of love, food, and laughter type of family. They made my first time to Sicily one I'll never forget and will cherish always.

And in case you're wondering, he and I stayed connected afterwards, and sometime down the road when I moved to New York City for school, he was the first person to help through his international connections and managed to get me set up with an apartment in Manhattan.

Crazy how things work out.

My whole intention in sharing this was to hopefully

inspire and expand your mind and idea of what travelling alone can be. And even if it's a single-girl's trip, just go for it, lead with an open heart, with a yes and attitude, and thank me later.

That summer was one of the best times of my life, no regrets.

Grazie, amore mio, per i ricordi.

Chapter Seven

LOVER'S LANE

SPEAKING OF LOVERS... who's ever had or considered taking one? Raise your hand because you're not alone, and you're not weird for thinking it. Until my absolute man arrives, I've learned how to balance enjoying the company of a chosen one in a completely unique and self-serving, typically sexual way, enter—the lover.

You might remember the idea of "taking a lover," which famously became mainstream by the fabulous Carrie Bradshaw in *Sex and the City* when referring to her Russian lover, Aleksandr Petrovsky. To which I say, if it's good enough for Carrie, it's good enough for me. Although I'm slightly kidding about drawing similarities between us, I'm very serious about lover's lane. Ever since I got the hang of how this special kind of relationship works, my lover success rate has been at a solid four out of five (there's always that one dud who fails to meet the mark, and by mark, I mean leave an impression).

Love it or hate it, it's a conversation worth having, and we're going to have it now.

Before anything, the *most* important step is to make sure that the person you may want to pursue is single and available. Do not accept anything less, including "I'm separated," or "It's complicated," or whatever. It's vital to know who and what you're dealing with before stepping into this world of extremes. We are not trying to be anyone's side piece. Hell, no! This arrangement only works between two consenting single adults; otherwise, you're the other woman or other man. Neither is a good look, and chances are you'll be the one getting hurt. Clarity is queen.

With that said, let's get into it! What's the difference between a lover and a boyfriend? I'm glad you asked. A boyfriend or girlfriend, for most people, is a monogamous commitment, a stable, comfortable routine. It's a relationship with someone who is there as a partner to support, encourage, and love you. Clear.

A lover is more like a pleasure playground without the promise of tomorrow; he or she could be considered a neutral safe zone or someone you have a deep desire for and sexual connection with but aren't necessarily looking for anything serious. A lover is there for a good time, not necessarily a long time.

I understand this may be a lot to take in and quite jarring for some, so I'm going to break it down step by step and play-by-play as best I can. Take what works and leave the rest; and if it's not for you, no problem, just enjoy the read and living it vicariously through my journey. I can only speak to my experiences, and here's what I know about taking a lover.

MASTER OF SINGLE

Still curious about this unconventional type of relationship, are you? Next thing to get clear about after the status situation is knowing the difference between your needs versus your wants and your head versus your heart. In simple terms, if your head is telling you what you *need* is someone with whom you can have regular sex, then a lover could be the key. But if your heart *wants* to fall in love, then a lover may be a dangerous and slippery slope. Lovers don't typically turn into boyfriends. I'll get more into that as we go on, but it's an important distinction to make. Recap: head=need for sex/heart=want for love. If your case is the latter, you're probably best to go the boyfriend route.

What I like about the lover option is that it comes with a sense of commitment but just a very loose one. Both parties agree on a set of rules that work for their situation while maintaining their personal autonomy outside the relationship. This means that when you're together, all eyes, attention, pleasure, and focus is on each other, but when you're not together, what happens on your own time is none of the other's business.

The only exception to this rule is that I require the person to let me know truthfully of any sexual activity outside our relationship that could impact my well-being, like having unprotected sex with someone else.

Lovers are great when you're not looking for a full-on commitment and all the bells and whistles that come with a traditional relationship. Being single doesn't stop me from finding clever and creative ways of engaging and satisfying my sexual wants. I recognize that this may not be the ideal situation for everyone; it's simply an option as part of the "in the meanwhile" phase of your single season. Think of it as an alternative option for those who dare to explore outside the box. I like having options and enjoy living outside the box; besides, who wants to be in a box anyway?

However, it's worth repeating that this is not for everyone. I'm sharing it because my lover experiences have been positive ones. I've done the heavy lifting on this subject, and I can recognize the value in this type of relationship when it's done right. Once you're clear about your want versus your need, it's of the utmost importance that you next clarify the terms of the relationship, or as I refer to them, the rules of engagement. When it comes to matters of the heart, things can get messy quickly, so think about what the rules will look like for you so that you can clearly communicate them when you find your lucky person.

I've seen it happen before. Once a man penetrates a woman, if she's not emotionally prepared, it can be game over. Women are emotional creatures (in a good way), and having a man inside us can stir up unexpected emotions, making us feel all kinds of crazy things that can easily blur the lines between love and lust. But fear not—it's nothing you can't handle if you're prepared. Remember, we hold the power, so if this is the lane you choose to explore, set yourself up to succeed and get real with yourself quickly.

Another important factor is having a clear perspective. In my experience, lovers don't typically become boyfriends, mainly because it can be difficult to reverse the original rules of the game back to something monogamous. That's why perspective is everything; love and sex don't necessarily have to go hand in hand. I'm not saying it's impossible, but heed the warning that a lover situation is what it is and usually doesn't change. But more power to you if you want to try to go for it. Just don't say I didn't tell you so. My best advice is to not overthink or try to make it something it's not; just enjoy being together and the choice you made to make yourself happy.

That said, we are only human, and for that reason I want you to make sure that you protect your heart by

MASTER OF SINGLE

establishing clear "rules of engagement" that suit you. Do not compromise, or you might find yourself in a "situationship," which is neither here nor there and can get messy very quickly.

Having these boundaries and guidelines will protect you, so make sure they're clear and respected by both parties, and for the love of God, try not to change the rules in the middle of the game. Once you start bending the rules, the entire structure and everything you've established can collapse like a house of cards. Both parties should feel assured that the rules won't change when they're least expecting it.

This spoken contract might include, but is not limited to, how comfortable you are being in public together, if at all, the number of times you communicate in a week, and where you meet to fuck. Pardon my brashness, but we're not "making love" here. Lovers are a hit-it and quit-it good-time situation. Don't be afraid to call it what it is; get comfortable with the verbiage and the truth of it.

Again, it's to protect yourself from yourself.

Maybe to start, you keep things neutral by choosing a hotel if you're not comfortable bringing him or her back to your place right away. Further conversations might include your sexual likes and dislikes and whether you prefer phone calls or text messaging.

You might have noticed that I'm not shy when it comes to saying what I mean and meaning what I say. When it comes to the importance of safety and my health, particularly these days during a pandemic, it's more important than ever to have good communication.

Don't be afraid to inquire about their last Covid or STD test. Be willing to ask the uncomfortable questions as it will only help you feel more at ease when the time comes to engage.

One of the greatest disservices we can do is to go into any sexual situation blindly or with lingering questions. Even after the conversations are had and requirements are met, most of the time I still require him to wear a condom, but that comes down to personal choice.

A smart idea is to carry condoms with you and have the conversation before things get too accelerated and heated. A lot of guys will try to sweet talk you out of making them wear one by saying that they don't have one or that it feels so much better without it. Which is true, but if this is one of your deal breakers, don't let anyone sway your better judgement. Be prepared and stay strong to your convictions.

Now that we've gotten the logistics out of the way, let's get into how to choose your person. My personal approach when choosing a lover is simple. The men I choose are typically not the same type of men I'd choose as a boyfriend. My lovers are usually very busy and are more on the transient side, meaning that they may be here one day and travelling the next. They typically possess characteristics that make them unable to sustain real commitment, and they're easily distracted, which works fine for this kind of relationship. This brings me back to my point of why lovers don't make good boyfriends.

A strong physical attraction is vital. You want to lust over this person. It should be all about the sex and how great you make each other feel. It may sound superficial, but that's the whole point of taking a lover. He's not your lover because he's intelligent (LOL). His brains are a bonus, but his sexy is a must. The other requirement is that he must respect and appreciate you, be open-minded, and make you feel safe and in good hands. That said, please send résumés and headshots directly to… ha ha, kidding (ish).

MASTER
OF SINGLE

This all begs the question: How the hell do you even find a lover? I wish I had a more sophisticated answer to that question, but the truth is, it's as simple or complicated as you make it. Here's a secret: lovers are just people like you and me. The key to landing one is having the poise and courage to let them know your intentions. Sometimes a lover can start off as a one-night stand that evolves into a longer-term sexual, lover relationship.

Listen, if someone catches your carnal eye, go to them like a boss, without overthinking. Don't stutter, fidget, or hesitate. Approach with confidence. An obvious place to meet a lover is at a bar or lounge, but really it can be anywhere people roam. If you're more comfortable online, there are apps that allow you to personalize your dating preferences, which might take a lot of the guesswork out by being able to state what type of relationship you're looking for.

If you're meeting someone face-to-face, start the conversation light and easy. Don't blow your wad before testing the waters first; go at your own pace. Remember, it's important and respectful to not impede on another woman's territory, so whomever you're pursuing, being single is an absolute must.

Once you're ready to make your move, start with introducing yourself and asking them how they're doing. Or break the ice by saying that they look like someone you know, and don't be afraid to offer a compliment, whether it be something about their cool vibe or what they're wearing. Flirting goes a long way, and don't forget about the power of body language. All the above will help you gauge his level of interest.

If you're feeling playful and bold, go up to your target and pull them in with a fun game. For example: "Hi, I'm Nicole. Want to play a game?" Don't wait for the answer, just start the game. Pick a number from one to five, and if you get it right, you buy me a drink; if you get it wrong, you buy me a drink. So cute and confident and most men love a confident woman and will indulge her playfulness. I mean, even I'd want to fuck that girl.

Based on his reaction, play your cards wisely, which also means having an endgame in mind even if that means walking away. Sometimes, despite your best efforts, the connection just won't be there. Don't take it personally; it's okay and no sweat off your brow. Exit gracefully and keep it moving. This is just one example of what I mean when I say be bold… Whatever that means for you, make it your own.

Another good option if you're not totally comfortable approaching someone is to send in a girlfriend to test the waters for you. I don't like when guys do this because I like my men to own their shit, and I know that's a bit of a double standard, but hey, suck it up, buttercup.

Normally I like to do my own dirty work, but if it helps you to take the edge off, then fine, send in reinforcement to test the waters for you. They might say something like, "Hey, my girlfriend wants to know if you're single. She thinks you're cute." Once they get the status report, depending on the answer, they can then proceed and ask if he'd like to join you for a drink. If he complies, that's a good sign, and be prepared to take it from there.

Other scenarios could be seeing someone interesting walking their dog in the park. I picked up a guy while walking my dog two blocks from my house, and within forty-eight hours we were banging each other's brains out; it was so hot.

Even riding on the subway, or maybe they are standing across from you at the gym, pumping iron while you're looking at him and wishing he was pumping you. No scenario is off-limits, and different situations will dictate your approach, but each time you should approach with confidence and own it.

Remember, it's supposed to be fun, and the goal is to start with establishing a mutual interest. Don't be discouraged if it takes a couple of tries and a few conversations to find the right person for the job. Your efforts will pay off in the end when you find yourself horizontal, saying their name. Take your time and keep your eye on the prize.

If you're really brazen, like me, you can cut to the chase altogether and just walk straight up to them and say plainly, "Are you single because I think you're hot. If you are, are you DTF?" It doesn't get bolder than that, then you see where things go. I've done it; it works.

Now, once you've established said relationship, at any point if you find yourself in a quandary and you start to catch feelings for said lover, stop what you're doing! If you become confused between your want and your need, and emotions begin to seep in and blur the lines of perception between lover and boyfriend, do not ignore the signs. *Run!*

Trust me, I know this all too well.

Unless you have good reason to believe the desire for more is mutual, lover's lane may just have hit a cul-de-sac. Of course, you still have the power of choice. You can choose to take the chance and put your feelings out there, but they are not responsible for that part of your heart as per the deal. You can hope they feel the same way, but you shouldn't expect anything back in return. Having no expectations beyond the rules of engagement can greatly reduce your chances of getting hurt, and I don't want to see anyone get hurt. In the same breath, don't let that scare you. This is when it's best to leave on a high note, protect your heart, and chalk it up to an experience. Call deuces. You're out. This brings us to my next story, a lover of epic proportions…

NICOLE JONES

When I think back to the lovers who've inspired me to believe it was possible to have great sex and connection without "true love" or a committed partnership, this next man stands out among them. Not only was he hot, but he was also kind, smart, funny, sexy, and a wild child—a dangerous combination for a lover status and almost verging on boyfriend material.

When we met, he expressed clearly that he was fresh out of an eleven-year relationship and wasn't looking for anything serious. He made his limitations crystal clear, and when a man tells you who he is, believe him the first time. In this case, it was clear that he would be strictly lover only, and that was fine by me.

He possessed a strong, manly disposition with a bad-boy edge, a killer smile, a great laugh, and had sultry eyes that brought me to my knees. I clearly have a thing for eyes; they're very telling about a person, and from what I could gather, his eyes were saying "Hello gorgeous, nice to meet you, cum on in." Yes, you read that right.

The slippery slope here was that we met at work (a corporate setting), adding heightened risk to the situation by mixing business with pleasure, so I would have to tread and tiptoe very lightly. I'd noticed him around the building, but the first opportunity we had to speak was at a company Christmas party surrounded by our co-workers, which acted as a buffer for us to meet naturally. By the time I rolled up on him, I'd had a couple of drinks, and my approach was about as subtle as getting hit over the head with a hammer. He was talking with another co-worker, who by the time I had arrived, they were walking away. Without mincing words, I said plainly that I thought he was hot, which was me throwing the bait out, the opposite of treading lightly, I might add.

Super important, know how to read the signs. A non-

MASTER OF SINGLE

reaction is also a reaction; thankfully, his response was that he thought I was hot too. Bingo!

Because this was a working environment and not an ideal situation for a hookup, I would have to first be sure he was someone who could hold his own way of separating personal from professional. A good rule of thumb is if your doubt is greater than fifty-one percent in either of you being able to maintain professional decorum, do not pursue or engage any further. Abort mission. The one percent that tips the scale is your instincts tapping on your brain and telling you to know better or to go for it. Listen to the signs or don't, but good luck with that.

After some good conversation and getting a sense of his vibe and attitude, I decided I wanted to get to know him a little more before making any decisions, so we exchanged numbers. And I immediately couldn't wait to see him again on neutral territory. We didn't waste any time getting together later that week. We met for a nice dinner at a place called Pica Pica (now closed, but so good), and let me tell you I was dressed to slay the night. No matter what happened, he wasn't going to forget me. I was giving him everything sexy I had in my bag of tricks. The dress… Oh, the dress I was wearing was such a tease—tight, short, and low plunging, not leaving anything to the imagination.

Those were the days I loved to show off my body, but not so much anymore. But on that night, I wanted him to see exactly what he had coming. I wanted for him to be so turned on that his dick got hard just looking at me, to the point he couldn't wait to get me home, bend me over, and show me what he was working with. He's welcome.

From the time we sat down, we couldn't wait to finish. Thank goodness we were in public or I would have done him right there on the damn table. But I'm a lady first—in public anyway—so we ate, drank, and laughed like civilized people, but eventually the suspense got the better of us and we couldn't wait any longer.

Much to my delight, I noticed when he got up that he had a hard-on, which excited me to no end. I'm getting warm inside all over again just thinking about it. It was so hot, and my kitty cat was ready for the cheque, please. Meow.

We got the bill in a hurry, jumped in a cab, and couldn't get back to his place fast enough. His hands were all over me, and I was wet in anticipation of his entrance into my pleasure dome. We kissed so hard and passionately that it made my nipples hard and my breathing heavier and heavier. We got out of the cab, and I kissed him some more while grabbing his cock at the same time, and I know a great cock when I feel it. I could tell his was going to be amazingly perfect in both size and girth. I couldn't wait to give him the best ride of his life.

Once inside his place, as hard as it was, I wanted to tease him and myself just a little longer before fucking him. With our eyes locked, I slowly lowered my body, unzipped his jeans, and wrapped my mouth around his beautiful tool, giving him a slow job he'll never forget, which means I took my time and made it count. He was delicious; I could have stayed down there all night. I love serving a great BJ.

I reached over and grabbed a condom out of my bag, ordered him to put it on, climbed on top of him, and slid all the way down his beautiful hard cock until the entire thing was inside me. He looked at me with those piercing eyes that reflected his naughty side; he bit his lip like he wanted to tear me apart and eat me whole, which he did.

He had me exactly where he wanted me—at his mercy and loving it. Oh, what a night!

Let's talk a little bit about where the sex takes place:

MASTER OF SINGLE

location, location, location. I mentioned hotels as an option, which is fine. I've done that before and it works. But if that's not an option, I personally prefer going back to his place. I'm weird like that and protective of the energy I let into my home, and to have sex with me in my bed is a privilege not to be taken lightly.

Using each other for sexual pleasure is one thing, but to get into my home space, that takes a little more time. Until then, his place will do just fine; besides, it's a good way to see how he lives. As well, I like the option to leave when I'm done and return to my little piece of undisturbed sanctuary. My home is my safe space, as my body is my temple, and I honour both equally and on my own accord.

Here's a better safe than sorry rule: if you decide to go back to a guy's place for a hookup, send a friend you trust a quick text letting them know where you are. It's just an added precaution.

I mean, if you get as far as going back to his or your place, you're probably trusting your instincts by that point, which is a good sign and very important.

After our initial rampage of sexual wildness, he attempted to play host by offering me a drink, but before he could pour the vodka, we were at it again. This time I was laid out on his kitchen counter looking up at his lovely ceiling, and he entered me with passion and vigour, and I love a good entrance.

Clearly our sexual chemistry outperformed the conversation. For hours we laid it down on every possible surface that would support our weight. We were so comfortable with each other, trying every position, submitting to each other's pleasure, and devouring each other until the sun came up.

Basically, we didn't stop fucking all night; it was a

marathon, not a sprint, and it must be said, his stamina was impressive.

Staying engrossed in the pleasure, which is a feeling, not the emotion, will help to keep your attention focused and clear, even after he blows your mind.

The key is to remember emotions don't run in coherent channels and will mess you up if you let them in, so leave them at the door.

I say this proudly that every traditional relationship I've had throughout my life has been monogamous, and to my knowledge I haven't had a boyfriend cheat on me. It's one of my hard rules in a committed relationship, and I expect the same in return.

The one thing I can't forgive is a cheater because that also means you're a liar—double whammy.

When I commit, I commit one hundred percent. I got his back and only have eyes for him.

Now, getting back to my hot piece of lover!

After our second, third, fourth, and fifth round of carnal pleasure (I lost count), we staged our own "occupy the bedroom" situation, where we remained blissfully for the rest of the day. Leaving only for bathroom and water breaks or to shower; otherwise, we were horizontal or vertical, and sometimes both at the same time—very notable I might add.

Eventually I decided it was time to go. I slowly peeled myself off the sweaty, dishevelled sheets that smelled of our glorious sex and started to collect my belongings. But as I got myself together, I could sense he wanted me to stay. To be honest, not only was I exhausted, but my vajayjay, cookie, kitty cat, pussy, or vagina—it has multiple names—had taken about as much as it could take. It needed a break and an ice pack. I was ready for food, sleep, and wanted to wake up in my own bed.

MASTER OF SINGLE

This is a great example of not getting too comfortable by maintaining your independence and not being afraid to leave a good thing.

No need to overstay my welcome or confuse the moment.

Sleeping over is a precarious situation. To maintain a certain emotional distance that allows me to stay within the boundaries doesn't usually include spending the night. My rule of thumb is that what happens in the night should stay in the night, although sometimes the night could bleed into the next day, but if you didn't sleep, it doesn't count. When he realized I wasn't staying, he said, "You don't have to leave."

I replied with, "Thanks, but I have things to do and prefer to sleep in my bed tonight, but I had a great time. Let's do it again soon!" It was clear, to the point, and left no room to argue or to be that guy who tried to make me stay.

Full disclosure: We were partying and using substances to prolong our endurance, which wasn't always the case, but sometimes it was, and that further explains why we didn't sleep.

On particular nights like that where the more heightened and savage the sex the better, we liked a little bump of cocaine before, during, and after to help us get there.

Which makes this a good time to pause for cause and take a minute to briefly speak to this side of my life on consumption. I want to be clear for those who may be curious as to how I was able to party and use drugs in this copious way without it becoming a problem or allowing it to dim my light, because it didn't.

First, by the grace of God. Amen.

It's true that in my plentiful party life, I've indulged for the sake of indulging, but I've also had out-of-this-world experiences that changed my life in incredible ways.

For example, having the honour to share in a secret ayahuasca ceremony and most extraordinary spiritual journey guided by an experienced shaman.

It's a medicinal plant that's boiled down and prepared into a tea (very bitter) and is commonly used among indigenous people in the Amazon as part of their spiritual practice.

It's an event that's difficult to explain. Like a journey that allowed me access to my inner being and to see myself unobstructed in all my power, pain, potential, and glory.

I mean, I was different in the most unexpected but welcome ways, stronger, healed, more connected to the universe, clearer, and grounded.

And the effects have been long lasting.

I've also had the good fortune of being at the forefront of unique experiences with one of the most advanced and sought-after scientific minds, who on a personal level made the study of psychedelics his life's work.

These tremendously privileged experiences I can only say were of another dimension that transcended me beyond this reality. I took everything incredible I experienced and applied it to my life, expanding and elevating me on all levels of consciousness.

So yeah, there's that too.

Granted, those were rare and special experiences, but it wasn't always like that.

I still think it's a little bit of a miracle there were some wild times, but the saving grace was having the ability to never forget who I was amid it all. Amen.

MASTER OF SINGLE

Also, I never lost sight of my addictive personality; staying cognizant of that helped to keep me in check and within boundaries, most of the time.

Then there's my strong will and an even stronger head with a character that isn't easily manipulated or allows myself to be controlled.

Somehow I was able to compartmentalize things in my mind, understanding on a soul level the difference between having fun and having a problem.

As crazy as it sounds, much like the seedy world of exotic dancing didn't break my spirit, working in nightlife didn't steal my soul nor did the trauma I suffered growing up dim my light.

Through the grace of God, this was one more part of my life I was able to keep in perspective and stay mindful to not let it use me.

And when I would slip—because sometimes I would—I'd catch myself using to mask the pain from past trauma that wasn't healed and didn't want to feel. Ultimately, that made it worse, and as hard as it was, I'd face whatever it was and find a better way of coping with it.

The one thing I could never do was justify letting myself become a victim.

People, whether they admit it or not, are dealing with something—a vice, an addiction, a compulsion, or a habit—whatever it is, it doesn't make you bad or wrong.

I believe the important thing is to stay self-aware because these things tend to stem from somewhere, and if a problem, instead of masking it, face, deal, heal, and move on from it.

It won't always be easy, but here's the secret: you are the secret; that's the secret.

Mind blown.

Clearly I'm not perfect, and thank goodness, by no means am I trying to be anyone's role model. However, if one person can learn from my life experiences or what I've learned, then it's worth sharing. But I want to be clear. Never would I encourage or promote using any type of drugs.

I absolutely realize not everyone's built like me, and this subject can be a dangerous gateway and slippery slope for most.

I'm sharing this unmasked part of myself with all my party people as an important reminder that nothing should ever have that much power over you.

And if it, he, or they do, then check it immediately and get the help you need.

If this is speaking to you, I'm praying for you.

My experiences may be specific to me; however, my message of love thyself and be in a relationship with yourself first are for everyone and transcend every subject matter.

I've often said that if I knew then what I know now, I'd do it all again, minus a tweak or two.

Sometimes I think to myself, *Nicole, you might not have gotten married yet (not even sure I want to) or had the blessing to birth a child, but girl, you have been blessed to live the life you designed for yourself. A life worth loving and not to be lived in vain.*

One thing for certain, I am not headed for a midlife crisis anytime soon. Every stone on my journey thus far has been turned, and I haven't missed a beat to my own drum.

With that said, beloveds, lover's lane isn't over yet…

The next day I woke up in my bed, thinking about him, mostly because I was bruised in places I didn't even know could bruise. I was so sore down there and everywhere that

MASTER OF SINGLE

it hurt to walk. Flashes from the previous night and all those hard surfaces and contortionists' positions came flooding back in a hurry, qualifying the hurt-so-good pain I was in.

Over the next few weeks, we continued to see each other for sex, mostly at night and usually at his place. As time moved on, so did our connection, which continued to surprise me. I've mentioned before that I don't like to get too personal with lovers because it puts me in a vulnerable position emotionally, but there was something about him. I could sense that I was beginning to feel oddly comfortable beyond lover's lane. That said, it was my work to keep things in perspective—lover, lover, lover. Period. Focus, Nicole!

And then the unthinkable happened. He extended an invite to join him and his friends for drinks, and I accepted. This went against every rule of engagement, and I knew it. Everyone could see that there was a strong connection between us, so much so that they questioned why we weren't taking our relationship more seriously. It was uncomfortable and awkward to try to explain, so we didn't try, and eventually they just let it go. But it forced me to look at what they were seeing, and that was even more awkward for me.

Our time together as lovers went on for almost two years without incident, until somewhere along the way he became my soft place to land. The intimate nature of our conversations humanized us. He no longer was just a hot piece of ass; he was a real person who was a good listener and a good guy who supported my dreams and had become a close friend. That was a huge sign that things were shifting into uncharted territory.

We were becoming strangely close and connected, both leaning in a little more every time we saw each other, and in my mind, I knew his limitations. But my rules and boundaries were beginning to feel so far behind me that it was concerning to say the least. Falling for him was not part of my master plan. I'd rather catch a cold than catch feelings for an emotionally unavailable man.

But, in true masochist style, I continued to play the role of lover as best I could, but I felt butterflies when I was around him. Those feelings weren't anything to take lightly; they were rare and special. I could feel myself wanting more, and it scared the hell out of me. I had no idea what to do, and I'd wished I'd gotten out sooner.

My only recourse was to separate myself from the situation for however long it took for me to regain clarity and perspective, which was a difficult but necessary next step for my emotional and mental well-being.

Of course he called, wanting to see me, and I'd make excuses for not being able to meet him. I was terrified of my own feelings but even more terrified of being rejected. I don't have suggestions beyond running for when boundaries fail and become matters of the heart. Those emotions tend to have a mind of their own, so yeah, if you go through that door, good luck. It's every single girl for herself.

When I finally felt strong enough and mustered up the courage to see him again, I did my best to go back to the carefree, easy, breezy lover he had come to know and appreciate. But really, I was just a girl whose heart was affected by a man I was beginning to fall in love with. Shit.

I wanted to abort, but I was in way too deep.

One night after being together and struggling to keep my feelings inside, I felt that if I didn't say something, I was going to implode. The whole situation had me feeling awkward in his presence, but I realized that everything I was feeling was happening in my head and my own heart. He was merely getting the residual effects and didn't understand why I was acting so weird, and that wasn't fair to either of us.

So the next time we were together, I tried again to mask my emotions with sex, taking a deep breath and saying to myself, *Just enjoy this man you love being with.* It was an internal dialogue that worked for a minute, but the greater reveal was that I was no longer the same person I started out as in this relationship.

Every time he entered me, my heart felt the emotion of every thrust. Kissing him was like kissing the man I loved, so ready or not, I had to decide. It was time to tell him what I was feeling.

I waited for the closest thing to the right moment and said to him in one shot, "I think I'm falling in love with you, and I want more than just a lover relationship." I went on to say how much I respected his boundaries but that my feelings were my feelings, and that's where I was. I'd never been so brave to go after a man and reveal my truest heart.

After cracking open and pouring my heart out, I looked at him for a reaction. I could tell immediately that his non-reaction was his response. I could hear my heart break. He managed to get a few words out, expressing his deep appreciation for me and our relationship (pause for more heartbreak), but his hesitancy to pull the trigger and take the next step was painfully clear. He didn't feel the same way. It was tough to be in that moment and be okay.

I knew what we'd signed up for, and I couldn't fault him for not feeling the same.

Fighting back the tears, I looked at him and said, "Hey, it's okay. I understand. I was just saying… but it's all good." I knew this was probably the end, so I said, "I'm sorry. I tried not to feel the feelings, and this is my problem, so I'll deal with me. I just hope you understand that I can't continue to see you because I need time and space to fall out of love with you."

I could tell that he felt horrible to see me so sad. He forced a humble half smile, and I knew there was nothing left to say, so we didn't say anything; instead, we quietly and naturally reverted to what connected us in the first place. Sex.

We spent one last night together, but this night was different. We didn't fuck like savages, and we weren't high on drugs. It was tender, intimate, and special, like two people who truly cared about each other, and I even slept over.

The next morning came with the dawn of a new light. I had sadness in my heart, but things were at least clearer, and I felt surprisingly okay about everything. As I got myself together to leave, few words were shared between us. We both knew our time and this chapter of our story had come to an end.

I appreciated his honesty in not just telling me what I wanted to hear, and although he couldn't meet me where I was, I knew that he also appreciated my honesty. And knowing he'd never intentionally want to hurt me made it a little easier for me to move forward.

Over the next few days, I did give in to my own little pity party. It was short-lived but necessary for me to purge and decompress from everything that had just happened. Within a couple of weeks, I could feel myself coming back to me. I was able to rise above my heart and appreciate our time together.

It's not the fairy-tale, happily-ever-after ending I would like to be writing about, but it most certainly was a fairy-

MASTER OF SINGLE

tale lover relationship and friendship, and he still holds an important place in my heart and probably always will.

At the end of the day, what's a girl to do when stuck between the heart thing and a hard thing? The only card to play is the truth, and no matter how difficult the truth is to say, be brave because it's the only thing that will set you free.

The lesson here is that lover's lane isn't a perfect science; it's what you make it and how you take it. And although it doesn't always go the way you want, the greater victory is the experience and taking the chance. The only regrets are the chances you don't take.

Class dismissed.

Chapter Eight

TO RING OR NOT TO RING

As a single woman moving through the world, I'm quite vigilant when it comes to looking for the ring on a man's finger before initiating any sort of engagement, let alone flirt.

But admittedly I've had to learn from my mistakes. Too often, I've found myself in situations where the guy who's flirting with me or vice versa is not wearing a ring. I understand that no ring doesn't necessarily mean he's not in a relationship. And if he is, he shouldn't be flirting with me, and I would expect if I was flirting with him, that he would be the one to tell me he was not available. Makes sense, right? I don't think that's asking too much.

In all my years working in the service/nightclub industry, rarely have I seen men put their relationship before flirting when flirting was standing in front of them. I know this because I've seen these men in action, and I know a lot of their girlfriends or wives. Just saying.

And the ones who do respect their relationships, I can count them on one hand, and that's not shade, that's just the nature of the beast.

When a beautiful woman is flirting with a man and you add a couple of drinks to the mix, very few men will have the integrity to stop the flirt out of respect for their relationship.

I hate to be the one to give it to you straight no chaser, but I'm about that girl power, and women should know the truth of what happens behind their back.

That's why when it comes to what you need to know, my single society, ask the questions. Don't expect anyone to "man up" and honour their relationship. Most men will even offer to buy you a drink just to keep the flirting going.

It infuriates me to no end when a man wastes my time, knowing very well that he's not available but says nothing about it. Not only is it disrespectful to me but also to his significant other. Men, you must do better.

Like I've said, we are a new breed of single women, and this kind of game playing just doesn't fly. Come correct or don't come at all.

I think we can all agree that wearing a ring is a clear sign to everyone of your commitment to another, as well as saying to the world that you're not available. But fewer men are wearing rings, unlike women. In fact, I know very few married women who don't wear their wedding ring proudly, every day.

For singles, this is yet another challenge to be aware of on an already turbulent dating scene.

In a social situation, a single person's energy is vastly different from someone in a coupling, meaning singles tend to be more open to meet and flirt, touch, dance, even exchange numbers. But how much of the responsibility should be on the single person to assume the job of getting to the point of full disclosure about the guy's status?

As an active single on the scene, I can tell you that it's tough enough to meet someone you connect with, that it's asking a lot to expect us to always have our Nancy Drew investigator hat on too.

So what's a girl to do? You meet a guy, you do your due diligence and look for the ring; there's none. You give him every opportunity to disclose his status short of interrogating him, and he continues to engage while perpetrating the flirt. At some point you don't look for problems where there seemingly are none. Most people would just keep things moving, because no, we're not Nancy Drew.

With that said, here's a suggestion guys: if you're married, please do us singles a favour and wear your damn ring. Even better, do it for your wife. And if you're in a relationship, may I suggest having the conversation with your significant other on what the boundaries are when it comes to flirting with others. Because from what I've noticed, the rules appear to be quite blurry.

Hopefully, post-pandemic we'll see a noticeable difference on the single social scene. Ideally, it will come back improved with a new energy. Perhaps this unprecedented time has given men a chance to appreciate the worth of a good woman. Equally, maybe women will be open to giving the good single men out there a chance to step up and let themselves be seen.

Respecting the power of the ring is one of my non-negotiable hard rules for my own personal integrity, having lived and learned from my mistakes. It will be a cold day in hell before I knowingly go after or get involved with another woman's man. Not today, Satan, not today.

There are enough single men and women on the planet that nobody needs to be doubling down on someone else's person.

That said, I'm also not trying to stay single forever, so where do we go from here?

Before ringing in this next single-girl story, which will put this introduction into context, remember that we are always in control of what we do and nobody can make us do anything we don't want to. That said, despite our best efforts to avoid the traps, sometimes our best efforts aren't good enough.

One of my many jobs in the service industry included working as a head hostess at one of my favourite restaurants, Jatoba, a gem of a place in the heart of downtown. I loved my job (mostly), especially the entertaining the guests part of it.

One night, a handsome stranger (I love a handsome stranger) walked in solo and right away caught my attention. Upon first scan, it was lust at first sight. He was my A-type of man; tall, dark, and handsome, stylish, and well put together. His physique was strong-looking, rugged, but still polished, like he could chop logs for the fire and then close a million-dollar deal.

When he first walked in and our eyes met, there was an obvious spark between us. But playing it cool, I addressed him much like I would any other guest, asking if he had a reservation. He replied that he didn't and that he was alone. I appreciated the way he slid that in, and for a half second, I imagined what else he could potentially slide in, but it was too early in the game to determine if he would be slide worthy or not.

I suggested seating him at the bar. He agreed. There were available tables, but seating him at the bar kept him within my peripheral vision so I could keep an eye on him. Yup, single girl on the loose, not just pretty.

Still playing my cards cool and with strategy on my mind, I walked him over to the bar and set him up to succeed. I took a couple of extra moments to suggest some of the popular dishes on the menu, giving him a chance to notice me too.

I also used that opportunity to do the standard glance down, looking for a ring. Much to my delight, there was no ring to be seen. So far so good.

Being the accommodating hostess I was, I said to him, "Enjoy your dinner and I'll be back to check on you soon." He smiled and said, "Okay." As I turned to walk away, he offered to buy me a drink. I didn't want to be rude, but I also didn't want to look too desperate. I said, "I'm busy right now, but maybe when things slow down, I'll let you know. Thanks." I walked away feeling pretty good about how I'd handled the situation.

Returning to my post and pretending to be busy, I had many questions running through my head. Was he single or married but just not wearing a ring? Was there really a spark, or was it all a figment of my imagination? Curiosity had me by the kitty cat, and I needed more information. So after a reasonable amount of time had elapsed, I returned to check on him and take him up on his drink offer.

In a rare opportune instance, I tapped into my Nancy Drew, leading the investigation in the case of the handsome stranger.

The delighted look on his face when he saw me walking towards him was warm and welcoming. Our conversation took on a life of its own, and we found out we had a lot in common. I also learned he was from out of town, that he lived in Quebec City, and travelled back and forth as a successful commercial real estate agent.

Throughout our plentiful conversations, there was no mention of any relationship or counterpart or anything that would have raised a red flag. He even mentioned he didn't have kids. I gave the man every opportunity to say something, and he never did.

Like I said, one doesn't look for problems where there seemingly aren't any.

Welcome to the life of a modern-day single girl.

Let's break this down from a single's point of view to help you better understand what I mean when I say "single, beware." Observation one: no ring, not even a tan line to indicate a hint of commitment once removed. Two: there was no mention, indication, or suggestion of a relationship. Did I ask? No. Three: Why the hell should I have to ask? Yes, I could have, but why should I have to is my point.

So you tell me, what's a single to do? He seemed too good to be true, right?

By now he had drawn me in, hitting all the marks of a potential person to pursue. I know it sounds crazy, as we'd just met, but I was secretly asking myself, could this be my man?

He had all the trimmings, bells, and whistles and possessed a lot of my physical and personality must-haves. I was hard-pressed to find anything I didn't like about him.

Every time he casually touched my knee when I made him laugh and the way he looked directly into my eyes when he spoke to me felt real.

He was generous with his compliments, talking about how pretty and funny I was and curious to know more about me. All signs led me to thinking that I wasn't alone in this flirt or feeling of connection.

I finished up my shift and had one last drink with him. When it came time to leave, he offered to walk me out, and once outside, we found ourselves looking into each other's eyes under the moonlit sky. Sweet moment. He asked if he could call me the next time he was in town and take me out for dinner. At that point, I felt confident he wasn't in a relationship.

I accepted and gave him my number, then he asked if he could give me a kiss. Of course I said yes, and that was by far my favourite part of the night. He leaned in with his luscious lips the kiss was just wet enough, sensual, and hard but soft at the same time. It was delicious and certainly left a lasting impression, giving me a lot to wonder about until we'd meet again...

As soon as we said goodbye, I knew I wanted more.

Over the next week or so, we communicated via text and phone. As promised, the next time he was in town he took me out for dinner. I tried to focus, but I couldn't help but wonder what he'd be like in bed. It had been a while I hadn't engaged, so his arrival came just in the nick of time.

As the night unfolded, our chemistry intensified. I love the buildup, knowing you're about to have incredible sex with someone you're hot for, and add to that the *je ne sais quoi* factor of hotel sex. There's just something about those extra-crisp white sheets, the DO NOT DISTURB sign, stocked minibar, and room service at your fingertips. It's the perfect scenario for a night of sexual misconduct.

Hotel sex in your own city is so fun. It's like a sexy staycation with all the pleasure and excitement that comes with having sex on vacation. Only difference, no beach and you get to go home afterwards.

Once back at his room, it didn't take long before we tore each other's clothes off and I had this gorgeous specimen on top, looking down at me with his deep, dark brown bedroom eyes.

NICOLE JONES

I was in hotel heaven.

We had incredible chemistry, and being the team player I was, I did my part to make up for the lost time from the week we'd been apart by respectfully having multiple orgasms, which he responded to with more of the same. This went on throughout the night. I even slept over, which by now you know goes against my own hard rule of not waking up together. But this was an exceptional situation, and one must know when to bend their own rules accordingly.

Plus I had waited a long time to be with someone I liked, and I planned on getting as much out of him as I possibly could before he left again. Good to the last drop, as they say. And he certainly was.

He had to work the next morning before heading back to Quebec, so we managed to get a couple of hours of shut-eye, but it was really nothing to speak of. Every time our body parts touched, the animal in one of us awoke, and without fail, sex would ensue.

That night, sleep was optional.

As exhausted as we were the next day, the pleasure of our amazing night together pushed us through the fatigue and morning light. He got ready for work as I wandered the room, collecting bits and pieces of myself, nylons, panties, bra, sprinkled a little everywhere—a good sign of a successful, sex-filled night.

It felt natural and good waking up with him, and I loved watching him get ready for work. The business side was as much of a turn-on as his sexual side.

We shared our plans for the day and then walked out together holding hands. We kissed each other goodbye, knowing we wanted to see each other again. He said he'd call me later, and I left with an extra skip in my step that day and with a glow that only a night like ours could inspire.

MASTER
OF SINGLE

I tried to not get in my head, but he seemed perfect—almost too perfect—and I hate that feeling like you're waiting for the other shoe to drop. I wondered how he was even available—successful, handsome, smart, funny, sexy, mature, no kids, charming, and a stallion in bed. I mean, come on, guys like that aren't just randomly roaming around. He was a freaking unicorn.

I began to question what might be wrong with him, but then I immediately stopped myself from spinning and instead shifted to looking at what was right.

After all, I deserved a "perfect" man, so why question what I knew I deserved?

Here's what I know about being too good to be true. I'm the epitome of too good to be true. But I exist and I am the real deal, so why couldn't he be? It was a shift in my internal dialogue and all I needed to calm my nervous system and keep it moving. If I exist, so could he. Period.

He headed back to Quebec, we stayed in touch, speaking or texting almost every day, but this time something was different. Our conversations brought with it an energy I wasn't quite feeling. He was often rushing off or sometimes couldn't talk on the phone. He used work as an excuse, but something wasn't sitting right. As much as I tried not to, my instincts had me questioning the situation further. I wanted to trust him and be all in, but I couldn't ignore the unsettling knot in my stomach.

Yes, he existed, but was he for real?

I needed more information. My soul was telling me that I needed to ask him straight out and hear him say the words "I'm single" before I could allow myself to fall any deeper down the rabbit hole. I didn't want to believe he could possibly be in a relationship, but you know what they say about a woman's instincts—they're never wrong.

I felt so nervous about asking him, and I wanted to do it face-to-face. Unless you're a habitual liar, then it's much harder to lie to someone's face.

But when we finally saw each other, I buckled, and before I knew it, we were horizontal. So yeah, that night we did everything but talk. I know… I was weak and I think a little in denial. I justified it by telling myself that we'd come that far, so what was another hour or two or four.

Post-session, we lay naked in bed, both of us trying to catch our breath. With my hand across his chest, I could feel his heart racing, and at that moment something illuminated inside me. Everything became real. I knew I liked him, a lot.

The time had come. I had him just where I wanted him, vulnerable and present. This was my moment to ask the question.

With my head nicely snuggled in the nook of his neck, I turned slightly to look up at him and asked, in my sweetest voice, "How is it possible you're single?" I was expecting to get a quick response back to clarify my question, but instead, there was an awkward pause, and that knot in my stomach tightened.

I waited, but he didn't say anything, which made me sit up real quick and look straight at him, this time without the sweetness in my voice or even a stutter in my speech. I said, "You are single, right?" A second pause. Oh boy. By now I was looking at him with daggers in my eyes like you better speak, motherfucker, and you better say the right thing right now! But be careful what you ask for because I wasn't ready for what I got.

When he finally found his manhood enough to look at me, the fear in his eyes was all telling, like he knew he was

MASTER OF SINGLE

about to die because he was about to tell me something horrible. The words "I have a girlfriend" spilled out of his mouth like hot lava, burning a hole in my brain.

I thought I was going to vomit.

I wanted to punch him in the face; he's lucky I don't resort to violence, but I was so livid and embarrassed. I felt used, and an avalanche of emotions came flooding in without warning. I wanted his truth but first had to look at my truth. I had trusted him blindly and too quickly.

I lost my composure and then totally lost my shit. Naked, screaming, and cursing, throwing F-bombs at him: "What the fuck do you mean you have a fucking girlfriend? How fucking dare you do this to me!"

I mean what kind of person drives a Rolls-Royce off a cliff?

It was horrible. I held back my tears; he didn't deserve to see me cry. But how could he do this to me? How could he sleep with me and lead me on for weeks, knowing all along that he had a girlfriend? I couldn't think straight beyond feeling like he'd set me up to fail by putting me in a position to sleep with another woman's man. Wow, brutal. What a bona fide fucking asshole.

I was beyond furious. I couldn't breathe. I just needed to get out of there.

It wasn't the exit I'd come to know with him, sweet and romantic holding hands, this was more like a 911 abort-and-vacate-premises situation.

He tried desperately to explain himself, but it all sounded like white noise, talking about his relationship was complicated, he wasn't happy, he really liked me, blah, blah, blah… He tried to apologize, telling me that he was sorry he didn't tell me… "Please, please let me explain." Nobody, especially me, cared about him wanting to come clean now.

My response was crystal clear. "Go fuck yourself, or go fuck your girlfriend, or go fuck whoever you want, but you will never be fucking me again. Boy, bye."

There was nothing on God's green earth that he could have said to stop me from getting out of that room; in fact, the more he spoke the more enraged I became.

Before he could get another sentence out, I was half-dressed and out the door, still cursing. I managed to hold it together long enough to get through the lobby without making a spectacle of myself, but when I got to my car, I just broke down.

I was so mad at him but also mad at myself for letting things get that far.

I went home and buried myself in my bed and cried myself to sleep; it was all too much for my single girl heart to handle.

Over the weeks that followed, he had the nerve to continue reaching out, wanting to explain himself, persisting with texting and voice messages. This went on for two or three weeks before I was calm enough to even consider hearing him out.

I eventually let him say his piece, but I mostly did it for me, not him. I needed some sort of closure to understand how he could do this to me. I'd never been played before, and I didn't have any tools in my box to deal with this level of betrayal. I listened to him explain that he was in a loveless relationship but he couldn't leave her because she was going through some deep depression and emotional issues. He went on to say that he never meant to hurt me, that he felt alive when he was with me, and he didn't want to lose me.

For what it was worth, which wasn't much, I could hear what sounded like sincerity in his voice, but by now it was too little too late. The damage was done; the trust was broken.

One could argue that technically, he hadn't lied, because I'd never asked him directly if he had a girlfriend, to which I would say, don't get it twisted. He had deceived me by sleeping with me without giving me all the information that would have empowered me to decide for myself whether to be with him or not. Liar!

Had I known about his situation, I absolutely wouldn't have engaged with him in a sexual manner. I don't do messy, and I'm not that trifling hoe who goes around opening my legs to every sad-stuck boyfriend in a loveless relationship.

What he did by playing with my dignity and integrity you don't come back from.

Here's the lesson: Benefit of the doubt is earned. Don't give it until the person unequivocally deserves it.

The deeply hurtful thing that I needed closure on, besides the entire deceit part, was that I really did like him, and after what happened, I wanted to hate him, but I didn't have hate in my heart. Plus I didn't want to stay bitter or let him represent all men. He'd already taken enough from me. I wasn't going to let him also take my trust in men too.

I knew that for my own well-being and to be able to move on, I would have to forgive at some point—not forget or pardon his actions, but forgive him and myself so that I could move forward in a healthy way. In a text to him before deleting his number, I wrote, "You really hurt me. I'm going to forgive you, not because you deserve it, but I don't deserve to hold on to this. You are the antithesis of what I want in a man. You made me the other woman, and that goes against everything I stand for. How dare you! I'm nobody's side piece, and you will never have me again, so go take care of your girlfriend and leave me the fuck alone."

Fool me once, shame on you; fool me twice, shame on me. But in this case, it was plainly shame on him. Period. Next.

Fast forward a few months, he's now a thing of the past, a mere chapter in my single-girl season. Then one day guess who pops up in my text messages. It was him; I couldn't believe it either.

Because I had deleted his number from my phone, it came through as an unidentified person, and it said, "I'm single." I knew right away it was him.

I won't lie—it made me feel a little good inside to think that maybe he finally understood what he had lost. Idiot.

Stone cold I replied, "Who dis?" It was the perfect diss and dig at the same time. It took a few minutes before he replied with his name. This time I replied, "You don't exist. Don't text me again." And then I blocked him. He's lucky I even gave him the time of day to reply, but it was the final piece of closure I needed.

I'll end this story with a message of solidarity to all my singles and the women whose men don't wear their ring and move through the world not honouring their relationships.

Singles, always respect the ring or the relationship—your integrity is too valuable not to—but just know that to ring or not to ring doesn't mean a damn thing.

And to the women of those men who are out there trifling, good luck. All I got for you is make sure you know your man because what he does in your presence isn't nearly as important as what he does behind your back. Okur.

Ring, game, wrap. Now what else is going on?

Chapter Nine

Charming is Alarming

Some of my favourite life moments are those spontaneous interactions you often don't see coming and couldn't have predicted. This is where knowing how to pivot on a dime and adjust accordingly when those wonderful but sometimes off-putting moments present themselves is clutch.

I spent two tough but amazing years as a student in New York City, pursuing my dream of becoming a New York trained actor with the Tom Todoroff Conservatory program.

After my experience, I'd become a little more jaded and slightly more cynical than when I started. Noticing nothing much surprised me anymore, and I didn't believe everything I saw, even with my own eyes.

Living in NYC you see every type of character and offbeat situation on any given day. I think that's why New

Yorkers are some of the most desensitized people due to the sheer nature and madness of their environment.

That said, it's still one of the most incredible and exciting cities in the world, but don't be fooled by its bright lights and big-city allure. It will make you or break you before you know you're even broken or made. I heart NY.

But I adhere to the idea of "never let them see you sweat." (Stay cool no matter the circumstances.) This brings me back to the importance of being able to pivot and change direction at a moment's notice. Why is this important? Well, life is unpredictable, and especially living in NYC, a good pivot will save you a lot of time and trouble. Think of a pivot like the pick-and-roll move in basketball where you post up and literally roll off your opponent to make yourself open to get clear. Same move, different game.

When any of life's many unpredictable situations catch you off guard, you owe it to yourself to not let the situation own you. Remember, you hold the power, and like many before me have said, my mom included, it's not what happens, it's how you handle what happens that matters.

No matter what the moment is, you always have the power of choice. Choose to be a person who knows when and how to pivot with poise.

Finally, let's remember that every situation good or bad offers an experience and a lesson that's yours to lose. Each one of your experiences writes on the blueprint of who you are, and that blueprint is how we see ourselves and I believe largely determines who we will become. Don't deny yourself, it all counts because you matter.

Without further ado, here's a pivot story just for you…

Sometime after returning home from NY, one of my jobs was working as the manager at yet another hotspot restaurant in the heart of Old Montreal, this time for a charming establishment called Scarlet.

If you've ever managed a restaurant, you know the importance of being able to multitask and wear many different hats at the same time. One busy Saturday night, I stepped in to help the hostess at the front manage the high influx of guests. Among them was a group of guys from LA, in town for a bachelor party. Because the restaurant was in the middle of all the action, (clubs and other hotspots), it wasn't unusual for groups like this to have a nice dinner at our establishment before hitting the party scene.

These LA guys... no, scratch that... this group of LA men rolled up in full force in a good mood, hungry and ready to get their night started. Collectively, they had an undeniable bromance between them. It was strong and their vibe was infectious, which we caught immediately and served right back on a silver platter.

We received them with a smile and asked the name of the reservation, much like we would any other guest, but I couldn't have been prepared for what happened next. Before getting the name of the group, the front man who was talking to someone behind him turned around to address my question. But it was his reaction to me that had me blushing to the heavens and pivoting where I stood.

As he turned my way, without batting an eye or so much as a stammer in his voice, he looked straight at me and exclaimed, "Holy shit, you're gorgeous!" It was such a visceral and spontaneous moment that it hit me right in the solar plexus and almost knocked me off my heels. I stood there for a second, feeling discombobulated and admittedly a little embarrassed by the attention.

Remember I said that nothing much surprised me anymore? I was wrong. I was surprisingly swayed by his charm and obvious good taste. All eyes were on me. Not quite sure how to respond and wanting to keep it professional, I smiled back and said thank you. I proceeded to grab the menus and escort them to their table. On the walk there, he offered yet another compliment, this time about my outfit, a sophisticated cream-coloured fitted one-piece jumpsuit situation with pockets and a sheer white panelled back. A gorgeous piece by Montreal couture designers Tavan & Mitto. Amazing! Clearly this guy had no problem expressing himself, and I wasn't mad at him for it.

Humbly, today I can say that I've become much better at receiving compliments, which wasn't always the case. For a long time, if someone gave me a compliment, instead of simply receiving it, I would deflect it by giving one back right away. My mom was the person who taught me that people don't have to take time out of their lives to stop and give me a compliment, so just say thank you.

Working in the nightlife biz, it's not unusual for men to throw accolades a woman's way; it's part of the game and who men are. It just so happened that night I was in a playful mood.

I'd been in the biz long enough to distinguish the difference between blowing smoke up my hookah and a sincere compliment. For what it was worth, he came across as sincere.

The entire time I was walking them to their table, I could feel his eyes piercing the back of my head and the heat of his body only inches away. When I turned around to make sure the group was all together, there he was right behind me, eyes locked on me and smiling like a kid with a crush. It was cute.

I would be remiss not to mention how handsome he was. Yes friends, yet another handsome stranger... It's my thing, so leave it alone, LOL. He had a nice, easy casual style about him, looking sharp in his red-and-black-plaid shirt, distressed jeans, combat boots, and a little scruff to his beard. His hair was short and caramel colour, and his skin had that LA sun-kissed glow.

He was tall and his physique was strong and stout, which I loved, and he had beautiful hazel eyes that seemed to sparkle when he looked at me. Okay, maybe that part was in my head, but he did have beautiful eyes and a smile that would melt any woman's heart.

Once the group was settled at their table and in the care of their server's capable hands, I wished them a bon appétit and went back to work, but not before exchanging one last smile with my not-so-secret admirer. As I walked away, I could feel myself blushing, but I reminded myself to take everything with a grain of salt; after all, what did I really know about this guy? Yes, he was good-looking, funny, bold, and clearly had impeccable taste in both fashion and women. But for all I knew, he could have been a serial charmer and I was just another charm on his belt. You know, the type of guy who gets off by getting women off with his compliments and charm, leading them to think something could be there, but in the end it's all fun and games to him. Before getting ahead of myself, a lot more recon would have to be done, so I played along until further notice.

Midway through the dinner, I went back to check on the table and with a little something up my sleeve, but the surprise once again was on me. I arrived at the table to a clapping and unanimous, "Hooray, she's back," from the entire table.

Once again feeling flattered by the attention, which was becoming a common and welcome occurrence with this group, I said, "Thank you" with a cute bow, like a queen addressing her subjects... You know, a typical Saturday.

Then I hung around for some fun banter with the boys and waited for my surprise to arrive—a round of shots which they appreciated greatly. We raised our glasses to the bachelor in a resounding congratulations, and with that, it was bottoms up!

Since I was at the table, I took the opportunity to purposely position myself next to my GQ jock and asked, "What's the plan for the rest of the night?"

He answered, "After this, we're heading to a club not too far from here. You should join us."

My first thought was, *I'm not dressed for the club.* The sophisticated jumpsuit looked great for work but not so much for a nightclub. Reluctantly I said, "Maybe." I was just about to leave the table when the group decided to order another round of shots and insisted that I stay and join them. Not a difficult sell.

What happened next still reigns as the best and worst line I've ever heard in my life, and I've heard my fair share of pickup lines. The shots arrived, he turned to me and grabbed my hand, pulling me in closer and looking deep into my eyes, and said, "Would you have one shot, two shots, three shots, come home with me and wake up in my T-shirt?"

Everyone at the table went wild, applauding their boy's bravado; meanwhile, I was caught between feeling insulted by the audacity of his boldness and imagining waking up in his T-shirt.

It was surprising, and how dare he say that in front of everyone!

But I wasn't going let him have the last laugh at my expense. So in my best sex-operator voice just loud enough for his friends to hear, I said, "I bet that line works on a lot of women; your problem is, I'm not a lot of women."

MASTER OF SINGLE

Pivot, hair flip, eye roll, and goodbye. I got a standing ovation from the table. You're welcome.

I couldn't make it that easy on him; after all, he was in the house of the pivot queen and needed to know he wasn't the only one with a quick wit in the room. Note: never let the guy hold all the cards; you must know how to play the hand you're dealt too.

Shortly after shot gate, the boys were ready to pay their bill and get their party on. As they made their way out, thanking everyone along the way for a great evening, my guy stopped one last time to invite me to join them. I was taken by this beautiful man with the cheesy lines and his not once, but twice invitation, so I said, "I'll see how I feel after I'm done working."

He kissed my cheek and said, "I really hope to see you there." His charm was not lost on me; in fact, it was quite alarming.

There was no question I was thinking about joining him, but if my past experiences had taught me anything, it was that I had to be sure before taking even one step forward. This too-good-to-be-true situation felt all too familiar.

He also lived out of town, and for all I knew he could have had a whole family waiting for him on the other side. It was still to be seen whether he was just playing to play or if he was being serious. No woman wants to look like a fool or be embarrassed by misreading the signs. But I also didn't want to miss the opportunity to know what was really on the other side of his intentions.

After some thought and careful consideration for my time versus my interest in him, I made the decision to go ahead and meet him at the club, which was just down the street.

I wrapped up the night and walked over to the club. The

usually ten-minute walk felt like it was taking forever, and my feet never felt so heavy. In a weird cosmic way, it felt as if I were going against an energy that didn't want me to go in that direction.

But being the hardhead that I am, I kept moving until I was inside the club, looking for him, and they weren't hard to find. They were the rowdiest table and the hottest guys in the place, turning up, popping bottles, and surrounded by beautiful women. Surprised? Not at all.

It was a little awkward making my way through the harem of women to get to him, but when he finally spotted me, his face lit up. He immediately got up and reached for my hand to pull me through the crowd to get to the table. That was the moment I hoped he wasn't like all the others. I knew one of two things was going to happen—either he'd confirm my suspicions that he was a player, or he'd surprise me by being the real thing. I was about to find out.

Once at the table, he said loudly over the music, "I'm so happy you came." I could tell he'd had a few more shots because he was quite touchy-feely. I knew right then that I wasn't going to waste any more time than needed getting to the heart of the matter. Was he single and available or not? That was the only thing on my mind, and I wanted to know before having one more drink. It wasn't the best place to have a conversation, but I didn't care. I leaned in and asked him, "Are you single?"

He jerked back with a quick motion, like he wasn't expecting that question. I gave him a moment to collect his thoughts while staring at him, waiting for his answer. After a longer than normal pause, which by now we know is never a good sign, he took a sip of his drink and replied, "No, I'm not single."

I leaned back the way you do when you be like, "Exsqueeze me? Can you repeat that?"

MASTER OF SINGLE

Another pause before he looked at me and said, "I'm married, but it's complicated. I can tell you're an amazing woman, and in another life, you would have been my wife."

WTF? Was I supposed to be flattered by this degrading-to-your-wife-and-my-sensibility comment? Who did he think he was? I can tell you who he wasn't—he wasn't a man who deserved me.

So please, take your complicated ass back home to your probably unsuspecting wife and spare me the probable shit show that comes with you and any future headaches.

Here I was again, dealing with a man in a complicated relationship. Lord, what lesson didn't I learn that made you send me the same type of man a second time? Was there a new strain of men out there I wasn't aware of? These complicated assholes in relationships who can't keep their damn flirting and compliments to themselves! I was as annoyed AF but sadly not surprised. Men can be the worst type of hoes. They will do, say, play, lay, and pay to get what they want. That's the real talk, the 411 and the 911 rolled up, wrapped, and delivered in one perfectly teachable moment.

What was the point of all the energy he'd put into winning my attention and ultimately getting me to come to the club? That's a rhetorical question. I know he was thinking booty call. I guess my showing up was the hopeless romantic in me secretly looking for my person. After losing all interest and my lady hard, I turned to him and said, "You need to respect your wife and stop being that guy who doesn't. I'm out of here."

I put my drink down and didn't look back, even when he called my name. I was gone with the wind and so was my treasure. Of course he wanted me. I'd want me, but that doesn't mean you can have me. Part of why I'm single is because I know my worth and thanks to guys like him, I'm not easy to get.

Days later, I shared what happened with my girlfriends. They were angrier at him than I was, which clarified that he had absolutely led me on. Their confirmation that he was wrong offered some comfort, but that's what good girlfriends do. They will drive the truck that runs him over and will keep running over him until you feel better, ha ha.

Once I got past being bothered by it, I sat with the situation and asked myself what I needed to learn from it to hopefully avoid getting into the same scenario again or attracting the same type of shady/complicated man.

I concluded that I had to slow my flirt and check myself, to accept my responsibility in that I chose to go to the club. He didn't owe me anything; he was just a guy being a guy with asshole tendencies. I didn't have any regrets. The whole thing was no skin off my teeth; he wasn't worth a second thought.

This is what singles go through and what makes us so resilient. We're willing to put ourselves out there in hopes of following the rainbow to the treasure waiting on the other side.

He tried it but got the wrong girl, and it certainly wasn't my loss. I walked away knowing that every night I go to sleep with the real treasure, me. And that's no line; it's forever.

But damn, his line: "Would you have one shot, two shots, three shots, come home with me, and wake up in my T-shirt." I have to say, it was good enough to get him in the book, it just wasn't good enough to get me.

Chapter Ten

THE GUY WITH NO NAME

AFTER HITTING A couple of dating road bums... I mean road bumps... I decided it was time to shake it off, shake it up, and have some fun. There have been times after going without sex for a couple of months and when masturbation is no longer cutting it that I begin to unravel just a little bit, and that's when I need that itch to be scratched. I don't do well being sexually frustrated because there's nowhere to release the frustration. When I get to the point where I'm masturbating more than four or five times a month, that's a sign that I'm overdue for sex. Being sexually frustrated affects my mood in a negative way. I have less patience, become irritable, and eventually hit my boiling point. That's when all I want to do is find a guy to bang it out with for a good session of uncomplicated, don't-call-me-I'll-call-you, less-talking-more-fucking kind of sex. And I know you know what I'm talking about. You might call it something different, but we're on the same page.

When in single Rome, there's only one thing I know that can satisfy such an insatiable urge. Unless I have someone in my life to whom I can turn to for sexual relief, like a lover, the good old one-night stand is my best go-to get-laid plan.

This is when I tap into my sexual alter ego, whom I affectionately call Lady Slay. She's one badass bitch who gives zero fucks and doesn't apologize about getting what she wants—a heightened, bolder version of me, if you can believe it. LOL. When Lady Slay rears her sexually frustrated head, boys beware, because she's coming out and coming atcha.

And that's what this story is about. What lengths a single girl will go to scratch that sexual itch. Sometimes you must meet yourself where you are and adjust to your circumstances, even if that means taking matters into your own hands.

I want every woman and man to know (especially women because we can be judgemental with ourselves), that a one-night stand doesn't make you a slut or easy or any of those negative labels we often put on each other. Until you've walked a mile in a single person's sexually frustrated shoes, do not judge.

One of the challenges of being single is that regular sex isn't guaranteed, so if you don't go after it, you can go a long time without it. God forbid you forget how to use it, and bless you if you're able to withstand the clock and go without the cock. Slow applause... I have great admiration and curiosity about those people who can go several months, sometimes years, without sex. In my eyes, that's remarkable. I don't know how they do it, but I know I couldn't.

I think sex makes the world a better, happier place. Haven't you ever seen a girlfriend who's just glowing and smiling ear to ear? When you ask her why she's so happy, she replies, "I just had sex." I mean, life is just better when you're getting laid. Period.

MASTER OF SINGLE

Not to mention it's a necessary and natural part of life's pleasures, so to simply go without it because you're not in a relationship doesn't fly with me.

I realize that for some women, and perhaps men, the sex drive dips at a certain age, or the interest in having sex lessens because it's harder to get when you're single.

And in those cases, with few options to exercise, one might simply accept and settle for a sexless single life.

As painful as that sounds if that's your choice, then okay, fine. But if it's a result of you just giving up, I personally want more for you. With that said, I don't want anyone thinking that they're doing anything wrong; engaging in sex or not is your choice, and I respect that. However, if I can provoke another alternative, then I'm here for it.

The moral is, if you want it, have the tenacity to go out there and get it, period.

For what it's worth, I think there's something fierce about that woman who knows what she wants and is motivated and driven to get it. Love her! Now that I've gotten your attention, hee-hee...

I stated earlier that masturbating was my go-to release to help carry me through the off-season and thank goodness for it. Can you imagine if we didn't have masturbation? I mean, I would have imploded a long time ago.

In fact, masturbation can also be the best way to learn about your body. Once you know how to please yourself, you can better teach someone to pleasure you too. I'm not afraid to tell a man what I want and how I like it. If I'm giving it up, you're damn straight I'm going to get out of it what I need. But if you don't know your own body, how can you teach anyone to navigate your waters?

NICOLE JONES

My masturbation preferences have evolved over the years from freestyle—meaning hand to kitty cat, which for the longest time satisfied me just fine—to the cutest hot pink vibrator, which I named my "Yes boy." He's the perfect size... and yes, size does matter, but so does motion. He's ribbed with three speeds and is the perfect yes and partner.

I think of his settings as his different moods, sometimes he's more playful, and other times he goes in for the kill. Now if I could just figure out how to turn my vibrator into a boyfriend, because it's honestly one of the best relationships I've had. Everyone has the right to sexual pleasure, and there's almost no greater pleasure than the pleasure of knowing how to please yourself. Nice to meet you.

I fear that a lot of women aren't comfortable with the idea of masturbation, or their own bodies for that matter, and I hope I'm wrong. But if you are that woman who hasn't explored her own treasures or tapped into the power of your personal pleasure, I'm sorry, but why? And what are you waiting for exactly? I really hope you feel inspired enough to step out of your comfort zone and get into your box.

My box is the only box I will ever want to be in. In fact, put this book down right now, find yourself a little mirror and a quiet place, and go meet yourself. And if you need a little stimulus to get you started, don't be shy. That's what porn is for.

There, now you have all the information. Please do yourself this favour and get your release on... I'll wait.

You're welcome.

I'm so proud to be able to speak with such playful confidence and conviction about sex; it's very empowering, especially because at some point in my early life someone

MASTER OF SINGLE

tried to take that power away from me, but I'm a survivor. I've worked hard to rise above the trauma to take my sexual power back. I grew up vowing that I wouldn't let my past determine my future, not when it came to sex or anything else. Nobody will ever take my power from me ever again.

I wish for all women, regardless of their past or sexual history, or wherever is their sex life, to own their sexual power. It's yours to lose.

Say this with me: "I am the captain, CEO, MIP (most important person) and head boss in charge of my kitty cat. Meow." And exhale.

Finally, my sexual deviants, now that I have you where I want you (wondering and hopefully wanting sex), I leave you with this before settling into the next sexy single-girl situation: Sex isn't always love, and love isn't always sex (refer to chapter Lover's Lane.) Love can be its own beautiful beast, while sex, if you allow it, can simply be the beast to your beauty. Now go get laid!

One enchanted evening, I was feeling hot, like zazazoo hot. Led by my sexual cravings and desires, which had a grip on me in the most affecting way, I could feel the urge for sex bubbling up inside, rearing its head like peekaboo, we want to play. I answered the call to action, got myself together, dressed to slay as always, and headed to my favourite nightclub hotspot and pleasure playground, Flyjin, where hot men roamed like cattle grazing in an open field. And to make things sweeter, it was also where my favourite man and one of my best friends, Jam, worked (he has his own chapter, Single is the new Jam).

He worked the door, and nobody got into the club without going through him first, making him the best person to know the inventory of who was inside, and he was always willing to help me get laid. Yes, girl, yes, everyone needs a Jam!

NICOLE JONES

To know him is to love him, and if for some strange reason you don't get along with him, I would think it's you, not him, because he's a good one from the inside out, so chances are you're the problem. And we probably wouldn't be friends. That's what's up.

I arrived at the club, coming in *hot*! It didn't take but a minute before he saw the look in my eyes that I was on the prowl and some lucky guy was about to get eaten alive. He looked at me and laughed, maybe even rolled his eyes, and said, "Oh Lord!" No words necessary, I winked back, nodded, and made my way inside. My mission was clear, my mind was right, and my sights were set on sex. Go.

When it came to the "who" I was looking for, I was on the hunt for a young, sexy stud who didn't have much to say. Remember, less talk and more sex kind of vibes was my approach. As I swept the club like a cat on the prowl and looking for her prey, no single man was safe. Between Jam's help and my prowl, there was nowhere to hide.

I positioned myself within the vicinity that had the most potential prospects. In the meanwhile, Jam was also scouting for me. He'd find guys he thought I'd like and bring them to me for my consideration. Yes, you read that correctly. He would literally bring me options, unbeknownst to them what was going on, and position them in front of me. Then he'd walk away with a "You're welcome," and I would take it from there. Best wingman *evah*!

If I liked them, I'd ask him to stand to the side and sit tight. I know it sounds crazy, but even crazier was they mostly would do what I asked. If they weren't my style, I'd simply smile and say, "Nice to meet you. Thanks for stopping by; have a good night." Very much like an audition process. I admit it was shady and a double standard, because if a guy did that to a girl, he'd get

MASTER OF SINGLE

demolished about how sexist he was being. But you know what? For all the times I've watched men sexualize women, it was a little taste of their own medicine, and I didn't feel bad about it for a minute. Honestly, you'd be surprised at how many guys would just take directions and wait. I found it quite hilarious and very entertaining.

It was only a matter of time before I narrowed down my top three potential finalists, none of them sure of what was going on exactly or that one of them was about to literally hit the jackpot. They were just hanging out in the designated waiting area, curious enough to stick around to see where this was going. They all were similar in looks: dark hair, handsome with chiselled features, medium height with good bodies and a face I wouldn't mind looking at from different positions. Check, check, check.

Before making my final choice, I did a last lap around the club to make sure I hadn't missed any potential persons of interest. I wanted the best candidates for the job, not to mention the one I felt would be the most deserving of having me for the night or at least a few hours.

As it turned out, they were the best options, but by the time I returned to where they were waiting, one prospect had left. Quite frankly, I was surprised any of them stuck around that long, but one down, two to go. They were both interesting in their own way, but one of them had a slight edge over the other in terms of potentiality and personality. I went to him first to feel out his vibe. He was cute and looked like he'd be dirty fun in bed, but just as he was about to take the prize, he dropped the ball (aka he fucked up).

As we were getting ready to leave, I noticed him flirting with another girl standing close by. I know what you're thinking. Karma much? Fair enough, but still, how rude. Total mood killer. The irony wasn't lost on me. I was playing games with them, and now I was getting played, but still, this was my game, I made the rules, and Lady Slay does not like to lose, especially not at her own game.

Still with one solid viable option, I turned to him to say, "Let's get out of here," but to my shock and dismay, he wasn't there, and now I was pissed. I had wasted my time on bozo number one, who turned out to be the wrong choice, only to lose the one who probably deserved me the most. Rookie mistake.

After all that, I ended up walking out alone, feeling like "WTF just happened? I had everything plus options, and I'm leaving with nothing." It was beginning to look like the only *yes* I'd be getting would be from my vibrator.

As I made my way outside, feeling discouraged about my night, I noticed a souped-up, fully loaded, lowered suspension, rimmed-out black Range Rover sitting idle at the end of the alleyway. The window slowly rolled down, and guess who it was? It was him, the second of my top two picks (also one of Jam's picks for me), who I thought had left. But nope, he was waiting for me to come out. Well played, player.

Leaning on the middle console and looking like a piece of meat on a stick, he signalled me over, and of course I complied. Once there, I leaned into the open window and said, "Are you waiting for me?"

He said back (in French), "You want to get out of here?" It was the panty-dropper moment I was hoping for. Clearly he knew what was up and that I was worth waiting for. (#andthewinneris)

It's not often the game gets turned around on me, but I quite enjoyed and respected how he played it to his advantage. It showed balls, so congratulations, he won and now he got to collect his prize.

Because I'd driven to the club, I suggested leaving my car

there and driving with him, which was the smart thing to do, considering I'd drunk quite a bit and would have taken a cab home anyway. I got in his ride and pointed the way...

It was unusual for me to do that, but I suggested we go back to my place, only because he lived far away, and by the time we would have gotten there, my nice drunk buzz would have worn off. So by default and in another rare instance, I offered up my spot. The ride took no time at all, and very few words were exchanged. Perfect. Before I knew it, I was in my bed, having amazing sex with a hot, young stud. Success much?

Lady Slay strikes again!

The things I enjoy most about young studs in bed is their stamina and that they have a short recovery time before they're ready to go again. They're also more motivated and interested in pleasing the woman, especially a woman with slightly more experience than them. It's like they have something to prove. No arguments there, and I'm a great teacher.

By the end of our "sexcapade," we had exhausted ourselves to the point that neither of us could put a sentence together, neither in French nor English. That's when I realized that the sun was coming up and he was still in my bed. Flag on the play, this was not normal protocol. Remember my hard rule of what happens in the night stays in the night and no sleepovers? So much for that. Before I could ask him to leave, he turned to me and said, "I'll drive you to your car when we wake up."

I wanted to say *No get out*, but I also kind of loved that he didn't give me the choice about him sleeping over, and I didn't have the energy to argue, so he did and we slept. Besides, he was right I'd need a ride to pick up my car, and I was better off driving with him than cold cabbing it with a hangover.

And what a hangover it was!! The wake-up was brutal, but when I turned to my right and saw this stellar piece and hunk of a man naked and sprawled out across my sheets, I instantly remembered why.

Again, few words were exchanged. In fact, we really didn't talk much at all the whole night, which was perfect... We got dressed to leave, and I don't think I even offered him a coffee, but maybe a glass of water... It seemed like the least I could do.

He drove me to my car, and there was a slightly awkward silence, but I do remember asking him what he did for a living. He told me that he sold luxury cars, which explained why he was driving such a sick ride.

Finally we arrived at my car, I gathered myself, looked at him, and said a cordial, "Thanks for the ride (wink, wink). It was fun. Goodbye." I opened the door to get out, and that's when it hit me: I didn't even know his name!

I started laughing so hard I almost peed my pants. Halfway out the door, I turned back to him, barely holding in my laughter, and asked, "Sorry, what's your name?" He chuckled, and then we both laughed at the situation, but he was a good sport about it because I don't think he knew my name either.

He said his name, I repeated it, smiled, and thanked him again. I closed the door, still shaking my head at the fact I didn't even get his name. Oh my God!

As I walked towards my car, still dying of laughter, I couldn't believe my own audacity and what I had just done. *Is this what it's like to have sex like a man?* I felt nothing. I conquered what I'd set out to do and didn't care about anything else, not even his name. Wow. Who am I?

Oh yeah, I'm Lady Slay, it's Friday night, and I just got laid. Heyyyy!

MASTER OF SINGLE

Listen, I understand especially in this unprecedented time we're in that reliving this story is high risk and unlikely, but the point remains the same. When it comes to your pleasure in all areas, nobody's going to care more about you getting what you want out of life than you.

Do what you got to do, and be the best at doing it.

And may we all go on to live happily ever after to slay another day, whatever that means to you.

Chapter Eleven

SINGLE IS THE NEW JAM

How much do I love this chapter? Let me count the ways! I've mentioned Jam before, but this is his chapter and the story of how we met, dedicated to celebrating that utmost important and special relationship between a straight single woman and a gay man.

Titled after the man himself, Jam, like strawberry, he jokingly says, is not only my favourite flavour, but he also reigns as my favourite man. *Amore*.

I trust him with my most intimate and vulnerable secrets. He sees me and loves me unconditionally, and he's always forward thinking for me, just a couple of reasons why I love this man so much.

With his consent, I'm using his name, but unlike the other chapters, this is a different kind of love story. It's a story only we could tell and I could write.

Here's a little backstory to set the stage of how we came to be. The year was 2014, and I had just returned home after living in New York City for two years. I mostly loved everything about a real New York acting/student-life experience. But I will say this—as tough and sometimes gruelling as it was, I'm happy I did it when I did. It was always a dream of mine to live and study in NYC, and now years later, I'm not sure I'd have the same strength or courage to go through that today.

The big takeaway and my absolute message to you is not to wait to do what you love or dream of because tomorrow is not promised and life may not offer you a second opportunity. Don't hesitate and leave your dreams to fate. Check the boxes and start crossing things off the list while you can. If our global situation has taught us anything, it's to take nothing for granted, especially time.

Fast forward, post-graduation, I was working tirelessly to stay in the States to further my experience, but nothing I did worked. Visas were near impossible to get, and marrying for papers wasn't an option for me, so in the end I was left no choice but to return home to Canada. That's when things went from bad to "What the hell do I do next?"

Short of my friends and family, there wasn't much left for me to come back to. After eight years, I'd resigned from my job in television and given up my apartment. I'd sold my car and most of my valued possessions, all to help pay for school.

Not to mention I was on the heels of turning forty, grrreat! I mention age only because for a single woman of a certain age to give up a career and security that's taken years of hard work, blood, sweat, and tears to build, is a big deal. The combination of being forced to return home and feeling like I'd let so many people down was hard to digest.

MASTER OF SINGLE

Disappointed with myself, broken-hearted about having to leave New York, and thinking about starting over again was too much for my heart to bear.

Although I knew I could do it because I'd done it before, in that moment I was exhausted to the core, depleted, and felt defeated. Just the thought of it all made me exhale and sigh out loud, sound effects and all. My greatest blessing in this time was my incredible support network and the universe that's always had my back.

From within my circle of sister friends, a series of phone calls and communications ensued regarding my situation. Without a moment's hesitation, one of my beloved sisters swooped in like an angel and invited me (more like told me) to stay with her and her family.

She and I share an incredibly special bond, fifteen years strong. It's one of deep respect, mutual love, and admiration for who each of us are as strong women and good people.

She's part of my core framily and my heart, and so are her family, including her beautiful mother, phenomenal father (RIP), and kind-hearted brother. As well as her amazing and generous husband along with their incredibly smart and beautiful children, I simply adore them with my full heart.

When I think about what they did to help me, it just blows my mind. They offered me the nanny's quarters and asked the nanny if she could find another place to stay for the summer (which she kindly obliged), giving me three months to get back on my feet.

I mean, how do you even repay something like that? I do with my unconditional love and loyalty to the family.

It was the perfect place to transition and heal on the down low, not seeing anyone or really letting anyone know

NICOLE JONES

I was back in the city. I used the time to regain my focus and figure out my next steps, but the best part was the joy and laughter of the children. They brought me back to life.

By the end of the summer, I was ready to fly again, and that's when I flew right into the arms of Jam.

As I slowly resurfaced into society, only a few friends knew I was back, including one of my good girlfriends. One day I received a call from her, at that time she was dating the owner of a nightclub called Flyjin, the same place I've mentioned in previous chapters. She'd thought of me because her boyfriend was looking for someone special to fill a new position within the club family. She was vague about the job description but said it had something to do with customer service. It sounded interesting, so I took the bait and met with the owner.

He explained that I'd be working the door, helping to filter the crowd as well as taking care of the VIP clients. I remember him also saying that I'd be working with someone named Jam, and then every sentence after that had Jam's name in it. I was going to love Jam, that Jam was cool and he would be training me, and ultimately, I'd be working under Jam. In my head I was like, *Okay, I got it, Jam. Good, got it.* By the end of the conversation, he'd said Jam so much that even though I didn't know him yet, I wanted to smear him all over a piece of toast. And with that, we ended the conversation, sealed the deal, and I started a couple of days later.

On that first night, I was feeling a little nervous, knowing I was going to see a lot of people for the first time since being back from NY, but I was also excited. The return was a good one. I was working at the hottest nightclub in the city with a position of respect and authority. But don't call it a comeback; this was a callback—a call back to my city and my roots.

MASTER OF SINGLE

Alas, it happened—the moment I will never forget that set my heart to fluttering and my eyes to twinkling. Finally my turn had come to be introduced to the one and only... drum roll.... Paul! Ha ha, kidding! I met Jam! I can hear the heavens now singing in all their glory in remembrance of our first meet. What can I say other than the boss was right and it was love at first sight! I'd never experienced love at first sight until that very moment. It was like a shot through the heart where for a fraction of a second you're thrown off-balance, but you catch yourself just in time to save yourself from yourself. Yup, love at first sight. There was just something about Jam. His energy was unbelievably palpable, and the way he carried himself was so attractive. I loved the kind tone of his voice and how he spoke *to* me, not *at* me. He exuded a confidence like he woke up like that with a vibe and style personified, and yes, handsome from head to toe.

When he shook my hand, I felt his energy transfer up my arm. It was real and instant like we'd known each other in another life and were picking up where we'd left off; it was that familiar. Divine intervention was revealing that we'd be friends, but what I didn't know was that our soon-to-be alliance would also be the saviour to my single-girl life.

Working the door at a place like Flyjin, with a limited capacity and everyone thinks they're a VIP because they know someone, can be annoying. But I noticed that no matter what or who happened, Jam never flinched and didn't let status or pressure affect how he did his job. He was steadfast and ready without hesitation, guilt, or apology. It didn't take long for me to understand why he was such an asset. People loved him, but more importantly they respected him even when they didn't want to. His presence commanded their respect just by way of his disposition, which is an invaluable combination to find in one person. Did I mention how funny he was? Always cracking me up with his matter-of-fact kind of humour.

I knew I could learn a lot from him, so I appointed myself as his protégé. He was the best, and I wanted to be the best too.

Working the door and tending to our VIP guests proved to be a lot more challenging than I'd imagined. The nightlife biz is a tough gig. Aside from the late hours and being extremely demanding, it's an industry where keeping your cool is essential. You must be willing and able to take a certain amount of shit, expect to deal with bad attitudes, and be ready to troubleshoot from all sides at any given time. Pivoting is a crucial skill in this biz!

The saving grace was having Jam in my corner. His calmness kept me centred and collected, especially in those times when I just wanted to tell asshole clients to go fuck themselves. But being the studious student that I was, I learned that keeping my cool was not only part of the job, it was also part of the look.

The more we worked together, the closer we became. It wasn't contrived or forced; it wasn't even planned. It happened very naturally. Okay, maybe I was secretly plotting in my head and conspiring with the universe to unite us in friendship, but let's not split hairs and just call it: meant to be.

The days turned into weeks that seamlessly melted into months and then years. We'd met each other's friends and family, all of whom I've come to love and care about deeply, among them his proper family who reside in Paris, his sweet husband Anthony, and my beloveds Elias, Kenza, and her hubby Mich. A collective group of beautiful souls.

It wasn't long before we were making time and space

for each other in our respective lives. We shared the same values and morals, and most importantly, we respected each other and that was everything. (#framily)

I'm not typically the type of person to let people into the fibre of my life so easily, but I'd never met anyone quite like him. He was a rare find. I knew it and appreciated it.

I cherished who we were together as something special, and the fact that he was gay just meant that we'd never have to worry about blurring the line between friend and lover, and the best part, we'd never go after the same guy. Brilliant!

Learning about his sexual preference didn't faze me for a second. If anything, that built-in safety net further confirmed that what made us different would also work to our advantage in solidifying a long-lasting friendship.

So now that you know how we met, I'm excited to share the best part; why "Single is the new Jam."

Here are just a couple (it was hard to choose) of my all-time favourite "jamazing" stories with this beautiful man.

Starting right here at home with all the crazy, fun party nights, particularly his ubersuccessful event called Drama Queen, a monthly party for the gay community that brought out the best crowds, sickest DJs, and was open to all people. He's always found creative ways to give back to his community, and this much-anticipated event was a prime example of who he is at his core.

He birthed an idea that came from a place of love, to create and inspire more love.

And then there's Ibiza. By now you know how special and important my Ibiza family and the island are to me. When I'm there, I feel like the best version of myself—unfiltered, plain to see, openhearted, grounded, blissful, and calm from the inside out. Sounds good, right?

It's my happy place, and not just anyone gets invited to come with me.

If there was a monarchy in Ibiza, my family would be the royal family—in my eyes anyway. I couldn't imagine the island without them. Their home (my home away from home) is a utopia and breeding ground for love, creativity, culture, family, and bringing people together with an energy and happiness that I protect with my heart and soul. Although I know they would welcome whomever I brought with me, the list of people for my consideration is very short, and the requirements are very high. I can't risk anyone killing my Ibiza vibe. Selfish? Meh, maybe, but my motto is Ibiza, I care enough to bring the very best.

But when it came to Jam, I was so excited for them to meet, I just knew they'd love each other and both would bring something special to the other's life, and I was right. Within thirty minutes into his first visit, he was interacting, laughing, and playing with the kids.

And if the kids liked you, you knew you were in.

In true gentlemen form, he arrived with gifts, three of the most adorable Adidas tracksuits I'd ever seen, one for each of the boys. They were so excited to receive them. Now that's a heart that thinks in service of others with an intention to bring happiness, with nothing to gain but everything to give.

It's a great example of why we vibe so well. I'm the same way, and that's why they say show me your friends, and I'll show you who you are.

When you read that in thinking about your friends, do you see yourself in them, or does it leave you questioning them? Food for thought.

No surprise, Betta and Ray just adored him without a second thought; basically, he became an instant part of the

MASTER
OF SINGLE

family. The kids lovingly called him Jamón, which means "ham" in Spanish but looks like Jam. It was the cutest thing, and he just rolled with it as they called his name non-stop, "Jamón, Jamón, where are you, Jamón?" Later that day I walked into the living room to see him helping the oldest brother, Sebastiano, with his French homework. I just about melted where I stood; it showed me that he knew how important my boys and my family were to me, and that was everything.

Once the kids were asleep and all tucked in, the adults came out to play, and boy oh boy the island was not ready for us, but ready or not, enter the Montreal invasion.

There are so many great memories and good times had at the most exclusive parties on the island with the best DJs in the world, including one of our favourites: Black Coffee.

You had to be there to truly catch the vibe, but I'll tell you this. Even in a sea of people we stood out, taking our space on the dance floor and graciously sharing our energy with everyone around us. When we were in our dancing zone, you couldn't touch that. We heart Ibiza.

I can say with one hundred percent certainty that the relationship between a straight single woman and a gay man is the gift that keeps on giving. There's something more expansive about the way he thinks and sees things, offering a fresh perspective to situations that not even my girlfriends could bring. It's truly one of the purest, most gratifying, supportive, loving, and real types of relationships a single woman could ask for and be blessed to have.

He needs me, and I'm there; I need him, and he's there. Just one more reason single is the new Jam.

But it's not just about the partying or the good times. There are also those real-life, tough moments when you need a friend who knows you well enough to help you through.

NICOLE JONES

The year my mom died, I was in a deep depression for a while, and her first birthday without her was a soul-crushing day. Knowing I was suffering through an extremely difficult time, he showed up at my door, holding the biggest, most beautiful framed photo of my mom and me, taken during a photoshoot I'd done with her years back as a Mother's Day gift.

It was her favourite photo of us because that day meant so much to her. I get emotional just writing about it.

He reached out and handed it to me with loving care. It was the most touching thing anyone had ever done for me. I had no idea how he even got the picture, but it didn't matter because in that moment, it was exactly what I needed to remind me that everything was going to be okay and that my mom would always be with me, and so would he. I mean, who does that? Jam does.

I later found out that he had tracked down the photo through my girl Patricia who had taken it, and they worked together to manifest that magical moment.

I'll never forget because on that day, he saved me from total devastation and grief, and today the photo hangs as the centrepiece on my wall and in my heart.

Not to make light of such a perfect moment, but how many straight men do you know who would have the wherewithal to think and love like that? I know a lot of straight guys, none of whom would even come close to having that idea. It goes to show when you love, you pay attention to what your friends need.

Now, I'm not saying that straight men aren't thoughtful, so please don't write to me telling me how great they are. I acknowledge that they're special and play an important role in their own way. It's just different; that's all I'm saying.

My secret wish for every single woman is that they too

have a Jam in her life (but you'll have to get your own; this one's taken).

I would be remiss to not extend my circle of impressive men of the gay persuasion to include my beloved Elias and sweet Youssouf, aka Youyou.

I met Elias through Jam, and my first impression was what an original individual. As our friendship blossomed, so did my love for him. He makes my heart smile, he's framily, and I love to love him. We freely exchange love and light between us, his pure and beautiful soul is plain to see, and he reserves the best parts of who he is for the ones he loves.

And then there's my Youyou, who's just the sweetest addition to my boys' crew and is like a little brother to me. Kind, sweet, real, so stylish with grace and poise and much love to give.

Single women and gay men are the new black, and if you didn't know, now you know.

One of the numerous things I love about my gay male friends is that they're honest almost to a fault sometimes, but I wouldn't change it for anything. If they don't like what I'm wearing, for example, they'll tell me I look a fool, but with my girlfriends, it's hit or miss if they'll say anything.

We've all had that experience when you see a group of girls out together and one of them is looking a hot mess and you think to yourself, *Her girlfriends lied to her.*

It's not because they don't care, but girlfriends tend to be more careful to not hurt feelings, whereas gay men are not typically feeling first. They're truth tellers first and will console you later when the truth hurts. We all need friends in our lives who are willing to tell us the truth and then buy us a cocktail afterwards.

Before closing this chapter, I'd like to address one more thing. I grappled with even mentioning this because it's a personal choice and it's never my intention to push my agenda or thoughts onto anyone else. However, seeing as I'm here to share and I have your attention, why not?

It's about straight women labelling their gay male friends as being their "gay husband."

There's something so wrong about that, to my ear and sensibility, that makes me cringe when I hear it.

What does it even mean, "my gay husband?" You're not bound by legal contract. They aren't sleeping with you or obligated to pay your bills or take out your trash.

I guess I just don't get the connection; it's an oxymoron.

I also feel that in some shady way it discredits actual husbands. Marriage is a special union in and of itself, so why bring one into the other?

They are not our husbands in any regard, but they are our friends and deserve the same respect we'd show any of our friends.

Again, this is only my opinion, so if you're yelling at this book, arguing your case about your gay husband, don't bother. If he's not offended and you're good with it, then keep it moving.

I personally think women use that term carelessly, not thinking about what it really signifies, instead thinking it sounds cute, but no.

As a black woman and minority, I'm hypersensitive about being labelled or put in a box, and maybe that's why I see things differently.

If the roles were reversed and my gay male friends introduced me as their "black wife" or even their "black friend," I would lose my mind and be really offended. Would you introduce your lesbian friends as "my gay wife?" All I'm saying is your relationship/friendship should be enough, no labels necessary.

Now before anyone gets all up in arms about this, I realize that I've given Jam the title of being my favourite man, best friend, and even my *amore*, but they're not labels, they're facts. Unless there's a marriage certificate between you, keep it real. They are not your husbands; they're your friends, and that should be respected accordingly.

So there you have it, my thoughts and feelings about a label-free world. Take it or leave it.

In conclusion, if you're a straight single woman and haven't found your Jam, Elias, or Youyou, it's okay. Don't despair. They are out there and open to meeting you too, much like your person is waiting to meet you.

Honey, it's 2021 and we are reinventing all the single rules one relationship at a time, and that's Jamazing!

Chapter Twelve

THE REBOUND GUY

OH LORD, NOT this guy (eye roll). The rebound guy—a story far too many of us have experienced and would rather forget. I'm pretty sure we can all relate in some capacity to having slept or gotten involved with a guy or girl way too quickly after having broken up with someone else, or at least we know someone who has.

Rebound sex can be a tricky and messy thing if you don't pay attention, so please pay attention as we learn from my mistakes.

Unless you're a unicorn living in some mystical forest or magical land where rebounds become the love of your life and you skip off into the sunset, following the yellow brick road together, then I'm happy for you. But here on earth, frogs are frogs and rebounds at best can be considered a moderately good time for a drunken one-night stand. Welcome back to reality and the single brick road.

There's a saying that goes "The best way to get over someone is to get under somebody else." I'd like to amend that to include a point that nobody's talking about—the fact that you don't want to be that "somebody else." Honestly, who really wants to be that random, wrong time, wrong place chick who gets lured into the trap of being the rebound?

It's important to note that there's a grave difference between having a rebound and being the rebound, so if you're having the experience, it's vital to know which one you are.

The person having the rebound, whom I'll refer to as the "rebounder," has a clear endgame in mind. It's one-sided and driven by their own selfish needs with a goal to get off sexually. Period. People usually rebound to purge themselves of their last relationship. The problem is, most of the time the person on the receiving end isn't aware that they're being used as the rebound, and that's when it becomes not so cool for them. This is typically a "hit it and quit it" before you can even exchange numbers kind of situation.

The person being used as the rebound, or the "reboundee," often doesn't have all the information going into the situation. They're swayed under a false pretense and blinded by the lure of the flirting and the charm of the rebounder. The facts are stacked against the reboundee, so unless you knowingly agree to being that person, beware. Without all the information, this will be crushing for a lot of people and difficult to come back from.

I suppose some people would argue that rebound sex is fine and that they're cool with it, but I suspect that if they're honest with themselves, they're not okay with it.

There's nothing prized about being used as a rebound. There's no big lesson or takeaway, and it's nothing to brag about because he's not the guy you're going to take home to meet the parents. The only reward, if any, might be the fleeting sexual pleasure in a blurry haze of losing your head, but when that moment passes (and it always does), it will likely leave you with a heavy heart, an empty bed, and some level of regret.

But I guess you can't have one without the other, right? To have a rebound experience, someone else must be on the receiving end, so yeah, there's that. I admit that I'm one hundred percent guilty of having been the "rebounder" and seducing some guy into a rebound situation, knowing full well that I was just using him for sex.

I'll even admit to enjoying the rush of the chase and releasing my sexual frustrations in the heat of the moment.

That said, it's hard for me to complain about it, having also been on the other side when I was the one being used by a guy and didn't know it. It really sucked, but hey, what goes around, comes back around.

In my defence however, I did know the person I chose to rebound with. Knowing he was single and DTF made him the perfect target. I just didn't communicate to him that he was being "used," but I think he knew and didn't care. I mean he was about to sleep with me and I'm no consolation prize, okur. It was more like an unspoken agreement between two consenting adults where everyone wins.

In these low moments when all we want is to feel "instagood" and don't care about how we get there are also the times when we sell ourselves short. My only advice is you can do whatever you want—nobody's judging you—but whatever you do, make sure you're able to look at yourself in the mirror and still love yourself the next day.

Live free, learn quickly, and rebound wisely.

I did a little research for my own curiosity to find out what the experts had to say about rebound sex. What I discovered was exactly what I already knew. I guess that makes me an expert.

Some described it as a desire to ease the pain of losing one's partner. No surprise there, but I also came across the idea of revenge sex. Slightly different and much shadier, it's when you have sex with someone your ex knows, just to get back at them—ouch!

Shady, shady, shady is the person who has sex for revenge out of spite. Not a good look.

It's not always easy to gauge who you're dealing with or what baggage they're bringing to the table, but listen to me: If for whatever reason you do find yourself caught in the web of a rebounder, don't be too hard on yourself. It's not your fault. How could you know? People on the rebound can be great at manipulating you to get what they want, so don't beat yourself up if you mistook their flirting for genuine interest. They should feel shame for deceiving you, not the other way around. The bottom line is that rebound situations are disasters waiting to happen, and you must stay vigilant about who you hook up with, or things could end as a bad romance novel.

Finally, remember this golden rule, people will treat you the way you allow them to treat you, so hold your self-worth high to the heavens and don't ever let anyone take you down.

Of course, this wouldn't be a complete chapter without one of my delightful—or in this case, not so delightful—single-girl stories. My biggest hope in sharing this story is to educate and hopefully spare someone else the agony that was my underwhelming rebound experience.

Welcome to the time I was rebounded…

MASTER OF SINGLE

I've always considered myself to be a person with good intuition and who trusts my instincts especially when it comes to gauging people and their energy. So when I was introduced to this next guy and my single-girl intuitive antenna turned up to full-frequency mode, I was intrigued.

The first time I saw him was at my workplace. He'd come in with a friend, but he was the one who'd caught my eye. I remember being behind the bar, making myself a drink, when I looked up and saw this handsome man standing there as fine can be, the epitome of the strong, silent type, which only made him more fascinating. The quiet ones always are.

It wasn't just his cool and effortless style that caught my eye, nor was it his edgy appearance with his salt-and-pepper goatee and fauxhawk haircut. It wasn't even his great smile and dazzling pearly whites or the fact that he looked age appropriate in terms of potentiality.

It was a mixture if at all, but the most interesting thing about him was that I'd never seen him before, and working in nightlife not much got by me by way of the single-male landscape, which made him all the more interesting.

Most single men I meet are one or two degrees of separation from my friend group, which I consider too close for comfort and not an ideal situation for dating. It does make it more difficult to meet people, because it narrows down the market, but it's a chance I'm willing to take. I don't need anyone I know and their mother up in my business, metaphorically speaking, so keeping my romantic life separate from my personal/friend/work life is tricky, but it's important to me.

There's also the possibility that things don't work out, and then your ex is within your friend group and proximity at any given time. No, thanks. The risk versus reward, in my opinion, is not a sane bet or a risk I'm willing to take.

An ex should never be that close to home, just saying. That said, my third eye is always open, checking for the new kid on the block or the needle in the haystack, whichever comes first. In this case, my intuitive side was really feeling what this guy was giving off, and yes, he was another beautiful stranger. Can't say I'm not consistent.

That night I was in a particularly good mood and looking forward to meeting up with Jam at the club after work. That was the plan before you-know-who walked in.

With my shift coming to an end and said person of interest still in the place, I was feeling a certain kind of way about leaving without more information, so I started to plot.

By now, I've learned my lesson inside out, upside down, front to back, and whatever else you got. To ask the questions before thinking, committing, or initiating any sort of engagement beyond friendly conversation. Period. Lesson got. Thank you. Next.

The plan was to take a last lap around to check on guests, including him and his friends, and when I arrived at the table, he was surprisingly much more talkative than I'd observed him to be, which was nice. After a shot and some friendly conversation that included eye contact, he revealed that he was single, and then he dropped the bomb. No kids! What? A clean slate. Where do I sign up?

Those words came out of his mouth. I heard them with my own ears. I was like, *Damn, it doesn't get any more confirming than that.* Are you kidding me? He was new blood, of a certain age, handsome, charming, sexy, and built like a mountain I'd like to climb—a rare breed that didn't often come along. Of course I thought to myself, let me get in there before someone else.

Without even thinking, I pulled the trigger and invited

him to join me to meet Jam at the club. I didn't know what to expect because he was with his friends, but he said yes, he'd be happy to tag along. If I was looking for signs, that was a good one. I just wasn't sure yet what I was going to do with him, but I was confident that I'd figure it out as the night went on. I was just happy he accepted my invitation.

The walk to the club gave us the chance to talk a little more, and call me crazy, but I detected a mutual interest budding just by the way he was engaging me, warm and playful.

By the time we arrived, it seemed more interesting to continue our conversation than going inside. I was there to turn up and maybe dance with a hot guy, but here I was bringing sand to the beach, albeit beautiful sand, which was counterproductive to why I was going in the first place. With him in tow, I wasn't interested in meeting anyone else.

As we approached the back entrance through the dark alley towards a lone light in the distance, walking shoulder to shoulder with my beautiful stranger, it felt very film noir, and I was living for it.

As per usual, there to meet us at the door along with the security (#bestsecurityintown) was Jam and his style. I was excited to introduce them, and I could tell that my guy was getting curious to know who this friend was he was about to meet. As soon as I introduced them, Jam said hello and then looked at me as if to say "Girl, he's hot. What are you doing coming to meet me when you have a piece like that?"

Then he leaned in and said those exact words, and we both laughed because I could read his mind. Now that's a friend—someone who will break the plans you have together so you can go get laid.

I gave him a look back that said, *Are you sure you don't mind?* Because I was equally cool with seeing how the night played out, but he doubled down. "Girl, you better take this man and get out of here." Subtle much?

I laughed in agreement, leaned over to my guy, and said, "You want to get out of here?" He said yes, and I left with my beautiful stranger, who by the way had been such a good sport that whole night, rolling with the punches and happy to let me lead.

He earned some cool points just by his attitude, and I was looking forward to being alone where we could talk and get to know each other better… or just get to know each other better, whichever came first.

He mentioned that he lived quite far outside the city limits. In fact, I didn't even recognize the name of the place when he said it. All I knew was that it was too far out for my comfort zone, and there was no way I was going back to his place. This is when you need to know how to amend your own rules. In this case, bringing him home was the best recourse, and he seemed worthy of making an exception.

With that we headed off, direction pleasure dome, aka my home.

We both had vehicles, so he followed me, and on the ride there, true to single-girl form, I started asking myself if my place was presentable and on point to receive a gentleman caller.

I'm a little crazy about my home being clean and organized, especially when I have people over.

It's something I got from my mom, who took great pride in her home. Whenever we were expecting guests, the house had to be cleaned to her standards first.

I remember as a kid not being able to use the

washrooms or mess up the living room until the guests arrived.

I'm not as stringent, but I also wasn't raising and running a house full of rambunctious, messy kids.

Plus that night I was in a rush when I left my house, not expecting to have anyone over, which reinforces my point to always stay ready on the go so that when opportunity arrives, you don't have to get ready. Note to self: take my own advice. Dirty laundry lying around or an unmade bed, which is rare but it happens, dirty dishes left in the sink, even my vibrator left out were all possibilities in this spontaneous moment.

Sue me. I'm a busy girl on the go.

Much to my delight, my place was on point and nicely together to receive company, avoiding any embarrassing single-girl moments, which was a relief.

He seemed to bring a nice and warm energy with him, and I liked the way he looked in my space—comfortable and handsome as he opened and poured the wine.

You know when your food tastes as good as it looks? Well, that was him. He looked delicious and good enough to eat, and I could only imagine how good he tasted.

We talked and laughed a lot, and it was surprising we didn't get to sex right away, but we were enjoying the conversation, which acted as foreplay. The more we talked, the more I could feel my mounting sexual appetite wanting him.

Eventually it was enough conversation and he came in for the kiss, which was divine, just as I'd suspected it would be. One thing led to another, and before he knew it, my milkshake brought that boy to the yard. We didn't even make it to the bedroom; he took me right there on the couch.

He's welcome.

Taking off his shirt was like unwrapping candy; it revealed his beautifully tatted body, shoulder, and sleeve, which only elevated his savage card even further.

He was fire. I was loving it and wasn't afraid to tell him. It was very sexy how he handled my sassiness.

The craziest part of the night was when I heard myself invite him to stay over; it even shocked me. I don't know where that came from, but there was something about him and our night that had me feeling like I wanted to wake up next to him.

Unfortunately for me, he explained that he hadn't expected his night to unfold in that way, which was great, but that he had to leave to go take care of his dogs.

How could I argue with that? I'd do the same thing. Let no person come between a man or woman and their dog. I would never sacrifice Dior's well-being for anyone.

I understood but didn't pretend to like it and might have pouted just a little while naked in bed, giving him sexy pose after pose, hoping to get him to stay a little while longer, and it worked.

He couldn't resist. I didn't blame him. I mean, duh!

We had sex one more delicious time, which made it a little bit easier to let him leave, but I was still bummed to see him go.

The days that followed, I found myself thinking about him often and replaying certain parts from our conversation in my head, trying to figure this guy out.

Why was he single? At least I knew for sure this time that he was. I'd heard it with my own ears.

But instead of feeling reassured, it made him more mysterious, and I wasn't sure if that was a good or bad thing.

MASTER OF SINGLE

I promised myself not to get in my head with questions, concerns, or problems that hadn't happened; instead, I'd trust the process.

Let's pause here to talk about what it means to trust the process. Often, we say these great phrases, but we don't always know what they mean or how to apply them.

My definition of trusting the process is trusting that things are happening in the universe and will unfold in their own time.

Good talk.

However—there's always something—one aspect that didn't totally sit well with me was that each time I asked him about his past relationships, he was vague and closed off about the details.

At first I thought he wasn't comfortable expressing that part of himself, so I didn't push, but I did nudge enough to get something out of him. Unfortunately, I wasn't thrilled to hear what he had to say.

He confessed to having just broken up with his long-term girlfriend not long before meeting me.

That's when everything became clear, and I was like, *Oh damn, I'm the motherfuckin' rebound. This isn't good. Red flag.*

But despite the waving red flag on the play, I still wanted to believe what I wanted to believe and led with my "feelings," sharing with him how much I liked him, hoping that would change something. Rookie mistake.

Which is a mistake a lot of women make even when the red flags are waving in our face, trying to get our attention. And when things blow up, which they usually will, it's hard to justify being upset when we had the information but chose not to listen to it.

I should have left as soon as I found out that he was in rebound mode.

Lesson: No dick is that good to justify overlooking the red flags. The things you ignore in the beginning will be the same problems that break you up in the end.

No surprise that the conversation didn't go as I'd hoped it would. After that, he took a step back.

I had opened the door, but he wasn't ready to walk through it.

Still, I wasn't giving up. (#masochist)

It was rare to meet someone I liked that much, so I gave it a little more time, slowed my roll, and eventually managed to get him back in my bed and good graces.

If love is blind, lust is blurry, and my lenses were foggy.

After we reconnected, I agreed to respect his privacy about his past (huge mistake), telling myself that his past had nothing to do with our present and I would focus on the now.

Boy oh boy, was I wrong.

Did I mention he was fifty years old? Which only increased my hope and faith in him, thinking a man of his maturity surely possessed the skills and life experiences to get through this break-up in a timely and mature manner.

A couple days later I proposed he come meet me at work and we'd go out for a drink afterwards.

Later that night, he arrived already a few drinks in, which I didn't mind. In fact, I enjoyed seeing him have fun while I was finishing up. I even sent over shots for him and the clients he was talking with.

Never imagining in a million years what would happen next.

He came over to tell me that he was stepping outside for a minute. I nodded and said, "Cool. I'm almost done. I'll come meet you."

MASTER
OF SINGLE

Ten or fifteen minutes later, I stepped outside to join him, but I didn't even make it past the front door. To my absolute shock and dismay, he was standing in the entrance of my workplace with some employees and clients, smoking a joint.

Listen, I knew he smoked, but I was flabbergasted that he would do it in this way. I couldn't believe my eyes! What the hell was he thinking? To do something so careless and reckless at my place of work with staff and in my face. Not only did it show poor judgement but felt disrespectful to the highest degree.

I looked at him with sheer disappointment, surprisingly though he didn't look like he thought he was doing anything wrong. I wanted to kill him.

If you're going to represent me as my man, don't embarrass me, come to my work, and mess with my reputation and job. Naw, wrong girl.

I was fuming at his lack of awareness. With my jaw clenched, I said to him, "Put it out right now." I couldn't believe the smug look on his face as he took another defiant puff before putting it out. Rude to the bone. Wow!

I pushed past him, stomping off in the direction of the club, and with every step, I was trying to shake it off, but I was beside myself.

I wasn't sure how I would continue with the night after his stupid antics, but somehow I did. I went deep inside and found the will to keep it moving, thinking that motherfucker better fuck me like the queen at the end of the night. I walked in front of him to give myself a moment and a little space to cool down; he gave me that space, walking a few steps behind me, but I wasn't sure if he was remorseful or just ignoring the fact I was livid with him.

Once at the club, I was still hot and giving him a little bit of a cold shoulder because he hadn't yet apologized or taken responsibility for his unacceptable actions, and until that happened, I couldn't get past my anger and disappointment. We made our way inside where the vibe was on point, the music was great, and the crowd was popping, all of which had me starting to feel better.

As I headed to the bar, stopping to chat with friends along the way, I didn't introduce them to him. I just wasn't feeling it.

Maybe it was a little passive aggressive, but bad behaviour doesn't get rewarded by meeting more of my friends.

That said, I also didn't want to ruin the whole night with this bad vibe, so to change my mood and turn the night around, I decided to be the bigger person and ordered both of us a drink.

But when I turned to hand it to him, kind of as a peace offering (even though it should have been the other way around), that's when he totally lost the plot, and this time it would be the nail in his coffin.

I extended the drink, and he blatantly refused it, giving me the cut eye look of death. It was so bizarro world that I thought for sure he misunderstood, so I tried again and said, "Babe, this is for you."

"I don't fucking want it, and we're done!" he replied.

What? I'm sorry, what did you say? WTF was going on now. This guy was a loose cannon. No matter how hot he was, his behaviour was deplorable. He was doing a great job of putting out whatever flame I had burning for him. And then I couldn't believe it when he turned his back to me and started talking to another girl like I wasn't even there.

I was like, this guy is straight tripping. Who did he think

MASTER OF SINGLE

he was? Better yet, who did he think I was? Did he fall and hit his head on the way over? Because, hello, knock, knock, I'm Nicole Jones, you better ask somebody; nobody treats me like this and gets away with it.

To disrespect me not once but twice in the same breath, boy please.

He was displaying some wack-ass borderline psychotic behaviour.

By now, I had stepped away from the situation to collect myself because I was literally going to kill him, I was that irate. Once calm enough, I was ready to confront him, but before I could, I noticed he was walking towards the exit, so of course my ego said, go follow him. Dumb move.

I stopped him outside, thinking he owed me an explanation. I asked him, "What the hell is your problem?" I couldn't have been less prepared for his reaction. I should have been, but I wasn't ready for how scary and volatile he became.

He literally flew off the handle and snapped like a little bitchy twig, yelling the most erratic bunch of noise, none of which made any sense to me and clearly had nothing to do with me or us. He was talking along the lines of, "Nobody treats me like that! I'm not your fucking bitch (but he was sure acting like one). What do you think I am? I'll show you. Fuck you!"

I started to nervous laugh because I couldn't believe what was happening. You know when something is so not funny but you laugh to not cry? This was that moment. It was scary, and I wasn't sure how far he was going to take his outrage. I was sitting on cautious, ready to run. It was like something evil had taken over his body, or maybe it was him showing his true colours. My guess was that it was the former.

I acquiesced by once again removing myself from the situation and leaving him to yell and scream in the comfort of his own demons. This wasn't my battle or worth the fight, swords and shields down.

Be free—you're a crazy idiot, and if this were a film noir movie, I left before the tragic ending.

He had some serious toxic energy coursing through his veins, which was a shame because he had been so good in bed. Such a pity.

I don't know if I can even call it a break-up, because it was far from being an established relationship. Everything that transpired made it easier to let go of him physically, but I had unresolved emotional trauma. I didn't want him back, but I did want to understand what happened, so against my better judgement I reached out a couple of days after.

Remember in the chapter Lover's Lane, I mentioned if your instincts are leaning fifty-one percent and that one percent tips the scale? Well, I should have listened to that one percent that was telling me to just let him go.

Unless you're a sucker for punishment or like to learn lessons the hard way, never, ever, go against your instincts; they're always right.

In my text, I wrote, "Hi. Can you please explain to me what happened at the club and why you snapped like that? I'm very confused and didn't deserve the way you treated me. I was nothing but good to you, and I think you owe me an apology." Send.

Much to my surprise, his reply was swift and telling.

It said everything I needed to close the chapter once and for all. He said, "You push my buttons and bring out a side of me I don't like. You remind me of my ex, and our relationship ended in violence and trauma."

MASTER OF SINGLE

Whaaaaat? Was my internal reaction. He didn't take any accountability for his vicious, violent, and threatening behaviour. No sir, I am not your deflection.

This is a great example of why I don't let people into my home until I'm sure about them. I had to sage my house a few times to make sure it was clean and clear of anything toxic he might have left behind. Just to be safe.

In conclusion, pursuing toxic men on the rebound is like mixing tequila and red wine. You'll regret ever doing it. Oh, and age and maturity don't necessarily go hand in hand.

Living is learning, and being single is learning through living. May nothing be lost on you.

CHAPTER Thirteen

ONLINE DATING: YEA OR NAY?

BEFORE GETTING INTO this chapter, it's important to preface that since being in this pandemic, the subject of online dating has surely evolved in its value and acceptance. Hence, this chapter has been edited accordingly, but my opinion remains the same.

It's a delicate subject, which I will tread lightly to not offend anyone, because if online dating is your thing, then more power to you. I'm happy to encourage people and offer advice to help navigate through the process of finding love online, but as a personal choice, this is a hard no for me. I'm just not that online girl, and here's why…

It goes without saying that I value love and seek it in truthful and visceral ways that don't necessarily include communicating or making emotional connections through apps on my smartphone. Call me old-fashioned, I don't mind, but I need to see, touch, smell, hear, and vibe with you before investing my time and especially my heart.

Online dating comes with too many variables and breeds the potential for people to falsify who they are. It's too easy to tell me what I want to hear from behind a computer screen while they're telling ten other people what they want to hear. That doesn't feel special to me. It's not to say meeting someone in person will prevent them from speaking with other people, but it's not likely to happen in the same way as it would online.

There's also a little bit of pride involved with my choice, in that being a public figure in my city, I feel more vulnerable on these apps and opening myself up to people I would never consider dating. And I don't fancy the idea of allowing access to personal information that under normal circumstances I wouldn't imagine sharing with strangers online.

However, I'm able to empathize and put myself in someone else's shoes who might be struggling and considering online dating. So, personal feelings aside, as your self-proclaimed master of single, here's my best advice, and I hope it helps you on your journey to love.

The first thing I'd suggest is to choose apps you're comfortable with and that mirror your expectations. Once you start making connections to further establish that emotional connection that everyone's looking for, start with four or five people of interest, and eventually narrow it down to one or two prospects to focus on and further develop a connection with.

This will help ground you, give you a sense of control, and help you build that emotional connection.

Second, go at your own pace. Don't compare your journey to anyone else. Particularly during this unprecedented time, it's important to trust your process more than ever, which can sometimes mean removing yourself from an unhealthy situation. If someone or something doesn't feel right, swipe left, delete, block, and keep it moving.

Having a dating plan will help to empower you in terms of establishing your boundaries and give you the sense of being in control, as opposed to getting overwhelmed with the whole process.

In terms of connecting, perhaps start chatting on the apps, then exchange numbers for text messaging. From there if things continue to evolve, you might consider a potential FaceTime or Zoom date, wine included. It's a different way of getting to know someone, but the face-to-face might make it easier to connect.

It's so important to be confident and honest about where we're at and what we're looking for. This unusual time we're in has forced us to have uncomfortable conversation, but those conversations are a sign of the times, and it's our job to meet the times where they are.

Speaking to the idea of a person-to-person meeting, I believe even given the circumstances, it's still possible with the right preparation.

Perhaps you prefer both parties wear a mask if that makes you more comfortable, or what does social-distance dating look like to you? These are the questions you must ask yourself.

If you feel you want to take a relationship to a more physical level, perhaps there's an agreement between both parties to get tested and exchange results so that taking that next step feels comfortable and safe.

Although online dating may not be for me, the advice I offer comes from my research and a lot of common sense, and I hope these quick tips help bring a little levity to your process.

Good luck! I'm rooting for you.

So my position, feelings, and conclusions about online dating also come from a personal experience. I have tried it, which is why I feel confident in my convictions.

This next story I'm going to share is so crazy to me I still can't believe my dumb unluck, so grab your popcorn, again, get comfortable, and promise me one thing. If you laugh, laugh with me and not at me.

One eventful evening at my bestie's, we were hanging out, catching up, drinking wine, venting about men, and laughing about everything—a typical girls night in. At some point she started talking about some guy she'd met online. She was also single and fabulous, and at the time, she was a casual to frequent user of online dating, resulting in several face-to-face dates.

As a best friend, I have so much respect for her and the way she moves through the world as a fierce, successful, and busy businesswoman. So I'm able to empathize with the challenges that come with meeting people.

Many career-oriented women who are climbing the ladder to their success don't have time to go out and socialize. And the few opportunities they do have to meet persons of interest in public settings are few and far between, so I totally understand the value of online dating from that perspective.

It would also be irresponsible and inappropriate to ever judge or hold any opinions other than loving and supportive ones.

On this night, however, she was the one person I trusted enough to talk me into creating my first and only online dating profile. It was like pulling teeth to get there,

MASTER
OF SINGLE

but I eventually bit the bullet and said I would do it. Knowing the entire time that I wasn't feeling it but to shut down the conversation and appease my curiosity, why not, coconut?

The next day in the privacy of my home, I created my first profile and posted it to a free dating website. The idea of paying to be on an app just didn't compute in my mind; in fact, it felt like adding salt to the wound. Paying for a service for someone to meet me was laughable and where I drew the line. Yes, I said "to meet me" because I'm a prize and there's nothing wrong with being that confident about knowing who you are.

Call me vain, but that's my truth.

Queendom for life.

With my profile up and feeling very exposed, I closed my computer and started getting ready for work, not thinking twice about it. It's fair to say there are parts of me that I won't compromise just to adapt to society or any person, for that matter.

I love who I am, and any adjustments to my character or personality should be on my own accord as someone who is open to growing and learning.

I don't do well with pressure or people pushing their ideas or agenda onto me.

I proudly hold many of the old-school values I grew up with close to my chest, despite society evolving past them. I still believe in handwritten letters in place of a text message. I like phone calls, but people don't pick up anymore. I prefer standing in line at the bank to talk to and deal with a real person when it comes to my money, and I'd rather go into a brick-and-mortar store than shop online.

I've tried the online shopping thing and always felt cheated except if I was buying high-end.

Otherwise, when the clothes arrived, they were never as good as they appeared on the site, which is a great comparison to online dating in a nutshell.

A bunch of well-polished images, but when you get it in front of you, it doesn't fit, and there's no way you'd be caught dead wearing it. Okay, maybe the last one was extreme. On second thought, no, it isn't. You feel me? Online and me is like, meh? Can I get a refund for my time and troubles, and I'd like to unsubscribe please?

That's why personally I prefer the full-bodied, tactile experience, I like to get up close, feel the material, and look at the detailing, just like with men.

Before leaving for work, I took a quick glance at my profile out of curiosity, and I was surprised to see so much activity so soon. I mean, the picture I posted was nice, but it wasn't wow, and the information I gave was very basic to protect my privacy as much as possible. So yes, I was surprised by the traction it had gained.

In particular, I noticed one guy who was showing a lot of interest, and when I clicked on his profile to see who the creeper was, I was gobsmacked when I recognized him from the around the club scene. This reinforces my point that online dating is too close to home. My reaction to his interest was an instant hell to the no, no, thanks. I closed my computer and headed to work.

Once I arrived, I put "profile gate" out of my mind and went into instant autopilot mode, making my way through the crowd, smiling, entertaining, and playing the part of social butterfly, which is something I do very well. Just as I was starting to find my groove and get my stride, I hit a road bump that sent me flying around the corner and right out the back door.

You know the feeling that someone's watching you and

it makes you uncomfortable? Well, that's what was happening. From across the room as dark as it was, I could sense this guy trying to get a better look at me through the crowd. He kept moving into the empty spaces to get a clear line of vision—extra creepy. It reminded me of the *Mona Lisa*; his eyes felt like they were following me everywhere.

I kept doing my thing and keeping him in my peripheral vision. One of the things that makes me great at my job is that I notice details and pay attention to things most people wouldn't even notice, like a creepy client acting shady AF.

At some point, the moving lights hit him in such a way that I was able to get a clear view of him, and that's when I freaked out.

I connected the dots and realized it was the same guy from the dating app. Gurrrrl, you've never seen anyone in heels move as fast as I did, bopping and weaving my way through the crowd before he could recognize me or worse, try to talk to me.

I couldn't believe my dumb unluck. My first time using an app and the first guy to creep on it is the same guy creeping on me in the safe space of my workplace. What are the odds? I get that we live in a small city, but come on... this was crazy. And in case you're wondering, no, I didn't put my place of work on my profile.

Talk about solidifying what I already knew, the whole time I was creating that profile, I knew I was going against my grain. But I will say this—I'm happy that I saw the process through because now nobody can ever convince me to try online dating again. Case closed.

Once safely outside, I took a breath and a minute to compose myself and figure out the best way to handle the situation. Eventually I'd have to go back in, but I had no interest in saying anything to him or having him try to talk to me. I can't stress enough how much he wasn't my type and how exposed I felt. For the remainder of the evening, I'd have to be very strategic as I moved through the space, at least until he left… Fortunately, that was soon after I went back in.

The moral is, stick to what you know. Just because society says it's the thing to do, it doesn't mean you have to do it. And if online is not your thing, then it's not your thing.

Own your choice, and don't let anyone shape your decisions.

I know that I'm fine with continuing to kiss many frogs and take my chances of finding my king, my unicorn, and person in the real world.

Good luck, good talk, and happy dating.

Chapter Fourteen

But He's so into Me

IN THIS CHAPTER, we're going to deep dive a little further into my single-girl, New York student-life adventure that I've touched on a few times already. But before taking the plunge, allow me to preface with this little nugget of context.

Although my taste in men has evolved over time, for a long while I was all about Italian men. There was just something about their charm and that accent when they said "Ciao, Bella" or my favourite term of endearment, "*Amore*." Of course, their sense of style and innate passion for everything, even the way the wind blows, was all consuming, and I couldn't get enough. But more than that, I was drawn in and seduced by the country and the culture, from the food to the people and the immaculate attention to architectural detail. The cathedrals were always my favourite places to visit in every city.

I've been fortunate to spend a lot of time in Italy over the years, from Rome to Milan, Florence, Pisa, Sicily, Ghiffa, and Novi Ligure, two charming destinations in the north, also where I've spent wonderful times with Betta and her family at their gorgeous homes. I love them, a noble family who welcomed me into their home with open arms and treated me like a daughter, which I consider to be an honour.

But besides the men, overall beauty, and love I have for the country, there's an even deeper and more special connection to Italy that transcends everything. My Ibiza family, except for Papa Ray, who is proudly Irish, are Italian, and my beautiful godsons are a product of both.

This direct connection to Italy gave me roots and only made my alliance to the culture deeply family-based and part of my truest heart.

I love Italy so much that at my peak, when I was borderline obsessed, I wanted to get a T-shirt made that read ITALIAN: I EAT IT, I WEAR IT, I FUCK IT. Yup, I was that girl. I would still love to get that T-shirt made to wear around the house; it was such a big part of who I was for a long time. I heart Italy.

The purpose of this preface is twofold: my love of Italian men as well as for my beautiful Ibiza family... not necessarily in that order, but both are the cornerstone of this next story with a few unexpected twists that even I didn't see coming...

Which brings me back to NYC.

One much-needed and rare night out with a friend, we ended up going to a posh lounge in the Upper East Side where I was introduced through a friend to a guy who happened to be Italian—so he had that going for him. Unfortunately, that was about the only thing he had going for him in terms of my taste.

MASTER OF SINGLE

Let me be clear. Being Italian was an advantage and likely to get you my name if you asked nicely with your charming accent, but it wasn't the be-all and end-all. There were other factors I needed to be attracted to, which this guy simply didn't have. It sounds vain, and that's okay, I can be vain sometimes. He just wasn't the good-looking kind of Italian swag, hot, and virile type of man I was used to—but then again, those men have kept me single for this long, so yeah, there was that. Just saying, note to self.

He might not have been my type, but he seemed full of joie de vivre, a businessman who travelled between Italy and NY for work and pleasure and clearly liked to have a good time. From what I could tell when he looked at me, I fit into the pleasure category of his wandering eye, feeling like he was undressing me with his eyes, so I was careful to keep my distance.

That should have been the end of it, right? But nope, it was just the beginning.

Have you ever had someone pursue you so hard that even though you weren't attracted to them physically, their persistence and insistence became weirdly flattering and attractive? It's a mouthful, I know, but each word describes the next series of events.

This guy was not your average player. He appeared to be of a certain age, well-to-do, and I could tell he knew that he wasn't the best-looking guy in the room, so he overcompensated with his money. But he had a confidence about him, whether it was real or not, and he wore it like a badge of honour and posted up to the hottest, youngest, most attractive women in the room, me included, like he was some sort of Don Juan.

I had to respect his ballsy ways. It wasn't my way, but he owned it, and that was respectable. Just leave me out of it, please and thank you.

He was buying a lot of that manufactured attention with all the expensive bottles he was purchasing. Everyone knows big spenders have the advantage, making them more attractive with the ladies, especially the thirsty ones on the scene dressed to be seen and looking to catch a big fish. There's a whole breed of women out there who are happy to sacrifice looks and their own integrity for money.

This wasn't my first rodeo. I could see right through the game, which was entertaining to watch because I had no stake in it… or at least I thought I didn't, but he had me in his sights and was becoming increasingly persistent with his approach, asking me what champagne I liked and ordering it accordingly. Then he started insisting he take me out for dinner, which I must admit was tempting. I was starving for an outlet of lux in my hard-knock student life, but I just wasn't interested, so I repeatedly but kindly turned down his invitation.

Keep in mind that some men love a good chase, and I was beginning to think he was one of them.

Fast forward days later, I receive a phone call from him. He'd somehow finagled my number from our mutual friend who later told me he thought he was doing me a favour by giving him my number. Never cool to do that. If someone asks me for a friend's number, I'm going to ask them first if it's okay. That's respectful. I mean, what if the guy was crazy?

But he knew this guy and vouched for him as a stand-up guy with a big heart who loved to have fun and seemed really interested in me.

Again, the last thing on my mind while in NY was dating anyone. School was all consuming and about as much as I could handle, and even that was a struggle to stay on top of.

MASTER
OF SINGLE

I answered the phone a little annoyed, feeling like he'd invaded my privacy, but I listened to what he had to say, which was more of the same—pleading for me to accompany him to dinner. "Please come to dinner. I wish to see you again. Please, Bella, it would make me so happy if you come to meet me." Insert charming Italian accent.

Yet again, I said no, thank you, and please don't call me again, I'm not interested. And I hung up. But the fucking guy, he wouldn't take no for an answer. The next time he reached out was via text message. He was smart about it; he didn't call like I had asked him not to but found an alternative way to still reach out. He pleaded again desperately trying to convince me and each time to no avail. After the fourth or fifth text, I finally said, "Fine. I'll go to dinner, just please stop texting and calling me." *Basta!* (Meaning "enough" in Italian).

There came a point where I just said why not? He'd put in the work, and I could appreciate that. I also needed so badly to not eat my next meal from a deli or donut shop, which was about all my student budget could afford. I was dying to sit in good lighting, be served, and eat a meal using real utensils and a cloth napkin—anything that didn't come wrapped in plastic or in a paper bag, which had become my NY norm.

To say I was going through a lot of lifestyle changes at the time would be an understatement.

Despite living in Manhattan where over a million and a half people reside and having roommates, it's crazy to think that I was experiencing bouts of loneliness, which was tough to deal with. The grind and the struggle were a real thing, and I often missed my lifestyle and the support of having my friends close.

The feeling of loneliness is a tricky thing and can sneak up on you when you're least expecting it and have you doing and thinking crazy things, like accepting a dinner invitation from a man whom I wasn't interested in.

But everything about my life was my choice, and I accepted what came with my choices. I rarely take the easy road in life. I live a life by design on my terms, free-spirited and true to me, finding that balance between my dreams and self-care.

But it's not always easy being a constant goal digger. I guess that's how I got to be so tough; I'm always challenging myself and seeking to deepen my spiritual connection in pursuit of my purpose and highest self.

As hard as it is sometimes, it's rewarding to know that I'm genuinely satisfied and content in my life. If not for my single status, I wouldn't have been able to pick up my life and move it across the border in pursuit of my dream.

To me, that's an incredible freedom and power to possess and simply can't be denied as a viable and respectable status and position to live from.

This is why I call it our single superpower, and I strongly encourage all singles to use their time to take chances while their decisions don't affect anyone else.

That said, my temporary bout of aloneness in this season of my life was a real thing, which explains the crack in the window that allowed this man access to make his way in. We went to a chic restaurant and enjoyed a wonderful meal, which made me the happiest girl in Manhattan that night.

In my head, it was just a dinner, but I could tell by the wining and dining that he was in it to win me. Not wanting to burst his bubble or ruin our dinner, I didn't stop him from ordering the best champagne and wines and letting him fawn over me. It was nice and refreshing.

From our conversation, I learnt that he was a successful

MASTER
OF SINGLE

international tax lawyer who appeared to be very smart with a good sense of humour (important). He was single with no kids, which sounded all too familiar, but I was just listening and taking it with a grain of salt.

No matter what he said, in the back of my mind I wasn't planning on seeing him again. He was nice, but there was just no chemistry.

That night would be a one-off that came at the right time to fill a much-needed void and give me a little boost to keep me going, but I certainly wasn't looking to get distracted from school by a man I wasn't into.

After a great dinner and evening, I was ready to hail a cab and head home to curl up in my subpar bed and call it a night. But of course he had a different idea in mind, wanting to extend things with a nightcap. Throwing caution to the wind, I went with my instincts based on how well the night had unfolded and decided it would be okay to continue the evening, justifying it with my favourite rational: "I've come this far… what's one more drink?"

We hopped into a cab that took us to the Upper East Side, the "fancy" side of town. The cab stopped in front of a luxury apartment building, and I immediately questioned where we were. I was expecting to hit a lounge or bar, but he really did have another plan in mind that had nothing to do with what I was thinking.

Before I could say anything, he counteracted my reaction with a smile, paired with puppy dog eyes and a plea to join him in his penthouse apartment. He boasted having the best views of Manhattan and a special bottle of champagne he'd been waiting for the right time to open.

Normally it would have been a hard no. First, you don't trick me with misleading intentions and bring me back to your place. Not cool, and I did let him know that. But lucky for him, I was in a good mood and curious about this view and champagne, so I obliged. "Fine, one glass and I leave."

Once upstairs, I was happy to see that he wasn't lying; in fact, he was humble with his description, the 180-degree panoramic view from his corner penthouse was stunning for as far as the eye could see. The city that had been so hard on me suddenly looked calm and peaceful, which was a welcome change from how I'd been looking at it.

As I took in the view, he opened a bottle of vintage Dom Pérignon—a man of his word and I wasn't mad at my decision to accompany him upstairs.

But I must acknowledge the risk that I was taking by going up to a man's apartment in Manhattan whom I hardly knew. I don't suggest anyone do the same thing carelessly. In this instance, I trusted my instincts as well as the feedback from our mutual friend who vouched for him. But under no circumstances should you proceed if there's even a hint of danger or uncomfortable vibes, which in this case there wasn't.

It's also worth mentioning I'm confident in that if I ever had to defend myself physically, I could. I've always been a fighter, especially while growing up. I've been known to knock out a boy or two who were bullying my little sister. I have a mean right hook. Fact.

Furthermore, I gained a lot of confidence when I took a self-defence course (twice) for women. The specific techniques and tools I learned instantly became part of my muscle memory. I might look small, but much like my mom, I'm quite strong. God forbid I need them, but if I do, I know I have it in me to fight and protect myself.

Ladies, I highly suggest taking a self-defence course designed specifically for women. It's incredible what you learn and the confidence you gain.

MASTER OF SINGLE

The course I took was called "Pleins Pouvoirs," or "Full Power." Knowing how to defend yourself is something every woman, especially single ones, should feel confident in.

But this guy didn't appear to be threatening in the least—he was too busy trying to impress me to be dangerous. As I stood watching the city lights and taking in his gorgeous home, it was clear to see that this baller was balling next level, and it was slightly impressive.

We made our way to the sitting area, which was ten times bigger than the room I was renting—but who's counting square footage, right? He poured the champs and handed me a glass. I was aware that I was already tipsy from our drinks at dinner, so I made it a point to sit opposite him, not to send any mixed singles. I wanted it to be clear that this was merely a nightcap, not a feather in his cap. Touché.

We talked some more, and he was saying all the right things. On paper any single girl would be lining up to date this guy. I knew I wasn't interested, but I couldn't ignore the opportunity that was sitting in front of me (blame it on the champagne). The more he talked, the more weirdly interested I became, but let's not get ahead of ourselves. Physically he still wasn't my type, and nothing he could say would change that. When it comes to a connection, I look for the signs, and there were no signs, tingles, or sensations happening down there to promote any sexual curiosity, and I didn't try to force it.

I did, however, for a fleeting moment ask myself if I could maybe be with him for the lifestyle, but that inner dialogue was short-lived. The answer was no, I didn't have it in me to be that girl. Damn, if only I was a little shallower with a tad less morals, I'd be living in the lap of luxury, but I probably wouldn't like myself very much, so yeah.

We finished the champagne, and I could sense he wanted to make a move. That was my cue to call it night... this time for real. He sulked a little when I said I was ready to go, but he was mostly a gentleman about it, walking me down, hailing my cab, and then paying for the cab to take me home. Very gallant. Those types of acts are never lost on me. He sent me off with some final words that he hoped we could do this again. I just smiled politely, thanked him for the lovely evening, got in the cab, and headed home.

I had hoped he got the message that I wasn't into a second date, but I should have known from his track record that he wasn't going to give up that easily.

True to form, it was only a matter of days before I received a phone call from him asking me out again, but this time I wasn't swayed by the temptation of fine dining and vintage champagne. Not wanting to lead him on, I couldn't justify accepting his invitation a second time. One date? Okay. But two? Now I'm not being honest with him or myself, and that wasn't cool. I told him straight, "I'm not interested, but thank you. It was nice to meet you and good luck with everything." He seemed to get the point that time, thank goodness, and I went back to focusing on school and my new normal NY grind.

Fast forward months later to the end of my first semester, now heading into our summer vacay, and guess who pops up! Yup, Mr. Won't Give Up, but this time he'd upped his game and was on a mission. I was curious about what he wanted after all that time, so I answered.

After exchanging quick pleasantries, he proposed that I join him in Miami for one week, all expenses paid.

He begged me like I used to beg my mom to buy me the expensive running shoes that we couldn't afford. It was kind of sad to hear him beg, but in comparison, I always ended up getting the shoes, so maybe he was onto something.

MASTER
OF SINGLE

It was the end of a tough year, and I was exhausted to the bone and needed a vacation badly, so his invite was once again tempting, but the facts remained the facts. I wasn't into this guy, and I knew it. I hadn't even thought about him once since we last said goodbye. That's very telling, so as tempting as it was, I turned it down.

But he was like the little train that could. "I think I can, I think I can..." Despite his persistence, I continued to push back harder. Eventually he conceded and reluctantly accepted my answer. Once again, I thought that was the end of it, but clearly, he was so into me, which weirdly and secretly I was a little flattered by the attention.

After all that, still he had the balls to reach out a couple of days later but again to no avail. Nothing seemed to stop him. Then a fourth and fifth attempt... you see where I'm going with this? His persistence was his secret weapon. He was calling so much, I was sure my number must have been on his speed dial. Each time I declined or ignored him, but the last time he asked, something was different. I don't know what it was, maybe he just broke me down which he seemed to have a way of doing.

Or maybe I was just so delirious with fatigue from my gruelling school year, but whatever it was, eventually I caved and agreed to go to Miami. Boohoo, poor me.

Not many men will put that much effort into courting you, so why not enjoy a week in the sun? Lord knows I needed it, and who was I to deny him showing me a great time? I negotiated the sleeping arrangements and any other details I needed to feel comfortable, and of course he agreed to all my terms, happily. How did I know it would be a great time? Based on what I'd observed so far from our dinner date to his baller lifestyle, all signs pointed to him treating me like the queen he knew I was—for a week anyway.

The next thing I knew, I was off, ready to let him do all the heavy thinking while I kicked back and soaked it all up. I arrived in Miami to him waiting for me in a black Mustang convertible. It was a nice touch and a warm welcome. Driving with the top down and the sun up, I could feel all the stress of school melting away in the warm Miami air.

We drove to one of his two condos on a golf course where he had champagne chilling and a surprise gift waiting for me. *Off to a good start*, I thought, but I wasn't surprised. I had a feeling he was going to pull out all the stops and then some to impress me, much like he'd been doing this whole time.

We drank a bottle or two of champagne, and it wasn't long before I was feeling good in Miami. Nothing like drinking some champs in the sun to take the edge off.

He handed me my gift in a pretty Victoria's Secret bag. I looked at him like *Really? Victoria's Secret? Not even La Perla? Underwhelming and not very subtle at all, might I add.*

I reached inside and pulled out the cutest baby doll and matching panties set, and I know what you're thinking because I was thinking the same thing—this guy wants to get laid in Miami.

It took a lot of nerve to gift me lingerie on the first day. Normally I would tell him how inappropriate that was, but I was buzzed on champagne and didn't have the brainpower to get into it, so I accepted it.

There's also the caveat that I hadn't gotten laid in a while, so even the hint of sex knocking on the door of my libido worked to his advantage.

Just like that, this man who once wasn't even on my radar was suddenly looking much better than I remembered. His hard work and little-train-that-could persistence combined with feeling free in Miami had the tides turning, fast.

But the closer was when he got changed from his dress clothes to more Miami-appropriate wear, which revealed a body I had no idea was under there. He'd mentioned he ran every day and played golf religiously, but damn son, the moment had me feeling a certain kind of way.

And then a heat wave came over me, and before I knew it, we were locked in a passionate kiss, tongue and all. It was steamy and alive; my lady juices were flowing, and my panties were soaking wet. It wasn't necessarily that I wanted him as much as I wanted his piece, so I leaned into every inch of what he had to offer.

Have you ever slept with someone who you weren't into but was into you? This was a first for me, and let me tell you, it didn't matter who was attached to the dick. I just needed sex like Miami needs the sun.

Fast forward twenty minutes and we're in full sex mode, ravishing each other from head to toe. And excuse him, Mr. Freak between the sheets, doing everything and I mean everything to please me. Over compensate much?

At first I wasn't sure if I liked his style in bed; he was generous, but he was also a little too needy and a bit whiney. He made this weird high-pitched sound when he got excited, and that threw me off a little but not enough to stop my orgasm. That's when I took the lead and led us to the promised land.

By the time we were done, I had determined that he was a good lover who just needed some guidance, and lucky for him, I was a great teacher.

I don't know about anyone else, but I pride myself on being a great lover. I know I'm great because they tell me so, and even if they didn't, I know what I know.

Have you ever rated yourself as a lover? What would it be on a scale of one to ten, ten being the best? Think about it... I rate myself high on the scale, and I like my sex like I like my martinis—dirty to the point of almost insulting. It's so important to have confidence in bed and be comfortable in your body. Don't be too shy to direct the person you're with by showing them how to please you. It's all part of building that comfort and confidence with your body and yourself. Once you get there and experience total surrender, it's another level of pleasure. Can I get an amen?

After that first session, every time he looked at me he got a hard-on and was ready to bang it out at a moment's notice, and my sexual appetite was insatiable, which made for great sex the rest of the week. We did eventually make it out of the apartment, once having sex in the back of the car before heading to dinner, but we eventually got there... to the restaurant, I mean.

The rest of the trip was textbook lux/good times. We dined at the best restaurants, enjoyed cabanas at the beach, hotels for the day with spas treatments, clubbing at night, and of course shopping in Miami was the pièce de résistance. He treated me like I presumed he would—a queen.

All points for him.

By now, everything I'd thought about him, or us, was being tested. Every fibre of my being was engulfed in the question, "Had I counted him out too soon?"

Was there really something, or was it just because we were in our Miami bubble?

I was dazed and confused.

It was a weird place to be, like being caught between here and nowhere. I knew something was missing, I just wasn't sure what. With more questions than answers swirling through my head, it was killing me, so I decided for the time being to let it go.

The answers would come in their own time, and until they did, I'd nothing.

And with that, I put my woes behind me, stayed calm, and carried on in true Miami style.

Then one regular afternoon while chilling on the balcony overlooking the golf course, enjoying a nice glass of wine, he sprung the subject of kids and our future on me. I almost pivoted off my lounge chair. What? Excuse me? Where was this coming from? We were just watching golfers play. How did we get here?

Then he upped the ante asking me what I thought I'd like to do as work if I moved to Italy.

Wait, *scusi*? I must have blacked out for a minute. What did he just say? I was in a state of stunned without words or reaction, but the expression on my face must have been priceless.

My mind was struggling to formulate a sentence without laughing in his face because it sounded like a joke.

Should I be entertaining this? Part of my brain was telling me to consider him while the other part was like, hell no, he's lost his damn mind.

All I could think was that the universe works in strange ways.

I started to break it down. By all accounts he was a good man and a hard worker, he would be a great provider, and he clearly wanted to commit. But the idea of moving to Italy and having kids was the furthest thing from my mind. I was still in the gray zone about how I even felt about him.

What's a girl to do? I was feeling that Miami heat breathing down my neck.

He gave me a lot to think about. As wild as it was, it isn't every day one's presented with such an offer, and being single, almost forty, and open to love, he presented a good argument.

It was a lot to process in a short period. I'd need time and help to determine if this was just a fauxmance or could possibly be the real thing. I needed to know. And then it hit me!

Prior to Miami, true to form I had already booked my annual trip to Ibiza and was set to be there in a month. I decided my Ibiza family would be the perfect panel to help me through my heart's conundrum. Not only do they know me so well, they know my type and of course only want the best for me. They're also very specific about the men I date, especially my godsons, who have strong opinions about the men in my life. I love them for that.

The idea went from a thought in my head to the words flying out of my mouth, and before I knew it, I'd invited him to Ibiza. I know… What the hell was I thinking? But trust me, I was thinking clearer than I had been all week. Was I blinded by the lifestyle he could provide, swayed by his charm and potentially missing out on something I wasn't seeing? Also, the multiple orgasms were a big distraction.

I needed an impartial opinion, and there was nobody I trusted more than my family, plus I knew he was going to be in Italy, which was a manageable flight to Ibiza.

It seemed the perfect plan, emphasis on seemed.

My spontaneous Ibiza verbal diarrhea of the mouth shocked the moment into an awkward silence, which lasted for the time it took for him to say yes. That was it—no looking back now.

He seemed pleasantly surprised by the invite and right away started thinking it through, telling me about his hectic work schedule but that he would carve out some time to join me for a weekend visit. I was impressed he was willing to juggle his busy work and travel schedule to accommodate my request.

Fast forward to me arriving in Ibiza. I had already briefed my family, and they were curious, excited, and totally on board to help me figure this out. The timing of his and my arrival was uncanny; the only time he could come was on the same day I was arriving. I barely had time to put my bags down and give hugs and kisses before I was heading back to the airport to pick him up.

We'd stayed in touch via WhatsApp and FaceTime, but a month had lapsed since our last physical meeting, and a lot can change in a month. My biggest concern was that I didn't miss him like I would someone I really liked, so I felt a little nervous about that.

During the ride to the airport, I couldn't stop the questions running through my head. Would my family like him? Would I like him? Was he the one, or was this a huge mistake? My mind was freaking out and winning. I hoped for the best but was prepared for anything.

As I stood at the arrival gate, waiting for him, I had two thoughts: run and never answer his calls again or lock my knees so they wouldn't buckle under me. I chose the latter and braced myself for his landing. I couldn't believe this was really happening. Oh my God, what was I thinking?

And then the gates opened.

One, two, three… eight, nine people came through. Each one represented a skip in my heartbeat, and then there he was, wearing a gray suit with the jacket draped over his arm, sweaty and looking anxious himself. I can pinpoint the exact moment I saw him and felt my heart fall to the floor.

All those suppressed NY feelings and initial instincts I had about him came rushing back to remind me that he wasn't my man. The pit in my stomach was the size of a grapefruit. Seeing him, it was plain to see, no filter and confirming my worst fear, our Miami heat had fizzled.

There I was, nowhere to run and no plan B, so I slapped a smile on my face, threw my arms wide open, and welcomed him as gracefully as I could. After all, he had literally left a meeting, hopped on a plane from Italy, and flew to Ibiza just to see me and meet with my family as per my request. I felt terrible inside, like a bad person. What else could I do but fake it until I made it?

My options were few and my heart was heavy.

Meanwhile, he was so happy to see me. He grabbed me in his arms and came in for a kiss.

It took everything to kiss him back and pretend I meant it. So awkward, but I'd have to pull my girl pants all the way up and figure this out. My internal dialogue was, just be cool, go with the flow, and let's see how this all plays out.

Oh Lord!

On the car ride back to the house, I let him do most of the talking as I collected my thoughts and prepared for him to meet the family. We walked through the gate at the house, and my heart was racing. As soon as we entered, I could see the look of disenchantment on their faces. Of course, they greeted him into their home with a warm welcome, but it was clear to me, they weren't feeling him for me.

As per usual, he was charming and kind with the kids and fit into the Italian component of the family, so we had that going for us at least, and I was taking whatever I could at that point.

He noticed the distance between us, sensing something

was off for sure. I mean, how could he not? I was acting so weird. Of course he felt it.

I kept myself busy: helping in the kitchen, playing with the kids, anything to avoid more awkward kisses or interaction, still not sure how to handle the situation.

Thank goodness for Ray, who kept him company while I got some much-needed sister-to-sister chat time.

We met in the kitchen, and the look in her eyes was all too telling. I could see she was trying to be mindful to not hurt my feelings, but she didn't know I'd already come to the same conclusion as she had, that he wasn't the one.

In her ever-calming voice, she said with her beautiful Italian accent, "Yes, Nicole, he is nice, bah (accompanied by one of her signature hand gestures), but I don't think he is the guy for you."

I just remember closing my eyes and thinking, *She's right.*

What was I going to do for the entire weekend? He'd come with the best intentions and unwittingly got caught in my Ibizan maze.

Case and point why I'm careful who I bring to the island. This was killing everyone's vibe. At some point, I had to show him where he'd be staying, which was with me of course. It was so uncomfortable being alone with him; for all I knew he was just waiting to pick up where we'd left off in Miami. Once alone, it only took minutes before he pulled me close, but my body automatically resisted. So awkward.

I played it off with the old "I had a headache" excuse, which bought me some time, but it wasn't fair and I got no pleasure from treating him that way. That's not who I am.

I wanted to be nice, but I was scared he'd misinterpret my kindness for feelings for him; it was a delicate line to dance.

We all sat down for dinner, and I knew I'd have to set the tone so everyone could relax and enjoy the evening. So putting my feelings to the side, I was just kind to him, and thankfully we got through it without it being too uncomfortable. After all, he was a nice guy; he just wasn't the guy for me.

After dinner, unarmed and without a master plan but a glass of wine in hand, I was ready to talk. I pulled him to the side. "First I want to apologize. I'm sure you've noticed that my energy is different from the last time we saw each other." He acknowledged that he had and asked if everything was okay. I took a deep breath, hoping the right words would spill out, but what came out was a bunch of nervous jumbled thoughts, and he looked at me more confused than ever.

"What exactly are you trying to say?" he asked.

This was it. I placed my hand on his knee and looked at him, and as gently as I possibly could, I said, "I don't know what changed from Miami to now, but something's changed. I just don't feel a connection." I went on to express my regret for putting him in that situation, which was an ego bruiser for any man, but especially under those circumstances. He was so vulnerable.

He pulled his knee away, and I could sense his instant disappointment, then the anger came. He was livid, and I couldn't blame him. When he finally looked at me, he spoke with a tone of bitterness in his voice. "How could you do this to me? Why would you bring me here just to humiliate me in front of people I don't know? I feel like such a fool."

I couldn't do or say anything but sit there and take it. He deserved the right to vent and let out his frustrations, but he also deserved the truth. I just wished I'd arrived at my truth sooner.

MASTER OF SINGLE

In a final attempt to explain myself, I told him I thought he was a great guy and any woman would be lucky to have him, and that for a minute I thought maybe I could be that woman.

And unfortunately, it took me going through all that to realize that I'm not the right girl for him.

My secret hope was that he'd understand and we'd laugh about it as we watched the sunset, but that was only in my dreams. The reality was now we had to figure out what to do next.

He sat there, looking sad and defeated, and I felt horrible, so I did the only thing I could think of—I asked him if he'd join me downstairs. He begrudgingly agreed and followed me down to our room where I proceeded to strip down to my bare necessities and fuck him like a champion. I didn't leave him any option but to take it and love it.

I felt he deserved something for his frustration. After all, it was me who had gotten us into this mess. The sex wasn't romantic or intimate; it was rough and tough, like I hate to love you and love to hate you, but it was my way of saying, "I'm sorry; thanks for coming (no pun intended)." I just hoped, aside from his hard cock, that there would be no hard feelings.

When we were done, we both rolled over on our respective sides and passed out. There was nothing left to say.

The next morning, he woke up early, changed his travel plans, and left the island. Ray drove him to the airport, and I didn't get to say goodbye, which was probably for the best. With his leaving came a sigh of relief. I still felt badly, but happy that it was over and done. Being home with my family and everything back to normal, it didn't take long for my joy to find me again. I turned all my attention, love, and fun back onto my family and my happy place.

Singles, this was a huge reminder and a great lesson that the soul wants what the soul wants, and that can't be faked, forced, or bought. No money, fantasy, or illusion of smoke and mirrors can force your heart into submission.

CHAPTER Fifteen

THE THINGS I DO FOR THE D

FULL DISCLOSURE: THIS chapter was an unexpected addition that arose during the writing of this book. This story reminded me of the lengths we'll go to get that D.

My experience with this next hunk, our weekend fling, and his stellar performance, earned him a coveted position in these chapters of single adventures, lessons learned, and memorable men.

Blame it on the fresh spring air, but I was feeling myself like a budding flower needing to be pollinated. Or maybe it was simply meeting the right group of individuals at the right time under the most unsuspecting circumstances. Whatever it was, I was there for it.

It was a Thursday night at the supper club where I was working as the director of hospitality. Which meant that my job was to troubleshoot all the problems while hosting and keeping our guests happy and smiling through it. Good times. As we readied ourselves for the night, I noticed a group of bachelors from Los Angeles coming in to celebrate. Sound familiar? Oh Lord.

Montreal is a breeding ground for many things, two of them being bachelor parties and beautiful women. It's a blessing and a curse because we love the energy and money the boys bring, but the competition of the ratio of women to men is fierce, which is great for the guys, not so much for the women.

The reservation was running late, which for a supper club can be a disaster. Timing is everything because the restaurant turns into a club after dinner, so it's important to keep the pace as tight as possible. A late reservation can throw everything off in terms of resetting the room and preparing for the second wave of club guests. It can be a frustrating situation that just adds more stress and urgency to an already stressful situation. In their defence when they finally did arrive, they were very apologetic and sweet, which helped because most people don't care and can be real jerks about it. It also didn't hurt that at least two of them were hot. If you're going to be late, at least be hot.

However, their late arrival did cause some unforeseen issues with the kitchen. Most of the group unbeknownst to us were pescatarians. Given the options left on the menu besides a salad, they basically could only have the fish, excluding shellfish, but it was so late that most of the fish options were already sold out. With time not on our side and all the dietary restrictions, I had to think fast or those guys were going to be drinking on an empty stomach, and in my experience that never ends well—not for us or the guests. Nothing worse than a group of drunk, messy, starving men at a bachelor party. Okay, there are worse things, but still, this wasn't a good situation.

MASTER
OF SINGLE

As the server took their order, she realized the dishes they wanted weren't available. At that point we could have told them we weren't able to serve them, but because they were planning on staying all night and spending a lot of money, we pushed ourselves to figure it out.

They recognized and appreciated our efforts. That's when I went into troubleshooting mode. Thinking quickly on my feet, I arranged with the kitchen to make them a vegetarian pasta, which wasn't on the menu, but it pleased the clients and solved the problem.

After putting that fire out, I was asked if I could also pre-order before the kitchen closed for some girls who would be joining their table later and wanted to eat. Sure, no problem. I coordinated that with one of the guys who was taking care of the group and kept the food warm until the girls arrived. Again, problem solved. What else you got?

Despite a couple of hiccups, everything was still on track. The guests were happy, and the bachelor seemed to be having a great time. Finally the night was starting to settle and take shape. Just as we were finding our grove, the girls arrived, and among them was one with a rude and entitled attitude—a real problem child with her attitude written all over her face. There's a saying that goes, "People won't remember what you said, but they will remember how you made them feel." She had everyone feeling uncomfortable just by the energy she brought by walking in, acting arrogant with everyone who tried to serve her. I'm very protective of my staff, and I don't like when guests are rude to them, particularly when they're there to be of service. This guest was already tapping on my last nerve, and she wasn't even seated yet.

By now we were into the club part of the night, and to be serving food wasn't what we wanted to be doing, but in service to the bachelor party, who were very appreciative and constantly apologizing on behalf of this girl because clearly everyone picked up on her bad vibe, we kept rolling with it.

As a team, we maintained our composure and pushed through focusing on the positive, but when the food was brought out, nothing was good enough for this girl. She insisted on ordering off the menu. "Bitch, you know what time it is? The kitchen is closed," was what I wanted to say, but instead I forced a smile and said, "Unfortunately, the kitchen is closed, so this is what we have, and it was pre-ordered for you." She rudely dismissed the gesture with more attitude, like a spoiled kid throwing a tantrum.

Normally by that point I would have been on the verge of losing my shit. I do not wake up to deal with the likes of people like her. Who did she think she was to come and rain on everyone's parade with her piss-poor attitude? I liked this group of guys, and even the girls who joined were all supercool, except for her. The person taking care of the group could see that we were having difficulties, so he came over to help. That's when I found out that she was a friend of a friend of a friend, meaning she wasn't even really part of the group, which blew my mind even more that we had extended her so much grace. But a client is also a guest, and no matter how rude they are, we do our best to take the high road. That's what makes us so good at our jobs—being able to manage people like her.

In the interest of keeping the good vibes alive, I dug deep, giving her one more chance to fix her attitude. I also noticed that everyone was keeping their distance from her, like nobody was feeling this person who was sucking the energy out of the room.

I needed a pause from the madness, so I left everyone to eat while I went and took a breath. It's sad and telling to see someone act so miserably and disrespectful when they have every reason to be happy. In a case like that, the only person who can fix them, is them.

I eventually made my way back to the table. As I was walking around, I noticed a menu off to the side, so I picked it up to bring it back to the hostess stand and continued my rounds.

I went to check on the boys, still holding the menu in my hand, and then I asked the girls how everything was going.

Everyone was super happy except the one thorn in my side. She snarled and said, "I don't like anything. I want to order from the menu." Again—killing her with kindness—for the second time I told her that the kitchen was closed and what was on the table was all we had. It was like trying to reason with a rock.

And then the unthinkable happened. She must have lost her damn mind because that's when she legit grabbed my wrist and snatched the menu I was holding out of my hand. Now, I do not condone physical violence, particularly in a business where people will try to come for you just to get a reaction, and usually a good pivot will get me out of any situation, but putting your hands on me? That's where I draw the line, especially when it's not warranted in any way.

I was fuming, and the only thing that saved her was my being able to be the bigger person and set the example for my team. She was also lucky that I respect my fellow females, as well as myself, and never want to physically fight another woman. I'm better than that.

This, however, was beyond my ability to just let slide. Short of shoving my fist down her throat, namaste, I had to do something to make it clear to her that she had crossed the line and to let her know who she was dealing with.

After she yanked the menu from my kung fu grip, she leaned in and snarled at me. "Get me another server." Fuck the namaste, that's when I lost it. I'm not proud of it, but I did. I leaned in nose to nose, teeth and jaw clenched, looking right into her beady eyes, and said, "If you ever put your hands on me again, I'm going to put my fist through your fucking face. Do you understand me?" I left no room for her to question the validity of my promise. The look in my eyes was all telling, and the look in her eyes was pure fear.

Was it the right thing to do? No, but did she have it coming? Hell yes, and it felt good to check that bitch.

I didn't act on my intention, but I left it so that she wasn't sure if I would.

Checkmate. Her move.

Thank goodness the guy who was my point of contact for the group noticed what was happening and jumped over a table in a hurry to come and neutralize the situation before things popped off. That's also when my manager rushed over to pull me away from the situation to protect me and her.

By now I was in such a state. I was seeing red and mad at myself for letting her get to me, immediately regretting my actions because I knew better and she didn't deserve to take my power like that.

Yes, part of our job is to be immune to belligerent clients to a certain degree, but I'd rather quit my job or get fired than let some overprivileged spoiled brat put her hands on me and get away with it. After a good cry to let out my frustrations, I talked with my manager, which helped to calm me down. We agreed that I would go back to work and ignore said person, and that's exactly what I did. I wasn't going to let her ruin my night or the bachelor's party.

I chose to include this somewhat-out-of-left-field part of the story because I thought it was a good teachable moment to remind everyone that violence is never the answer, especially women being violent with each other. We're better than that.

All the decades of work and struggle that women before us went through to lay the foundation so that we would be respected and taken seriously in the world and in business, may that not be in vain. We must do better by each other and for each other as women united, not divided.

Even in the face of a lost soul as she was, it's incredibly important to have the skills that will enable you to walk away from any type of physical situation. As difficult as it may be, never let anyone take you down to their level. Be stronger than your circumstances and walk away. You don't have to like it, but you must do it. It will be the best decision you never regret.

Now that we got that teachable moment out of the way, let's move on to the better parts of the evening, including my beautiful... you got it... stranger!

When the whole debacle was over, I noticed one guy who hadn't said much since they'd arrived. He was also one of the hotties who caught my eye upon arrival and was the first to come up to me and ask if I was okay, commending me on how I handled the situation.

In my head I was thinking, was he my prize for walking away?

Still feeling a bit shaky from the ordeal and wanting to circumvent any further incident, I thought it best to avoid the table for a while. So I just hung out with him, and he was so sweet with his thick Middle Eastern accent. He offered me a drink at the bar, which I happily accepted. "Make it a double," I said jokingly.

To cheer me up, he told me that everyone liked me better than her, so not to worry. I was doing great and I believed him. I'd been nothing but cool, kind, and helpful and was invested in them having a great night. He also told me that the bachelor had been angry for the past hour because he was so mad at the chick for causing problems with me. It made me feel great that they acknowledged how wrong she was, as well as all the hard work we'd done.

With a little convincing, my beautiful stranger talked me into going back to the table, telling me everyone missed me. Being the bigger person, I put my bachelor client first and went back to the scene of the crime. The crime being her attitude.

Now in full club mode, the boys ordered their bottles, but despite all attempts to move forward, I could sense that the energy of the group had changed.

That's when one of them approached me and said they were thinking of leaving. This didn't surprise me, as it wasn't a very busy night and the vibe was kind of shit.

That's when I proposed that they change tables and get closer to the DJ, and because it was slow that night, we had some flexibility to play. I told them we'd take requests of their favourite songs and make the space theirs, creating a private and intimate party vibe.

I brought all the hot servers over to their table (when in doubt, distract them with beautiful women), and it worked. Before long, they were dancing, singing, drinking, and getting messy like bachelors should. Mission accomplished. God, I'm good. They don't call me "Queen of the Scene" for nothing. Okay, nobody really calls me that except for me, LOL, but I never wait for anyone to validate me. You should know that by now. I crown myself today, tomorrow, and every day.

Queen of this, master of that—it's just how I roll. You should try it; it's very empowering.

MASTER
OF SINGLE

Find your most skilled talent and crown yourself today.

With the tides turned, I was feeling much more relaxed, and the boys were off and running.

I spent the rest of the night hanging out with them and laughing as they made fools of themselves on the dance floor. And although we'd managed to turn the night around, I still didn't like the elephant energy in the room regarding that one misfit girl.

It was like a dark cloud over a rainbow; it just wasn't working, and I knew I had the power to change it.

As a final act of solidarity to the bachelor and his night, I went and found the chick who was—not surprisingly—sitting by herself and looking out of place.

I went up to her and said plainly, "Listen, we had a bad moment, you did some things and I said some things, but this isn't about you or me. It's about the bachelor. So with respect to his night, I'm willing to forgive and move on so that everyone can have a good time. What do you say?"

Moments like that remind me just how much I've evolved beyond ego to be able to align with my authentic self and know when I'm standing in the light.

The old me would have sent her home crying, teeth in hand, but the new me was extending the metaphorical olive branch. (#personalgrowth) You'd think a normal person would feel humbled, or at least softened by the gesture, but this girl came back at me with a shoulder shrug, barely a verbal reply, and some half-ass whatever eye roll. Girl bye. But the boys were so impressed and applauded my efforts, which was all I needed. And with that, the party turned all the way up and I left them to it.

At some point, another guy in the group came up to me and told me that his friend had a crush on me. I laughed because I couldn't remember the last time someone had a "crush" on me. It was cute. I asked who, and he pointed out the same guy I had my eye on who didn't speak unless he had something to say.

Normally I wouldn't let another guy speak on behalf of his friend, but I didn't think he knew his friend was speaking on his behalf. It seemed like he was trying to be a good wingman when really, his friend didn't need any help at all. I loved the intention and wasn't mad at the information, which I received and used wisely.

This is the perfect time to circle back to one of my initial points about self-care and being ready on go for when the opportunity for a possible hookup presents itself.

On this night, I was ready for anything. Shaved, plucked, and baby smooth from head to toe, and I was wearing a sexy, lacy bra and panty set. Prepared, able and willing to engage, and what a relief knowing everything about me was tight, ready, and right.

It's worth mentioning that it had been something like four or five months since I'd had sex; one of my longest stints without it. This was a result of a lapse of time during which I was focused on working on myself and sex wasn't top of my mind. I call it the drought of 2017, so trust and believe when I say that I was ready to get me some, and Mr. Strong and Silent type was looking like a snack attack.

As the end of the night got closer, the crew began making plans to move to a second location, a nearby strip club. As the guys were organizing things, my guy looked at me and said, "You want to go with them, or come with me?" Ah, duh… It was a no-brainer. Without a moment's hesitation, I chose him, and he was happy I did.

He took a moment with his friends, then he grabbed my hand and we were out of there.

My car was parked in an underground parking lot

nearby, but I didn't want to drive, as I'd been drinking all night. He agreed, so we cabbed it back to his hotel.

He was so cool, collected, and exuded a quiet confidence that put me at ease, and I was enamoured with his good looks and boyish charm, a young stud international soccer player. Yummy! I say boyish charm because he was twenty-six years young and… well… I wasn't. In fact, I was old enough to be the cougar to his cub and was ready to teach this cub how to become a lion.

Mind you he looked like he could also teach me a thing or two, absolutely my type, exotic with a strong athletic body and beautiful face. All I could think was, *I'm Nicole Jones, and I approve this moment.*

We got to his hotel, and it was effortless. We both knew why we were there. I excused myself first to freshen up, and then he went. When he came back out, I was posed on the bed, wearing nothing more than my pretty red lace panties and bra, and he was wearing tight, sexy boxer briefs (not white).

He mounted me and we kissed passionately and started to pull down my panties, and then in a hurry, but not rushed, he went down on me and ate me like a champ.

I held his head between my legs and enjoyed every moment of it until I came all over his face, almost choking him but releasing him just before. No apologies given.

He was a very good cub. What more could a girl ask for? That was a rhetorical question, by the way. I knew exactly what more to ask for and I wasn't afraid to ask for it. When he finally came up for air, my whole body was trembling. I wanted him inside me so badly I could hardly stand it, but first I wanted to return the favour and pleasure him; after all, it was the polite thing to do.

I know some women who don't like giving blow jobs,

and I get it that it can be a job for sure, but it seems like such a shame to overlook that part of foreplay. There's something so exciting about manipulating a man's penis to the point of getting so hard he can barely handle it. And that first contact when he enters you feels like the reward waiting on the other end of a "job" well done.

Eventually the rest of the boys made their way back to the hotel and started calling him. That was my cue to leave; besides, I had to get home to my doggie, Dior, who'd been alone long enough due to Mama's extracurricular activities. In true gentleman form, he walked me down and handed me a large sum of money for the cab as well for the parking garage the next day. It was a little weird accepting money under the circumstances, which felt very *Pretty Woman* of him. But the bigger picture was a sweet and thoughtful gesture because yes, parking and cabbing are expensive, so thank you.

The next day, feeling on top of the world and with an extra spring in my step, I started thinking about all the things I'd done the night before to get the D. It just wasn't like me to make so many concessions, but his D had me all the way bending the rules.

I did a lot for that D. I left my car for that D, I took a taxi for that D, I left my dog for that D, I missed the gym for that D, I left the club with a guy I'd just met for that D, and thank goodness it was worth all the trouble to get that D.

In the end, aside from the no violence teachable moment in the beginning of this story, there's no great lesson or moral to leave you with.

Except to applaud all singles who know the struggle and are willing to do what it takes to get the D, respect and well done! Crown on.

Chapter Sixteen

HOT BITCHES AND A BACHELORETTE

I'M SO EXCITED about this extra spicy chapter that features some of my favourite things: my sister tribe, Ibiza, villas, and exotic men who say exotic things… oh my!

What better destination to have your last hurrah and bachelorette party than in Ibiza surrounded by your best girlfriends?

And we had the perfect bachelorette to celebrate. She was a loving and loyal sister who was adored by all, and we couldn't have been more excited to show her the time of her life, because she deserved it, and we were all the way there for it.

From the start, our trip was aligned with the stars to be amazing. One of our sisters had asked a dear friend of ours who was also a very influential person on the island if we could please, please, borrow his villa to host the bachelorette party. Much to our elated delight, he generously agreed to allow eight girls to occupy his place.

Brave soul indeed. We were so grateful.

Located on the south side of the island, it was what many would describe as the most beautiful villa on the island, breathtaking and beyond magnificent. So stunning, in fact, it had made the cover of exclusive design magazines. As well as having a reputation for hosting some of the most elite and incredible parties, if you were fortunate enough to get invited, you knew you were lucky and privileged to be there.

We had the entire place to ourselves to celebrate our girl in the most fabulous way for a week of anything and everything. And the blessing of it all was not lost on us. We were so overjoyed and thrilled that we couldn't have asked for anything more.

One by one the girls started to arrive, with a couple of the crew already on the island preparing the terrain for the rest of the group and getting ready for the arrival of our bachelorette. Yup, hide your sons, Ibiza was about to be taken over by a French invasion, and make no mistake about it, we were a crew of professional partiers with one crystalized objective: to show our girl her best pre-marriage turnout before tying the knot with the love of her life.

But before marriage comes Ibiza—and a week she'd never forget, regret, nor quite recover from.

Sorry 'bout it.

Like I said, having the house was more than we could have asked for, so when we found out our friend was also allowing us access to his staff, security, drivers, and his yacht, as well as VIP access to all the clubs, we couldn't believe it. I mean, talk about setting us up to succeed to party as hard as we could.

The fact that everyone survived and lived to tell about it is a small miracle on its own. There was literally nothing more under God's blue sky that we could have needed or asked for. Nothing.

Okay, maybe one more thing, but he would manifest naturally and didn't come with the house.

The bachelorette was the last to arrive, and as soon as she landed, she was met by an eager crew of her favourite girls, who basically intercepted her at the airport with champagne and good vibes in tow. You know when you're experiencing something so special that it almost feels like living in a dream? That's how we felt, and to do it with our favourite people was such an incredible blessing. I feel humbled just thinking about it.

This was a once-in-a-lifetime experience that most people can only dream of, and we were living it. Now a decade later, I have the distinct privilege and honour to write about one of the best times of our lives. What a beautiful, full-circle moment. Amen.

The main thing we'd have to stay mindful of was to make sure that our bachelorette made it back to Canada in one piece and in time for her wedding. We unanimously agreed that would be our goal and we'd do our best, but we couldn't promise anything, LOL.

As we headed back to the villa where some of the girls were already getting ready for our first night out, the plan was to start with dinner at a spot called Planet Sushi and then hit the clubs from there.

When the driver stopped in front of the restaurant to let us out, the deboarding of the group from the vehicle was a show and a feast for the eyes—a non-stop lineup of stunning women from somewhere else in the world all dressed to kill. One by one, stepping out of our eight-passenger Mercedes van, just saying.

Girl, we were stopping traffic and disrupting people's meals just by way of showing up.

Montreal much? We didn't even make it inside before spotting the first exotic male target from where we stood on the sidewalk; that's how clear and sharp our lens was that night. Our group's agreement among us was that when it came to guys and hooking up, our bachelorette and the coupled girls would live vicariously through the singles in the group. We weren't trying to have anybody cheating or being scandalous. That wasn't the vibe. And us single girls accepted the mission to give them something to live for.

We knew our tribe was bound to get attention and more attention, so picking up guys would not be our problem. It wasn't our priority, but it was on the list of possibilities, and we proved that to be right on the first night at our first stop.

As we made our way into the restaurant, our beloved bachelorette stopped short, grabbed my arm with a gasp, and steered my gaze to align with the delicious piece of man that we noticed from outside. He was the epitome of sexy bohemian, looking like a pirate, very Johnny Depp, artist type, giving off easy, breezy island energy about him. Smoking hot. His beautiful, tanned skin and long, dark brown hair was just tousled enough to give that effortless, naturally good-looking vibe.

I didn't even mind his slight beard. It was all working for him, framing his chiselled face quite nicely. Dressed in beautiful linens that draped over his God-given sculpted torso and strong frame, he was a masterpiece in our eyes. Speaking of eyes, when his and mine met, forget about it. It was like a quiet introduction from across the room.

MASTER
OF SINGLE

In an instant, we knew each other existed.

And then one of my funniest moments of the night happened. Our bachelorette said something to me that I'll never forget. In her most matter-of-fact voice, she said, "Nicole, as my bachelorette gift, you have to fuck him for me." I laughed so hard. I didn't see that coming, but I liked it.

My first thought was, *Girl, I'm already ahead of you* and was honoured to accept the mission; after all, it was her party, and she could order us to have sex with strangers if she wanted to, ha ha! It was part of our unwritten contract, and who was I to break a contract or to deny her bachelorette wishes?

We all looked incredible that night, and I was feeling myself from top to bottom, dressed to entice in an all-white mini shirt with a crop top till you drop situation, giving legs, face, and hair for days with my eighteen-inch wavy extensions and heels so high I could touch the sky.

I dare you to not stare was the vibe of that look.

You know when you look as good as you feel and vice versa? That was us collectively; we all had our personal style, and each one was as beautiful as the next.

But that's Montreal women for you. We know how to do sexy better than most, and you can take the girl out of the city, but you can't take the hotness out of the girl. Bam. We've arrived.

With my mission clear, once inside and seated at our table, the games began. We ordered our food and got the logistical stuff out of the way, then I decided to take a little stroll to the bar, confident he'd come find me, and I was right. I watched him as he very casually made his way through the crowd and across the room, saying hello along the way but always keeping one eye on me.

I just stood there, taking in the view and enjoying my cocktail while waiting for him to finally reach me, and when he did, there was an instant connection. We both knew what the other was thinking. It was written all over our faces.

From the moment he said his first words in his sexy Italian/Spanish worldly accent and voice, I was dead. It wasn't a question of *if* we were going to fuck, but *when*.

The answer in my mind was sooner rather than later, please.

But as much as I wanted to pursue the chemistry with this hot Ibizan man, my loyalty to my girls and our first night out was more important.

I knew he'd wait; he was as into me as I was into him, and he wasn't blind. He knew that I was worth waiting for. However, creating memories with my girls couldn't wait and took precedence over everything.

Knowing your priorities is important, ladies, and you should never prioritize a guy (especially one you just met) over your best girlfriends, no matter how hot he is. The hard rule should always be your chicks before dicks.

So we exchanged numbers and agreed to meet later, which would be the much-anticipated part two of a long, sleepless night ahead, and I'd never been more excited to not sleep in my life.

Best bachelorette assignment ever!

Turning back to the girls, our night went on according to plan—zero fucks given and no holds barred, meaning we partied like it was 1999 and a motherfucking bachelorette.

Let it be known that everywhere we stopped it was noticed that we had entered the building. From clubs like Pacha to Space, we were VIP all the way and couldn't have imagined it any other way.

MASTER
OF SINGLE

We looked like bachelorette royalty, from the driver and all-access to everything, which made people stop and take note even more. They're welcome.

Let's just say we had a blast and we made it last throughout the night into the break of dawn and carry on. Imagine, this was only night one. Oh Lord, have mercy on our souls and on the island of Ibiza.

As our night wound down and the day began to peak, I couldn't help but think about my next stop. When I called to let him know we were wrapping things up, the conversation was short and sweet. He said, "Are you ready to meet, my lovely?"

"Yes, I am ready for you."

"Text me where you are. I'll come and pick you up."

"Okay. Hurry," I said back and I meant it.

The whole night was incredible. We couldn't have designed it better if we tried. Our girl was beyond elated and celebrated. The whole crew was vibrating at the ultimate sisterhood frequency.

Inside I felt fulfilled and grateful knowing we were making memories and a little Ibiza history that would stay with us for a lifetime.

By the end, the girls were so happy that I stayed with them but were basically kicking me out the door and excited for me to go meet my hot Ibiza man.

Of course they were. They wanted all the play-by-play dirty details the next day, and I was happy to be the one to bring it back to the family.

Ordained by them with their blessing, it was the perfect transition, and by all accounts, the perfect night. After a last shot and some sisterly love, off I went into the Ibiza night with my beautiful stranger. I'm obsessed with beautiful strangers.

It was finally time for me to honour and fulfill my duties and responsibilities to my sister the bachelorette, and I wouldn't let her down... or him, for that matter.

When it comes to what happened next, what can I say that you don't already know? I love sex and exotic men, and that night I had both. It was the perfect storm, and I was at the heart of it all.

His hotness took me a minute to process. He was just so fucking beautiful, one of the most beautiful men I'd ever laid my eyes on, and sexy off the charts. So cool and smooth that he couldn't have been a more ideal specimen for an island romance, one-night stand, throw caution to the wind, yes and kind of situation.

He set the mood with candles, burning incense and playing some sexy chill beats. The Ibiza air engulfed us. It felt dreamy, and he was making all my fantasies come true. That night ranks as one of the top three best nights of sex and connection I've ever had, and I've had some stellar nights with some incredible men. But he was in a league of his own, and I was grateful to be sharing the moment with someone who was as enamoured by me as I was by him.

As I lay there on his bed, wrapped in one of his sarongs with a cool breeze coming through the slightly cracked window, he looked at me with such inquisitiveness and desire.

Where did you come from? Where have you been all this time? How did you get here?

He paid attention to every detail; the smell of my skin and the curves of my body I could tell intoxicated him.

He took his time softly kissing the nook of my neck and along my collarbone while gently caressing the small of my back. I loved every sensational moment of it.

MASTER OF SINGLE

He took both my wrists, placed them above my head, holding them with one of his hands while his other hand teased and tantalized my now naked body. It drove me crazy.

After hours and hours and hours of giving each other pleasure, he looked at me like he'd just had an aha moment, and that's when he bestowed on me the title of *pantera*.

I loved it immediately and owned it proudly. "Say it again," I told him as I made my way down his sexy body to his beautiful instrument, in true *pantera* style with sexy and grace written all over my face, and repeat.

Meanwhile, back at the spot, the girls were chilling and living la vida loca without a care in the world and the world at their fingertips. Our bachelorette continued to be celebrated like the queen she was, deserving of every second of every minute of it. The days were long and time went by slowly, as it usually does in Ibiza.

One afternoon, we decided to have a BBQ at the house, and I invited my guy over to formally meet the rest of the tribe. I had spoken frequently and in detail to them about this man's skills, he wasn't a fucker, he was a lover.

It was time for them to put a face to the man and all his deliciousness.

On the flip side, I hadn't prepared him for what he was going to be walking into—not only the grandeur of the villa but the impact of seven other hot women roaming the grounds, perhaps some even naked, but I knew he could handle it. He was from Ibiza, after all.

I wanted to gift him the element of surprise upon his arrival to the queendom.

And what a welcome! He arrived at the most sickening villa and followed the yellow brick road to the beat of the music, which opened into a bevy of stunning female specimens, some dressed and others not so much. It was a moment that would qualify as any man's dream scenario, and he fit right in.

All the sisters were wooed by his charm and good looks and maybe were a little jelly that I was the one to have him. Only because he was so damn hot and everyone's sex drive was at a ten, but they were happy for me and enjoyed the additional eye candy I brought to the group.

The funniest moment occurred when he and I were lying on the grass, kissing, and wrapped up in each other just lost in our own world.

Then one of the sisters walked over to us very casually, topless, wearing a huge sun hat, sunglasses, and holding a glass of wine (totally normal).

With a slight rumble to her voice in her beautiful Argentinian accent, she said, "You know, it's not nice to eat in front of starving people." Translation: Not everyone's getting laid, so stop torturing us. Ha ha! We both burst out in laughter; it was such a classic line, but it wasn't just the line—it was the whole visual along with her delivery that made it the most hilarious, real moment, and I knew when it happened that I'd never forget it. So good!

As for the remainder of the trip, we did some shopping, relaxed at the villa during the day, and partied at night. We spent great times on the yacht cruising around on the Balearic Sea and basically didn't want for anything except for our girl to be blissfully happy.

Our vibe was no worries, no problems, all pleasure, all day every day and all the time, which is also a good motto for life.

So what's the takeaway here besides sharing this incredible time we had with our awesome tribe and how Ibiza will never be the same again?

MASTER OF SINGLE

As blessed as we knew we were to have experienced such abundance and to have been so spoiled, the bigger message was even if we'd celebrated our girl out of a cardboard box, the intention, love, respect, and unity we all shared had nothing to do with any of the above, as amazing as it was. It had everything to do with the loyalty of our friendships and the love we had for each other; that's what transcended everything.

The villa and the bells and whistles were the icing on the cake and the cherry on top.

And so I leave you with this. Hold your friendships close, celebrate your friends without any reason, and never let a good time pass you by without turning it into a memory you'll talk about for the rest of your lives.

Congratulations to the beautiful couple who have since celebrated ten years of blissful married life, love, and have brought three of the most beautiful and precious children into the world. They are one of the couples to whom I look to as a marriage and a love done right. (#couplegoals)

To my sisters and all the sister tribes out there, I salute you. Amen.

Chapter Seventeen
(The best for last)

The Greatest Love of All

Every end is a new beginning…
Hello, beloveds, and welcome.

I'm so excited that we've made it to the best and last, the greatest and my most anticipated chapter.

I hope you've enjoyed the journey thus far. This chapter is where I finally get to bring every lesson, experience, man, and introspection together in one message of solidarity and what I perceive to be the greatest love of all.

My journey in writing this book had me experiencing and sharing things I wasn't expecting to feel or reveal. I couldn't have imagined when I started the emotional and spiritual toll that would come with it, but the more I wrote, the more I leaned into it, no fear and allowing myself to be plain to see.

I've laughed and cried, healed, and sometimes felt

embarrassed, but I learned a lot about myself. And through it all, I've gained an even deeper sense of pride and ownership of my life and the stories that make me who I am.

Taking ownership of the good, the bad, and the ugly pushed me through when I doubted myself or my work or when I would freak out about putting my life on blast.

Nonetheless, as difficult as it sometimes was, I vowed to myself that I would be as honest, transparent, respectful, and as fair as I could possibly be while staying true to who I am and the message I wanted to share.

A message of strength and of love that is not manufactured by another soul but lives in each of us.

I've known from the beginning that I wanted my final message to be the most empowering one. Opening my life and letting you into my experiences wasn't meant to "expose" myself but to drive home the point that everything we experience matters. When it comes to our dreams, they say it doesn't matter where you come from—you can make it regardless.

I say it does matter where you come from because where you come from and what you've been through shapes who you are, and you can't have one without the other.

Everything matters. You matter. Your dreams matter. Your story matters. Your voice matters.

My fundamental message for singles is not to wait until someone comes into your life to live your best life or to find your purpose. Your life is your purpose, and that message is for anyone who seeks deeper meaning and higher love. The only thing standing between you and the life you want to live is you. You are the master of your life, and your past, regardless of the advantages or disadvantages, does not and should not determine your future.

Speaking of the future, fast forward to today. I'm grateful that after five long years and a lot of writer's block and procrastination along the way, I was able to finish writing this book during my quarantine amid a global pandemic. Which is crazy to me that it took something like this to quiet me and finish what I started almost five years ago.

This global collective experience we share has been overwhelming and brutal on all facets of our lives. It also forced us to decide if we were going to let it break us or rise above to find the blessing in it.

This unprecedented and crazy time has also presented us with an exceptional once-in-a-lifetime opportunity to stop and reflect. Take stock of what's important and what we truly want out of life. Perhaps this time has even inspired dormant minds to awaken to live a more connected and spiritually aligned lifestyle. Whatever it is for you, this is an experience no matter where you go, someone will relate.

For months we sat still, devastated as the world was on fire, bleeding, pleading, and crying for love, peace, justice, solutions, and hope. I managed as best I could with the issues as they were brought to task, putting my voice/actions behind what mattered to me.

One of the many things I thought about during my quarantine included asking myself if I was truly happy. I realized that many aspects of my life were happy but that I could still find more happiness.

I held that idea in my mind and ran with it.

In the craziness, I managed to find the blessings in disguise. Losing a job that was seemingly great on the outside but slowly robbing me of my joy on the inside. That was a huge wake-up call. I took it as a sign from the divine to let go of what no longer served me and took this time to be of service to myself. Redesign my life according to who I want to be in this world.

Enter, master of single. Next stop, author.

Now, mid-pandemic and editing my final chapters before I release this book into the world is one of the most rewarding, scary, and uncertain things I've ever done. But it's also the most exciting investment in myself, the biggest chance I've ever taken, and I've taken some big chances. And as close as I've ever come to giving birth.

My faith and understanding of how not to be attached to the outcome have allowed me to remain calm and enjoy the ride.

But I didn't get here without one major and probably the most important lesson I've ever learned… and that's what I've saved for last, one final teachable moment, from my heart to yours.

And with that, beloveds, the last dance and one step closer towards the single greatest love of all…

The year was 2016, and the event was Burning Man. One typical (open to interpretation) single-girl day, I received a not-so-typical phone call from a friend who doesn't often call, so it was a nice surprise but a curious one too. I answered the phone, happy to hear his voice on the other end. After a quick catch-up, he pivoted the conversation with a hard left, asking me if I'd ever heard of Burning Man.

I told him yes, I had heard of it, and then he proceeded to tell me that he and his lovely wife were strongly considering attending.

Admittedly, he caught me off guard because these

friends were quite posh and polished, professional businesspeople, dignified and refined. Which was a stark contrast to what I had heard about Burning Man in that the environment and conditions were quite harsh and not for the faint of heart.

Suffice it to say, I was surprised to hear that from him.

He explained that they were considering the experience but were feeling a bit intimidated by the prospect of being trapped in the desert for a week, and they had more questions than answers. They had friends on the inside who were seasoned burners and had invited them to join their camp, which he described as being established and well organized with a formidable team of leaders and fellow burners.

What I know now is that there's not only one way of doing Burning Man. The living conditions and choices are different for everyone. For example, some people choose RV life, others do the hut, and some live in a tent, or tepee. Point being the most important thing is that whatever you choose, you're comfortable committing to that choice.

In this case, it sounded like the camp he was describing offered a comfortable environment.

I thought, cool, sounds great, but as he continued talking, I still wasn't sure why he was telling me all this random information. That's when he dropped the bomb, proposing something that would have my head spinning.

He said, "Listen, you're someone I trust with my and my family's well-being." That confidence stemmed from his knowledge of my work ethic and taking care of him, his colleagues, and family members in my various roles in the nightlife industry where he witnessed my ability to manage hectic situations. Great, thank you, but I still wasn't making the connection between me, them, and Burning Man. He went on to ask, "If we paid for everything pertaining to your trip, would you join us and come to Burning Man?" Pause for reaction. What? What? Wowwww. Mind blown! I didn't know what to say at first. I mean, how do you even begin to process that request?

These friends were a bona fide power couple—successful, internationally well respected, loved, affluent, and influential. Not only did they have the respect of our city, but they had mine.

His offer was flattering but compounded with more confusion. Why did they want me to go with them? Then he explained: "Because we trust you; we'd ask you to go ahead of us, scope out the terrain, set up our quarters (the RV), and prepare things for our arrival. We'd feel much more comfortable knowing that you are on the ground organizing things prior to our arrival so that we can mentally prepare for what to expect."

Oh, okay, shit just got real. Are you kidding me? That was a ginormous ask and responsibility to take on, especially considering who was asking, but also given the fact that I'd never been there myself, which really upped the ante. For all intents and purposes, I would be responsible for two extremely important individuals who were also parents to two wonderful boys, as well as taking care of myself. All this in an unforgiving environment that I'd never experienced, surrounded by tens of thousands of people while living in an RV.

Sure, no sweat. Just another day. WTF!

I sat in silence as he continued breaking it down. "Should you accept, we'd make the arrangements for you to fly to Reno to meet with the core members of the camp I mentioned. From there, you'd join the team in getting all things together before heading to Black Rock City."

MASTER OF SINGLE

If there was one thing I knew, it was that I could trust his word. If he said they'd take care of me and that I'd be in good hands, I trusted that. Not only because of who they were in their integrity, but as my friends I trusted they'd uphold their end of the deal. I got the impression that he knew how big of an ask this was. I also knew there probably weren't many people like me that he could ask something of this magnitude, giving me a lot to consider. But before committing, I really had to think on it.

We ended the call with him saying, "Take your time, think about it, and let me know what you decide."

Perfect. "Okay, great," I said. "Thank you so much. I'll get back to you soon."

Time was what I needed to let this process land.

I sat for a few seconds in shock and feeling a little bewildered before bursting out into a loud cheer! I wasn't sure yet what I was going to do, but I knew enough to know this was exciting, nerve-racking, but exciting!

What was the universe trying to tell me with this offering? After a short outburst of unadulterated joy, I pulled myself together and started to get my thoughts in order, beginning with a phone call to my sister, Marie Eve, who I knew had been to Burning Man before.

She also knew me well and would be the perfect sounding board.

I got her on the phone and quickly broke down the details and then waited for her to respond. It didn't take but a second for her to give her stamp of approval. She was quick to say that I should take their offer and not look back, citing the following: Burning Man is one of the most incredible experiences you will ever have. The cost to do Burning Man right isn't cheap, and to be connected to a seasoned, well-organized camp is clutch. Between plane tickets, hotel room, the entrance ticket for the burn, supplies, etc., this was a deal of a lifetime, and without a doubt I should take it.

She also reassured me that she believed I'd be able to handle the responsibility that came with the invitation.

I felt a big sense of relief after that conversation, and her feedback pushed me to strongly consider his offer, but there was one more very important thing.

Weeks before receiving his call, I'd already committed to an important reporter job working for my best friend Judy's marketing company. It was for the Toronto International Film Festival, or TIFF, which is the largest film festival in the world.

For both of us, this was a crucial professional opportunity. I was asked to be the lead reporter on the red carpet, interviewing the world's biggest stars and celebrities. Goals AF.

After comparing the dates, I realized that the TIFF and Burning Man conflicted in terms of timing. Of course they did. The universe is very generous in its offerings, but it can also challenge you to do the work to be able to receive its gifts. I took the cues and the challenge and did what I had to do in terms of strategizing and thinking outside the box to make it all happen. Trusting that what was meant to be would be.

I got all my ducks in a row, including doing my research on the burn and weighing that against the work pile I had ahead of me to prepare for the TIFF. Once I felt I'd done enough research and spoken to enough people, I meditated on it, which helped me to decide. The next day, I called my friend with a few questions and discussed the particulars of my situation regarding the TIFF. I would have to leave the burn a day early to make it back to Montreal in time to get

MASTER
OF SINGLE

myself to Toronto. The idea was I'd go from Reno-Montreal-Toronto in thirty-six hours, or better yet, Burning Man, pause for cause to red carpet. Sure, totally normal.

For this to work, they'd have to meet me where I was. It wasn't the most ideal situation, especially for me, because it meant leaving before the most anticipated event, the burning of the man on the last night. But for this to work, something had to give. It didn't take but a second for him to reply. "Listen, we trust that you'll be able to do what needs to be done both for yourself and for us, so if leaving a day early helps you, then it's fine with us."

At that moment there were no more questions; everything became clear. I replied with an instant and resounding yes. I'd be honoured to join him and his wife for our first burn together. I thanked him for extending this incredible opportunity and for choosing and trusting me.

"Yes, yes, yes!" I proclaimed. He was delighted with my response, and, well, the rest is this chapter... Burn, baby, burn all the way home...

I hung up and did a little happy dance before hitting the ground running.

This was exciting, but the clock was already ticking, less than one month to countdown for both. The plan was to start studying for the TIFF while I was still in Montreal, and at the same time I'd begin preparing for the burn. Beginning with creating a shopping list of the essentials we'd need to help manage the unpredictable desert life—things like camel packs, goggles, dust masks, et cetera. You know, your basic desert survival gear and just another day in the life.

Next, I had to start my research for the TIFF. Now, keep in mind the magnitude of this job, which entailed learning over two hundred movie titles, plot summaries, actors' names, roles, and coming up with thoughtful questions for a red carpet.

The study guide provided by the company I was working for was as big, heavy, and intimidating as any book I'd ever pick up. That's when things got real for the second time. I knew immediately that this whole process would be a juggling act, a marathon narrowed down to a sprint to the finish line, but somehow in my idealistic mind I convinced myself that I could do it all if I just stuck to my plan. Well, ha ha, the plan and the joke were on me.

I underestimated how much time it would take to prepare for the burn. Just getting my costumes together was incredibly time consuming. Okay, my looks might not have been the top priority, but while doing my research, I noticed pictures of people dressed in all kinds of beautiful costumes as a form of self-expression. I knew right away that I wanted that artistic expression to be part of my experience. It was the one thing in all the things I was doing that I did for myself, making it important enough to become a priority.

Also, finding all the items we needed for the burn a more daunting task than I'd anticipated. I'd never been to so many army surplus stores.

Without even realizing it, the month had zipped by and I'd barely cracked the binding of my TIFF study book. And then before I knew it, I was on the heels of departing to meet the team in Reno, Nevada.

Okay, no problem, I thought. *Don't freak out. I'll just pivot and take my TIFF study book with me; after all, there's always the plane ride and an overnight stay at the hotel.*

There was also the RV ride from Reno to our destination of Black Rock City; surely I'd find time to study

MASTER OF SINGLE

somewhere in there. I knew I was lying to myself, but I was trying to convince myself that there would be time to get it done. By that point I had no choice. It would have to get done, so the study book was coming with.

But before going any further, let me take a minute to speak to my sick costumes and how my amazing and talented friends pulled off a small fashion miracle in getting me together.

With little to no time, they transformed me into a would-be desert warrior queen, "Burgin" (Burning Man virgin).

Credit and gratitude to Natalie @qualibling and Jason @instaglam, they both set me up to succeed in my artistic vision and expression for my first burn. I was beyond grateful. What each of them came up with independently was just stunning, from my gorgeous headpieces to a mirrored bustier, butterfly body chain, and tutu fabulousness for Tutu Tuesday in the desert. I even had a crinoline coat lined with LED lights that was perfect to be seen and keep me warm at night.

I wasn't sure what to expect from this experience, but I did know that whatever happened, I was going to look incredible doing it. To complete the look, my hairdresser Jackie (who's been doing my hair for twenty-plus years) created this super funky, cool half braid/half Mohawk hairstyle. It was the perfect look—functional for the elements but still sexy and cool. Collectively, they were my Burning Man glam squad dream team, and I couldn't have done it without them. Life note: Never forget the people who help you climb the ladder to get you where you want to be because you may just meet them again on your way down. Appreciate the people who help you shine because they don't have to help. Higher consciousness 101.

The day before my departure, I was packed with all lists

checked twice. I was as ready as I could be to start my journey to Reno to meet with the leaders of the camp, which appropriately enough was called Camp Epic. A fitting name for what would be an epic experience.

My friends had already briefed them as to my arrival, so all that was left was for me to get there.

I didn't sleep a wink that night; my mind was going a hundred miles an hour. But what was cool about this phase of things was the feeling of being excited about the unknown. Having butterflies in my belly and hoping the people I was about to meet were going to like me.

It was stirring up a lot of excitement and emotions that I rarely have as an adult. The start of this experience had awakened the kid in me, full of wonder and anticipation.

Getting to Reno was the easy part, and meeting the crew of Camp Epic was one of my greatest pleasures. It was so amazing to finally put faces to names, which really put everything into perspective. This was really happening.

I had the great fortune of meeting some of the coolest, kindest, funniest, most generous, purest souls I'd ever met. I think at first glance I appeared to be a little nervous, but they welcomed me with open arms, and our common friend acted as the anchor that grounded us in something familiar. They shared with me how much they loved our mutual friends, how happy they were that they were coming, and how grateful they were for me helping them to facilitate their experience. Basically, I felt at home from the moment I arrived. My friends were right—I was in good hands, and I couldn't wait to learn more about the next phases of our adventure.

That first night we dined together, I discovered that most of the team were seasoned burners who already knew each other from past years. There was me and one other

MASTER
OF SINGLE

person who were new to this crew, and he was also the person I instantly gravitated towards.

His proper name was Chundrea, but as per his consent, we called him Dray, and he was the coolest cat on the block. I was drawn in by his swag and the steadfast confidence he projected from every pore of his being without even trying.

He made no apologies for wearing his shades indoors; his vibe was on point, Zen energy out to the max in the best way possible, with all signs pointing to him being someone I wanted to know more about. Also, it was comforting to see another black person going to the desert. It's just not something you see every day, black people in the desert on purpose, ha ha.

I spent most of dinner, talking with him as well as others around the table, but something kept pulling me towards Dray, and it wasn't a sexual thing. It was more like a big brother/energy connection. It's not often that you meet someone who makes you feel safe around them without even knowing them, but that's what was happening, and it was cool, just like him.

Before the dinner ended, we were briefed about the next day and the final stretch to Black Rock City. They described a detailed plan of action from the time we woke up to the time we would arrive.

The team I'd be travelling with included approximately twenty campers and six or seven RVs that would be following each other. First thing in the morning we would complete any last-minute errands, including shopping for food and final necessities at the local Walmart. From there, we'd pick up our bicycles, which from my research and what everyone was telling me were a must. They would be our main means of transportation in the desert, aside from the camp's art car, which I would learn about later.

After the briefing, we went to our rooms to get some rest, but I was too wired with excitement, so I walked around the hotel grounds for a while and eventually met a few Epic members along the way. Dray was one of them. We gathered and chatted awhile. I got to know everyone a little better. Everyone shared their stories and burn experiences as I sat there listening with stars in my eyes and images of desert fairies dancing in my head.

Feeling full and inspired by their stories, it was time for me to get some rest. I bid everyone a goodnight and returned to my room to take advantage of the few hours left to sleep before showtime.

A short sleep later, I was up, bright-eyed, and ready to burn. We gathered for breakfast, and once done, broke off into small groups and started the process of checking things off the to-do list. We also set a time and meeting point for our departure.

At noon, we congregated as a team, assigned RVs for everyone to ride in, lined them up in a row, and we were highway bound to hit the road jack, not for a second looking back.

Direction: Black Rock City, Burning Man to dust. I remember trying to play it cool. I didn't want to come across as the girl who blew her load before the main event. But inside I was exploding with glee. I wanted to see everything, talk to everyone, and hear more about their experiences.

The ride, which I was told usually takes two to three hours, turned out to be much longer than anticipated. It appeared everyone heading to Burning Man had the same departure time in mind. By the time we hit the single-lane portion of the trip on the I-80 highway, it was literally bumper to bumper the whole way, with RVs for as far as the eye could see, drastically slowing us down. But by that point I was in such a happy space, nothing could ruin my good mood, not even insane traffic.

Let's remember for a laughable minute my plan to study for the TIFF somewhere between home and Burning Man. Well, let me say this for myself. I tried, I really did give it my best shot, but yeah, that plan didn't stand a chance.

At one point, I'd parked myself on the top bunk in the back of the RV with my big book of movies and stars, note pad and highlighter in hand, and did my best to focus. My efforts lasted all but an hour. My mind just couldn't focus; I was too distracted by the conversations happening in the front of the RV, even just looking out the window into the desert was more exciting than the idea of studying alone in the back of our RV on my way to Burning Man, for God's sake. So I made an executive decision to abort project study for the TIFF until further notice.

Once again putting it to faith, trusting that somehow down the literal road I would figure things out. Was it a risk? Yes, but I made the choice to be in the moment rather than worry about something that hadn't happened yet. My faith told me it would be all right, and that was good enough for me to close the book and return to being present in the moment.

What I realized in closing the book was that my journey had already begun. I didn't have to wait until we'd arrived; it was already happening. Even the traffic was part of the experience, and I was soaking it all up like a sponge does water. It truly is about the journey and not the destination.

When we chose our respective RVs to ride in, I knew immediately I wanted to ride with Dray, and I was so happy I did. We had such a cool crew to journey with, and we kept each other laughing and engaged, which made the long-ass ride that much easier.

But I knew straightaway I also wanted to use that time to get to know him better.

Let me say this about the traffic: it was moving slower than a turtle taking its time. I was often in awe of how many RVs there were and how long the road was to get there. There were times we sat in the same spot, not moving for thirty minutes or more, but everyone was making the best of it. People were getting out to throw footballs around on the side of the road while others opted to climb on top of their RVs to capture the iconic shot of them heading to Burning Man.

The energy of it all left me feeling so blessed that I was even part of it.

After several hours of being in this slow-moving traffic and with night starting to fall, people slowly rejoined their RVs to chill and continue the journey down the road.

On a personal moment of reflection, prior to leaving, I was already on a path of spiritual growth and seeking answers to the questions that would bring me enlightenment. Feeling like I was on the verge of some sort of breakthrough, I just wasn't sure yet what that was.

But something was telling me that I was exactly where I needed to be.

I started talking with Dray, only to discover that he was a bona fide yoga instructor, no surprise there. I'd already sensed that he was an energy magnet, filled to the brim with knowledge and tapped into wisdom and information from higher sources. He was like a safe place to fall only to be elevated again. I suppose through divine intervention, which is the best way to explain it, I ended up sharing with him personal stuff that I normally wouldn't even share with close friends, because it made me feel too vulnerable. But with Dray it was easy, and the words came naturally.

MASTER OF SINGLE

He was a great listener and allowed me to express my thoughts, worries, concerns, questions, and fears. He was generous, present, and just listened to me without judgement and didn't try to make things better or give advice. He just listened to how I was feeling.

I shared with him the secrets of my soul, of not feeling like I was enough in my daily life, as if I were missing a gene of happiness or confidence that would complete me. Like a caterpillar destined to become a butterfly, I wanted to be free to fly. Free of the feeling inside me that was becoming too heavy a burden for my spirit and soul to carry. I explained how for months I'd been working on healing from trauma in my past and how that trauma showed up and still affected me. I shared how I was exhausted from living in toxic cycles of self-destruction, sabotage, and fear, but that I didn't know how to change them.

It was a lot for him to take in, especially considering we'd just met and he didn't know me from Eve, but he never made me feel awkward or that I was annoying him.

He was simply amazing.

At the end of what felt like hours of talking to him and purging everything that needed to come up, he, like a true master, looked at me and said in the kindest way and with the most soothing voice, "Okay, well, that's a lot, but that's okay. Listen, just stick with me. I'll teach you something you probably haven't had the chance to learn yet and will help you tremendously to make peace with yourself and your life, but for now, just try to let it go and be here with us."

Pure magic.

Then he smiled the most genuine smile with the kindest eyes that pierced through the smoky lenses of his sunglasses, and that was a wrap. It was powerful and immediate how he pulled me from my erratic thoughts back down grounded on earth.

I took the cue and let it go, realizing that none of my life problems had anything to do with what was happening in the now. With that shift, we headed to the front of the RV to reconnect with our driver, co-pilot, and other friend, who had been doing a stellar job navigating us to the promised land. The promise of what? I wasn't sure, but it felt like a pilgrimage, and I was about it. Music up, good vibes activated, and mission burn still well underway...

Now into our tenth hour of driving at a snail's crawl—yes, ten hours!—I wondered if we'd ever get there, and then like a miracle in the desert night, like a glimmer of hope through the darkness, we spotted the first sign to Burning Man.

Seeing that sign energized all of us from tired and stiff to full of hope and excitement. I remember jumping up and looking around, squealing like a teenage girl. I couldn't believe I'd made it to Burning Man. It was amazing and magical, and the minute that long, paved road changed to a dirt road, it was on.

In the distance we could hear what sounded like explosion after explosion. That's when we noticed a massive torch sitting in the distance, perched high in the sky. Every few minutes it would let off this explosion, and fire would shoot into the air.

I was feeling all the feels.

The theme of that year's burn was Carnival of Mirrors, which was totally open to interpretation. I was so excited to wear my costumes and so happy to have them.

After about thirty minutes of making our way towards the entrance, a very happy-looking, colourfully dressed

MASTER
OF SINGLE

attendant came up to greet and welcome us home. She handed us a booklet of protocols, including a map of the site, and asked a few questions. We had to show our tickets and were subjected to a standard search of the RV (mainly for dangerous weapons). Once that was complete, we were ushered through the pillars leading into the campgrounds.

Normally, as a first-time burner upon arrival and before proceeding to your camp, you'd be initiated by way of rolling around on the ground in the playa dust. Playa dust is this light, dusty powder that sticks to everything and is almost impossible to get off once it's on your body, unless you take a shower, but it's also part of the experience. Fortunately for us because it was so late and everyone was exhausted, they forfeited the initiation so that people could get to their camps quicker. But they did invite us back to experience it at another time if we wanted to. We said thank you, and I kept it in the back of my mind, but I never did go back. Once I was in, I was in, and I got dusty enough just standing in the open air, so I was okay with missing it.

The next series of steps were as follows: Our posse of RVs followed each other to our designated campsite, and the first thing I noticed was how well done and designed everything was.

The masterminds behind the burn understood the need to make the grounds accessible as well as functional, creating a grid-like situation that made a half-moon-shaped campsite that housed upwards of seventy thousand burners.

It was many, many, many rows deep, and each intersecting corner had a number and a letter. For example, D214, which would be your address and how people would find you as they biked through the open desert land.

Once we arrived at our spot, everyone was given a parking position and would remain parked there the whole time. Other than authorized vehicles and art cars (which are creative, functional cars turned into pieces of art used to transport people usually from camp out to the playa), otherwise any other vehicles were prohibited.

The playa represents the outskirts of the camp in the open desert space. It's also where you'd find all the insanely creative and beautiful artwork, sculptures, and creations by some of the most talented and skillful minds. Each piece of art was a clear work of heart.

And of course it was where we'd play and party with some of the world's most renowned DJs.

Words can't do justice to the playa experience, surrounded by tens of thousands of vibrating dancing souls, as we watched the sun come up at the edge of the desert. It was a collective experience almost feeling like we were all one heartbeat.

Simply mind-blowing.

Back at the camp, now well past midnight, there was already so much going on around us.

The energy was intense, and my eyes couldn't keep up with everything I was trying to look at. Most everyone was scurrying around getting their camps set up.

It felt like a real dream or like I'd been whisked away into a foreign land, and I liked it.

Our fearless camp leaders, Lee and his wife Gaby (Gabriela), led a quick debrief meeting along with the rest of the stellar team and my soon-to-be soul connections—Jessica, Pacha, Antonio, Jeff, Steve—and the many more that made up our camp. These beloveds are still in my heart and will always be remembered fondly as being my Epic friends who popped my Burning Man cherry.

And then that's when a dose of reality hit me: I wasn't just there for fun. I remembered I had a huge responsibility

MASTER OF SINGLE

ahead of me—my friends, who up until that point had graciously held up their end of the bargain. So I shifted my headspace to start thinking about their arrival.

They set us up with a great RV, comfortable with plenty of room, and I did everything I could think of to make the space welcoming for their arrival, only thirty-six hours away.

I fixed up their master bedroom, unpacked and sorted all our perishable food/snack items, chose their bikes for them, and did anything else I could think of while trying to adjust to everything myself. I was pleased and proud of my efforts.

Before turning in, curious, I took a walk around close to camp just to see what was surrounding us. There was so much going on; it was overwhelming and too much for my tired self to process, so I decided to try to get some rest.

When I awoke to a bright new day, that's when things were really put into perspective. *Oh, my goodness... what the actual fuck? Where was I? This place was next-level insane.*

Those were just some of the thoughts going through my mind as I stepped out into a new surreal reality. People were dressed in the craziest, most beautiful costumes, and some weren't dressed at all. There were people riding their bikes while holding lacy miniature umbrellas, and everyone was happy and smiling from ear to ear. Earth to Nicole, we have landed.

My friends were right in that our camp was very well organized. I believe it housed approximately 120 burners and had common areas generously stocked with fridges, freezers, and all kinds of food and snacks, and there was a fully functional kitchen—very impressive. Another trailer was filled with every costume accessory and all the fun things you could imagine that was available to us to use at our discretion, with the condition we took care of it and returned it when done.

Our camp was very laid-back and quite cool, providing lounges and BBQ areas, hammocks, and even had stations to spray paint and personalize your bike. They'd created a calendar of duties and responsibilities that everyone had to participate in and follow to ensure that our camp ran smoothly but also to keep each of us responsible for taking care of one another. That's the heart of Burning Man: may no woman, child, or man be left behind or go without. The other underlining motto was "nothing left behind" or "leave no trace." Meaning we were all responsible for keeping the entire playa and campgrounds free from waste, litter, and garbage. It was part of the unwritten contract that every burner was expected to respect, with the thinking that the land we were on was lent to us and we must honour the grounds and not destroy them with careless behaviour.

As free as we were, we were not free of certain human and civil responsibilities to each other but mostly to Mother Earth and her desert lands.

Who knows what the post-Covid future holds for Burning Man? I pray it comes back reinvented and anew but with the same principles and energy. But I do know that I am blessed enough to say that I was there, and for that, especially given our new reality, I am deeply grateful.

If you ever dreamed of attending and the opportunity comes your way, I strongly suggest you go for the experience, if you dare. The feeling of liberation and self-expression was the freest I'd ever felt. To experience all love, all the time, no judgement, no prejudice, non-sexist, no fear, totally equality zone in a makeshift non-monetary society, is second to none. That imagination, creation, and manifestation of such a utopia doesn't exist anywhere else.

MASTER
OF SINGLE

It felt like a glimpse into what the "real world" should be but couldn't quite get there, so enter Burning Man as a stark reminder of how much better life would be if everyone was simply kind to one another and loved each other without condition and with a willing and free heart. Once you experience the love, generosity, and kindness of strangers at that level, you can't pretend you don't know it can exist.

I took much of what I learned and experienced back home with me and applied the same rules and principles to just love everyone, a beautiful addition to what my mom had already taught me growing up.

It felt very much like I was home, and I was happy to have a full day alone to get acquainted with my surroundings and have my own little mini experience before my friends got there.

Fast forward to the next day, I was so excited for my friends to arrive. I'd worked hard to make things perfect for them. I wanted them to be as happy as I was with my efforts and to show them that they chose the right ally for this mission. But when they finally did arrive, I was greeted with a surprise that left me feeling bewildered. I wasn't expecting them to show up with two additional friends.

In their defence, it was their show and they could bring whomever they wanted. I just felt a little caught off guard because I wasn't expecting it, and it would have been nice if they would have given me a heads-up, that's all. Not at all prepared for this surprise, I panicked. Was I expected to take care of them too? I didn't know them; I didn't know what to think, and obviously it wasn't the right time to ask. They all showed up, curious and excited, and if I'm being honest, I allowed my personal feelings about their friends being there to get in the way of the big picture, which was to support my friends and help make their experience a safe and great one.

I was caught in my feelings, no doubt. I could feel a wall of resistance building inside me in the face of their friends, and instead of processing it and allowing it to be, I tried to control and understand it. That was the moment that opened the door to my greatest lesson learned.

I know, it sounds selfish and not at all in line with the values of the burn, but to my credit, I'm only human and I was already a mixed bag of emotions. In hindsight, I realize I'd gotten so caught up in the idea of making everything perfect that when that idea was interrupted, I wasn't equipped to handle it well. Something inside me was telling me that this was my teachable moment and a very distinct experience that was mine to lose.

Admittedly, the vibe started off a little rocky. My first impression of the friends wasn't a good one. They came off a little pushy and demanding as they dissected everything about our RV.

I just stood there, not receiving their feedback at all and feeling slightly insulted at how they were nitpicking all the hard work I'd done. I could feel myself boiling up inside with everything they asked me to do, get, or figure out for them, but it didn't feel good to judge them or be critical of them or myself. It wasn't what I'd signed up for, and it bothered me to no end.

At some point things went left. I ended up arguing with the wife of the couple over something so stupid I don't even remember what it was. Their perceived attitude and approach left me feeling unappreciated and taken for granted, and those feelings fuelled the argument. After our heated interaction, I felt horrible. I was disappointed in myself, and I could see that my friends were disappointed in me too.

How and why was this happening? I was devastated.

MASTER OF SINGLE

I needed some space, so I walked off to clear my head, I happened to meet Dray along the way just chilling with not a worry in sight. He could tell I was visibly upset and asked if I was okay. I took a breath, pushed through my tears, and said, "No, I'm not okay." I managed to explain why I was so upset, and once again being the beautiful soul that he was, he listened, and then something so lovely happened. He gestured me closer to sit down beside him and said two words that would redefine and change my perception of things, not only for that moment, but forever.

In his laid-back and dignified voice, he said, "Self-love."

I snapped back and looked at him with a curious expression, not quite understanding what to do with those words. I just sat with them for a minute, and then he went on to remind me, "Remember, sis (I loved that he called me sis), on the ride here I told you I'd teach you something you probably haven't learned yet? Well, this is it. The friends aren't the problem; the problem is the way you're looking at yourself in the situation.

"When you have self-love, you don't let things or people get to you, and you don't let situations bring you down. You accept yourself especially through your mistakes and rise to the challenge because you love yourself enough to do so. That's self-love, not just in this moment, but in life."

His words hit me right between the eyes and were felt throughout my whole body.

It was like giving gas to a car that was about to stall, or in my case, feeding the human spirit information to heal, enlighten, and make it better, and that's exactly what it did.

I had heard the words "self-love" before but never really owned them or understood their true definition or power.

Dray must have felt that I was ready to receive this knowledge, and I was.

That void inside me that I'd been struggling with came full circle and to a cosmic close, and the feelings of being unsure, unfulfilled, unworthy, not enough all came tumbling down when I opened the door to this brave and beautiful idea of self-love.

Namaste.

He suggested I take a few minutes to gather myself and then go back and resolve my issue with my friends and their friends. I took his advice; I trusted him.

I loved my friends, and I didn't want whatever this ugly energy was to persist and wouldn't want to jeopardize our friendship, especially over a dumb misunderstanding.

Now armed with this radical new information, I went back and apologized to my friends first, explaining how I allowed my ego to sabotage my heart's intentions.

That I had created an image in my mind of how things were going to go because I wanted everything perfect, and when that image was disrupted, I didn't handle it well, for which I sorely apologized. Knowing my true heart, they said they understood how I could feel that way, that they recognized and appreciated all my efforts in doing a great job. They graciously accepted my apology, and with that I felt like a hundred pounds had been lifted off my shoulders and replaced with wings and an influx of love.

Then I went to see their friends, and in no uncertain terms I also apologized to them for making them feel uncomfortable in any way. I let them know that it would be my pleasure to do whatever I could to help them. I was pleased that they too were gracious enough to accept my apology. It was a fresh start and a welcome new energy that stayed with us for the remainder of the burn.

MASTER
OF SINGLE

Then I went and found Dray, excited to let him know that things were okay, but as soon as we saw each other, no words were exchanged. I just smiled at him. He nodded, and I did a little happy dance. He knew that I'd done the right thing, which set me free.

I could tell that he was proud of me, which was a great feeling, and then we just sat quietly taking it all in, just another day in the desert. Dray's... the... best!

In a series of divine moments, many astonishing things happened. Apologizing was healing, and saying "I'm sorry" was empowering. I started to realize that it wasn't about what happened with the friends. That situation was simply the catalyst that carried the blessing/lesson, and that's how it showed up.

In the end, this unexpected incident led to an incredible breakthrough and opportunity for growth. I felt it in my soul, and now it was mine and part of me.

With this newfound self-love in tow, (like a new best friend), along with my Epic family, we partied like desert queens and kings, spreading our love and shining our light the rest of the days and nights. I took as much in as my soul could take and wore as many outfits as humanly possible, ha ha, until it was time for me to depart, but I would never leave.

A part of me will always belong to the desert and Burning Man.

And in an interesting turn of events, I wasn't worried about the TIFF anymore; maybe I was overshooting my confidence, but after what I'd just experienced, I felt like I could conquer anything. Bring it on. I had the power, the fire, and the energy of the burn pushing me forward—red carpet, lights, camera, action, ready or not, here I come!

But before we get to the TIFF, please indulge me for a

quick moment as I'd like to pivot just slightly, adding a mini bonus Burning Man story from my second year, this time with Jam.

This is one of my favourite stories ever that I want to share, so before taking you to the TIFF, here's one more story for your burning heart... The year was 2017... round two.

As the story goes, I was already in Tahiti, and I would be travelling to the burn via Los Angeles, and Jam would be departing from home in Montreal.

Our communication was limited, as I didn't have great reception on the private island that I was on in Tahiti. Don't hate 'cause my life is so great, hehehe (ish).

The situation was that we were staying in different camps and arriving on different days.

We didn't have a plan of action for how we were going to meet once we got there, nor did we have information to exchange about our respective camps at that time. Any info we did have was very choppy at best, and knowing how challenging it could be to find someone in the desert without proper information was a big concern.

With little to nothing to go on and scarce communication between us, we'd have to put it to faith that somehow we'd find each other even though I couldn't quite see how it was going to happen. But I guess that's what faith is, trusting things will work out without really knowing how it will happen.

Fast forward to my crew's first night partying on the playa with our incredible host and group of beautiful souls with whom I'd just spent the most insane fun time with in Tahiti. We went from perfect crystal-blue Pacific Ocean views to desert sand for as far as the eye could see.

What an incredible juxtaposition, right?

MASTER
OF SINGLE

That night, we partied like rock stars and repeat... at some point it ended and we headed back to our camp. I remember being somewhere between lucid and loopy when I said to my girls (shout-out to my favs Natalia and Krystle), just as I was crawling into my bunk, that tomorrow we'd be on a mission to find Jam.

I knew by now he must have arrived, but with the dicey desert cell service, I wasn't sure how I was going to reach him. The girls had met Jam before and instantly fell in love—duh—so they were excited to find him too.

And so with that plan (ish) in place, I put on my eye mask, laid my head down, and passed out cold... and then the surprise of all surprises!

The next morning bright and early, with me literally half hanging off my bunk, drool running down my face and in deep REM sleep, I suddenly felt a tap on my shoulder and heard someone say, "Jones." I thought I was dreaming and continued sleeping, but then it happened again. "Jones, wake up."

Still thinking I'm dreaming, the tap then turns to a little nudge and firmer voice: "JONES, WAKE UP!" Startled, I lifted my head, recognizing it was Jam's voice, but I was so hungover and still dizzy from the night before that I wasn't connecting all the dots.

Discombobulated, I yelled out, "Jam, is that you?" I heard roars of laughter fill the RV. I must have looked like a straight crazy person. Then I repeated anxiously, "Oh my God, Jam, I hear you but I can't see you, oh my God, I can't see!" I started to panic in my bunk.

More and louder laughter followed, and then Jam said, so plainly, "Jones, take off your mask." Bahahaha! Oh my God, I'd had my eye mask on the whole time and didn't realize it, that's how out of it I was. I quickly removed it, and there he was in all his Burning Man glory, a feast for my eyes and an explosion of love in my heart.

My mind was blown that he was standing in front of me. I thought the girls and I were going to spend hours passing out flyers looking for him. I didn't think he even knew where our camp was. The most amazing and heartwarming part, other than everything, was that out of tens of thousands of people, he found me. When I asked him how, he just said, "I felt you." Amazing.

Sometimes life affords you moments that are so special you couldn't imagine them in your wildest dreams nor deny any devotion that one heart can hold for another. It's truly a beautiful thing.

Thank you for indulging that little detour. I'm so happy to have shared that moment with you.

Meanwhile, my departure to the TIFF and my goodbyes to my original burning family was a tearful one. I think I hugged Dray until he eventually peeled me off him. For a girl who started with so much to say, I found myself without enough words to express my gratitude to him for being on my journey and teaching me a lesson that would change my life. We exchanged smiles and energy before parting ways, but only in the physical world would we be separated; in the divine cosmos, I knew we would always be connected. I held on to every single second of my final moments until alas, I was at the airport, heading back to Montreal to prepare for round two and who knows what next?

Once home, the pressure was on. Twenty-four hours to departure, and by the hair of my little chin-chin, I managed to unpack my luggage covered in playa dust and repack for Toronto. There was so much to do it seemed impossible, but I had a new tool in my box, self-love, and that's what I led with.

MASTER OF SINGLE

I got this. I can do this. I am made for this. Go!

I was finally able to get some studying done at home but mostly used the ten-hour train ride to Toronto to really dive into studying, and surprisingly, I managed to get a lot done. In fact, by the time I arrived, my book was dog-eared and tabbed to death. But regardless of how much or how little I studied, I wasn't worried. I just knew I'd be okay.

I arrived and checked into my hotel room, and soon afterwards I met with Judy, who would be acting as the liaison between the client and me. Super important to note that we were going into this as the number one seeded underdog because we weren't representing a media outlet; instead, we were representing the automotive sponsor of the festival, who was also Judy's client.

She had suggested to them that they use the press pass that was included in their sponsorship package to put a reporter on the red carpet to capture content for their social media platforms. Brilliant idea, they loved it and had nothing to lose, and that's where I came in.

Knowing my background in television, Judy proposed me as the reporter, and they happily accepted.

But because we weren't a media outlet, the odds were hugely stacked against us that we'd even get any stars to stop and talk to us. Why would they? We weren't media, and they were there to promote their films.

Knowing this going in, the client's expectations were very low, which was fine, but we accepted the challenge and took it head-on

Determined to beat the odds, I started thinking, what can I do to stand out? I decided my best weapon would be to use my fashion and my looks to get their attention. This was no time to be humble.

NICOLE JONES

On every red carpet, I dressed to kill and showed up to get noticed, and it worked.

It was a little bit of torture, wearing stilettos and standing for hours in restricted, yet beautiful pieces, but it was all worth it.

Here's a great tip. Always use the skills you know you have and apply them to all the things you do.

I went in prepared, and I knew how to stand out. I also knew that confidence would get me noticed. I had it, so I used it.

Before every red carpet, Judy and I would strategize our pregame plan, including discussing who would be on the carpet and which stars we wanted to try to get.

And break!

Humble brag, I was so well dressed looking confident and cool that I'm sure some of those stars thought I was one of them, but more than that I had an energy and a smile that just couldn't be denied. Be so good they can't say no!

I was my own person on that carpet, not in competition with anyone except myself.

But I couldn't have done it without my amazing cameraman Bradley, who was incredibly quick and so on point quick. I was throwing that mic out in front of stars as they were walking by like nobody's business, and he was right there with me, capturing every moment.

My whole thing was, I wasn't taking no for an answer. You are going to stop, talk to me, or say something to my camera. Period and smile.

Maybe it was my fashion or the confidence I exuded, or my no-nonsense attitude, or maybe it was the residual burning fire still smouldering inside me from Burning Man. Whatever it was, I left it all on the carpet, and together, we murdered it.

MASTER
OF SINGLE

Sure, there were a lot of fleeting moments and quick replies from the stars, but I also got the chance to ask smart and relevant questions, and I was honoured to land some great actual interviews with stars who took my question or wanted to talk to me.

Including some of my favourites like Octavia Spencer, Morgan Freeman, Kevin Costner, Jane Fonda, Chris Rock, George Clooney, Denzel Washington, Sandra Bullock, Diane Keaton, Leslie Jones, and the list goes on.

Not bad for an underdog, right?

Even I was like, wow, that's serious.

The client was blown away and so was Judy, but she knew I wasn't going down without a fight. Against all odds, we rose to the occasion, and for ten days and nights, we shone brilliantly.

And that's a beautiful place to transition as we near the end of this incredible journey that's led us to the grand finale master of single message… I profess to you here and now that self-love is the greatest love of all!

It is the love that changed my life and brought me to master my single life, which I humbly pay it forward and share with you, and now self-love is yours.

I leave you with this…

Today, at the tender age of forty-five years young, here's what I know for sure…

I am my mother's daughter, and she is proud of me. I am a child of love and light, part of the divine vibrating in harmony with the universe.

Energy is everything.

I know that my story does not define me, but my story matters and so does yours.

The year 2020 has shifted the world. We've arrived at a

crucial inflection point of change, and to affect change we all must do our part.

It's been a long time coming. Black and Indigenous lives matter, and as far as I'm concerned, we always have and always will.

We must raise the next generations with love and to be strong and educated because they are the future and deserve a better, more just world.

I am a lovable, nurturing partner, and vulnerability is a strength.

I believe most people have good in them. Oftentimes they just weren't taught how to be good, and you can't be what you don't know.

I move through the world with intention and love and one hundred percent. The world needs more love. I have faith that love is on the way for me and for the world.

Trust God. Trust the universe. Trust the process. Trust yourself.

Everything is possible and anything can happen, but we must do the work if we want the reward.

Personally, I still have so many dreams to fulfill, from personal to professional. My dreams are endless, and my potential is limitless, and so is yours.

I'm a goal digger for life. Godspeed.

As it is written so it shall be said that until now, single has been the most underrated status and true happiness is a choice.

I've lived a remarkable life full of incredible blessings and have the best tribe in all the land, hands down! I love and cherish you all!

Nurture your family/friendships, know who your true tribe is, and don't be afraid to say I love you.

MASTER OF SINGLE

It's fact. Dior is raised in my image and is one of my greatest blessings. I'm obsessed with loving her.

Being of service is my calling, and I am living my purpose every day with every step I take.

And finally, I understand that I have learned a lot and I still have a lot to learn... but what I know undoubtedly, and put this in your pocket, is that self-love is indeed unequivocally the greatest love of all, and from a place of self-love, all things are possible.

Now, did I always choose the right guy? Ah, no. Did I always make the best choices? Absolutely not... Have I lived a life that I'm proud to take ownership of? Affirmative. Have I learned and grown from my mistakes? I sure have.

Do I own my story and love myself through it all? One hundred percent a resounding YES!

Do I know my worth? What do you think? Ha ha!

My taste in men has certainly evolved, but my self-love is unmatched, without waver, and is the same kind of love I'm prepared to wholeheartedly give to the right partner, in due time. The man who will get me will be the man who moves me because he sees me.

And when our stars align (lucky us), I will know it when I'm looking into his kind, loving eyes saying back to him, I love you too.

If I could mandate one thing for the world, it would be that everyone learn to self-love, because with it, you can't hurt others or yourself. It can change the world in that your compassion precedes you, your heart is open, and your soul is free.

It's healing, and part of it is having the ability to not believe everything you think, to not always listen to your inner critic, and as a basic human necessity, be accountable for your own happiness.

It allows you to accept your flaws which we all have and see them as strengths without pride or selfishness.

It's having the wherewithal to know how to set boundaries and have forgiveness for yourself and others. When you have that kind of love, you make good decisions for your life, and that's the energy that will attract the right partner and allow you to fully embody living with intention.

It is the greatest single lesson I've ever learned.

Which is why I say as tough as it sometimes can be, not to burden yourself about the how, who, when, or where your person is. You're doing great with yourself and you're exactly where you need to be.

My hope is that you're inspired to master your life, single or other, and for you to close this book and start writing your next chapters.

Dare yourself to see things differently, design your life, put it on a vision board if that helps, and live on your own accord, your person/partner will find and meet you where you're at.

But until then, focus on you, love doing your work and trusting the universe, which is full of abundance, knows that you exist, and the rest, beloveds, in the name of self-love, I truly believe will follow.

Can I get an amen?

All that's left to say, my beautiful single society, is to remind you that with every end is a new beginning, and never be afraid to start again. You are worth the wait… master of single at your service and serving self-love, the greatest love of all.

You're welcome.

Book Cover Special Credits

Book cover photographs—Patricia Brochu
@patriciabrochuphotographe

Hair stylist—Jacqueline Morgan aka Jackie Mo

Makeup artist—Lisa Sim @lisasimmakeupartist

Fashion stylist—Aime Elchab (aimejaymedia.com)

Wardrobe assistant—Stephanie Anne Gatien

Follow me on the Gram @masterofsingle

Thank you, dream team; it took a village.
(*Special thanks to the wonderful team at Victory Editing)

CPSIA information can be obtained
at www.ICGtesting.com
Printed in the USA
LVHW051710230321
682230LV00013B/2224